SPOILED

SPOILED

ASIAN AMERICAN HOSTILITY AND THE DAMAGE OF REPAIR

SUMMER KIM LEE

Duke University Press *Durham and London* 2025

Printed in the United States of America on acid-free paper ∞
Project Editor: Ihsan Taylor
Designed by Courtney Leigh Richardson
Typeset in Garamond Premier Pro and Peridot Devanagari
by Westchester Publishing Services

Library of Congress Cataloging-in-Publication Data
Names: Kim Lee, Summer, [date] author
Title: Spoiled : Asian American hostility and the damage of repair / Summer Kim Lee.
Description: Durham : Duke University Press, 2025. | Includes bibliographical references and index.
Identifiers: LCCN 2025009495 (print)
LCCN 2025009496 (ebook)
ISBN 9781478032052 paperback
ISBN 9781478028833 hardcover
ISBN 9781478061007 ebook
Subjects: LCSH: Asian American art—Themes, motives | Aesthetics—Psychological aspects
Classification: LCC N6538.A83 K56 2025 (print) | LCC N6538.A83 (ebook) | DDC 709.73089/95—dc23/eng/20250618
LC record available at https://lccn.loc.gov/2025009495
LC ebook record available at https://lccn.loc.gov/2025009496

Cover art: Julie Tolentino, *HONEY, 2024 (Final Iteration)*. Part of the Elemental Media Conference and the "Queer Durations" symposium. Courtesy of the artist and Brown Arts Institute at Brown University. Performers: J Tolentino and Stosh Fila. Photo: Peter Chenot.

Publication of this book is supported by Duke University Press's Scholars of Color First Book Fund.

For Mom and Hamii

CONTENTS

ACKNOWLEDGMENTS

In my dissertation, I included a quotation from Clarice Lispector's dedication to her 1977 novel *The Hour of the Star*, translated by Benjamin Moser, which I think about from time to time. She dedicates the novel to her blood, "to the gnomes, dwarfs, sylphs, and nymphs who inhabit my life," as well as to composers like Schumann, Beethoven, and Stravinsky. She writes, "To all those who reached the most alarmingly unsuspected regions within me, all those prophets of the present and who have foretold me to myself until in that instant I exploded into: I. This I that is all of you since I can't stand being just me, I need others in order to get by, fool that I am, I all askew." I hope this conveys, if only partially, the need and gratitude I have for family and friends who, comparable to Lispector's composers and fantastical beings, have taught me about myself, have made me aware of what I have yet to know and want to learn, and have provided a forecast of what a life as a person, a writer, a teacher, and a student could be. I have felt grounded and full—not *too* self-serious or anxious—because of the people named here.

I'm immensely grateful to the Department of Performance Studies at New York University, which has always felt like home. Tavia Nyong'o, Karen Shimakawa, Alexandra Vazquez, and Barbara Browning have modeled a way of moving through academia and the world at large with the knowledge, patience, and insight they have extended to me since graduate school. Noel Rodriguez and Laura Elena Fortes kept all of us messy graduate students on track and as sure as we could be of what lay ahead, beyond the nest of the department. When I write, a part of me wonders what José Esteban Muñoz would think and if he would like it. I hope that my writing in this book reflects my indebtedness to him, to the influence he has had and will continue to have on my thinking.

It feels like I moved through New York University at the perfect time. As an undergraduate student, I took all of Gayatri Gopinath's courses, and as a graduate student, I was her TA for some of those same courses. I try to put into practice everything I have learned from being her student. Thank you to Joshua Chambers-Letson, who has made sure to check in when I needed it most; to Ricardo Montez, who taught the first performance studies course I ever took; and to Leticia Alvarado, who suggested I consider applying for a graduate program in performance studies.

My time at Dartmouth College was a crucial period of growth. I thank Eng-Beng Lim for guiding me there, in a moment when I wasn't sure what was next for me. Alexander Chee welcomed me into the English department and helped me find my grounding. Israel Reyes took care of the Mellon postdoctoral fellows, encouraging us with his firm belief in our ability to succeed. Dartmouth had a wonderful postdoctoral community, and I'm so glad I got to be a part of it. After I left graduate school, Kelly Chung, Becky Clark, Kellen Hoxworth, Mingwei Huang, and Emily Raymundo welcomed me into a new cohort.

I feel extremely lucky to have landed at the University of California, Los Angeles. A lot has happened since I joined the English department in 2020. In addition to the pandemic, the graduate student worker strike came in the fall of 2022, followed by the Palestine Solidarity Encampment and another graduate student worker strike in the spring of 2024. Contrary to some accounts, the peaceful encampment did not interrupt campus life but remade it, transforming the expectations of faculty, students, and staff around what we collectively can and should demand from our institutions, and beyond them. In the midst of everything, the support and solidarity of colleagues in English and elsewhere at UCLA has felt reassuring, humbling, and inspiring. Yogita Goyal has been a constant as my mentor in the department. Danny Snelson has become a true friend and coconspirator. I derive such pleasure in talking about all things related to queer aesthetics and style with Uri McMillan. Saree Makdisi has been a supportive chair during extremely difficult times for the department. Thank you to King-Kok Cheung, Fred D'Aguiar, Jonathan Grossman, Louise Hornby, Sarah Kareem, Rachel Lee, Alex Mazzaferro, Kathleen McHugh, Ho'esta Mo'e'hahne, Rafael Pérez-Torres, David Russell, Justin Torres, and Cass Turner for their guidance, camaraderie, and conversation, however passing, in the department's hallways. My wholehearted thanks to Stephanie Bundy, Laura Clennon, Rizwati Freeman, Jade Lacy, Janel Munguia, Alondra Lizarraga, Marta Wallien, and Ana Wevill, who have been gracious, giving, and patient in teaching me how the department works. Beyond the English department, I'm so glad I've gotten to connect with Jacquelyn Ardam, Grace Hong, Elizabeth Marchant, Sean Metzger, and Wendy Sung.

I love getting to work with students. Thank you to Jo Alvarado, ren Mai Dinh, Lynette Dixon, Brett Driben, Salvador Herrera, Courtney Lau, Tony Wei Ling, Salem Martinez, Nicole Prucha, Janine Rogers, Evan [NAMI] Sakuma, Brenda Wang, Rebecca Wong, and Katarina Yuan for being in conversation with me, and for trusting me with their work. Thank you to those who were a part of the fall 2024 graduate seminar on contemporary Asian American literature and Asian Americanist critique. The rigorous discussion (as well as memes and baked goods) made the seminar some of the most fun I've had in a classroom. I'm exceedingly indebted to Austin Nguyen, whose meticulous attention to detail as an RA helped me finish this book (this "eczema manuscript"). He is my ideal reader, as are all the students I am fortunate to know.

The artists in this book have transformed and challenged my thinking. Without them, there would be nothing to see here. Thank you to Patty Chang, Jes Fan, Alison Kuo, Brooke Nicholas, Cato Ouyang, TJ Shin, Julie Tolentino, and Mila Zuo for meeting with me, corresponding with me, and scheduling studio visits and exhibition walkthroughs. I'm grateful to them for giving me permission to include images of their work here, as well as to Electronic Arts Intermix for permission to publish images of Wu Tsang's work.

After I completed my PhD, Tavia suggested I meet with Courtney Berger to talk about a book. I wasn't sure I had one (at the time, I definitely didn't), but over the years, Courtney has offered the advice and direction I needed to make what now, miraculously, can be called a book. I'm incredibly beholden to the readers of my manuscript, who understood the project and gave me a clear vision of what could be done to make it better. They shaped what the book has become, and I can only hope I rose to the occasion. Thank you to Laura Jaramillo, Ihsan Taylor, and Courtney Leigh Richardson for their communication and coordination with me throughout the production process, as well as to the rest of the Duke University Press team for all of their labor.

As an academic, you can feel like you're writing into a void. Therefore I have so much gratitude for readers and audiences that have offered invaluable feedback at Dartmouth College, Williams College, Wesleyan University's Queer Studies Research Collective, Post45, UCLA's Center for Performance Studies, the Americanist Research Colloquium in UCLA English, the "IMU UR2" symposium at

Stanford University, the New Work in Queer and Trans Studies series at the University of North Carolina at Greensboro, the "Object Relations" symposium at Northwestern University, the "Queer Durations" symposium at Brown University, and the Autotheoretical Turn conference at UC Santa Cruz. Many thanks to the *Social Text* editorial collective, the *ASAP/Journal* editors, and Alex Brostoff and Lauren Fournier for working with me on previous iterations of the material included here. I'm also grateful that this book has been supported by the UCLA Hellman Fellowship, a grant from the UCLA Council on Research, and Duke University Press's Scholars of Color First Book Fund.

It has been a dream to find myself among amazing friends, colleagues, and interlocuters, who have offered feedback and encouragement, shaped my writing with their editorial skills, published my work, patiently listened to me ramble nonsense, or else taught me something that I continue to carry with me. Thank you to Sareh Z. Afshar, Patty Ahn, Kadji Amin, Sampada Aranke, Christine Bacareza Balance, Nick Bazzano, Katherine Brewer Ball, AB Brown, Kandice Chuh, Chris Eng, David Eng, Jennifer Doyle, Malik Gaines, Jules Gill-Peterson, Laura Gutiérrez, Mashinka Firunts Hakopian, Lucas Hilderbrand, Leon Hilton, Jane Hu, Douglas Ishii, Sarah Rebecca Kessler, Jina B. Kim, Lazz Kinnamon, Marci Kwon, J. de Leon, Licia Fiol-Matta, Heather Love, Joan Lubin, James McMaster, Christine Mok, Amber Jamilla Musser, Ren Ellis Neyra, Ianna Hawkins Owen, Roy Pérez, Alex Pittman, Dixa Ramírez-D'Oleo, Sarah Richter, Juana María Rodríguez, Sandra Ruiz, Avgi Saketopoulou, Daniel Sander, Chad Shomura, Dan Sinykin, AE Stevenson, Beth Stinson, Kyla Wazana Tompkins, Jeanne Vaccaro, Anh Vo, Danielle Wu, Hentyle Yapp, and Mila Zuo.

With her brilliance and warmth, Vivian Huang teaches me what the sociality of study makes possible. Every conversation with Lakshmi Padmanabhan leaves me invigorated and much, much smarter. Sharing Airbnbs with Kemi Adeyemi and Kareem Khubchandani reminds me that conferences are, first and foremost, a time for being with friends—until the next Airbnb, long live the group chat. Karen Tongson's love and appreciation for popular culture, as well as her mentorship and friendship, have shown me the kind of academic and writer I hope to become. I lived in New York for over ten years, and some of the most formative years were spent living with Ari Brostoff. It felt right that after helping me bring my dissertation to the finish line, they would read parts of this manuscript and bring it to the finish line, too.

Whenever I catch up with Nijah Cunningham, I'm reminded of how much more I have to learn, and especially from him, a dear and old friend. Through his friendship, Ethan Philbrick continues to teach me how to be in relation to other people—I'm so glad I get to be in relation to him. In graduate school,

Joshua Javier Guzmán let me stay at his place when I had bed bugs in Brooklyn. Since then, he has continued to make space for me. Whenever I want to rave about anything—an episode of *Girls*, Rilo Kiley—I know I can text Iván Ramos. He always responds, ready to share his good advice and good taste. Let's get churros in CDMX again. I have had the best time sharing conference hotel rooms with Christina León, forever my GGG. In whatever way I have managed to succeed or grow as a feminist scholar, it is in no small part due to her.

I love living in LA and getting to see my family—Emo, James, Alexa, Brendan, Uncle David, Auntie Robyn, Alyna, and Westley. By the time I moved back, my grandpa—Papa—had passed, but whenever I hear "Edelweiss," I think of him and feel thankful for all that he's done for us, for his family. In LA, I also get to see friends I used to miss all the time. For years, Erin English and Hannah May have made me feel welcomed into their home and their family. I'm so happy I get to live in the same city as they do and to see their family grow to include Henry and Juniper. Ambrose came into my life during a pandemic and some of the worst LA wildfires. They soften my edges, calm me down, and slow me down (especially when I'm driving; sorry for that). I love our home and our life together with our girls, Kiley (Rusty) and Wednesday (Nadine). Ambrose, I remain in wonder of you.

When I was young, my stepdad, Adolfo, read books to me, like *Treasure Island*, and introduced me to Bob Dylan. We watched Alfred Hitchcock's films and romantic comedies like *His Girl Friday*. I'm grateful to him for teaching me what it means to love a song or a film, and to be passionate about one's politics and beliefs in how the world should be. I dedicate this book to my mom and my grandma, Hamii. It is hard to put into words how much my mom means to me. She read to me before bed even when she was tired after work. She took me to the library or brought home books she thought I'd like. She took me to New York on her work trips so that we could watch musicals on Broadway together. She sought out whatever made me happy and found a way for us to enjoy it together. She is the most beautiful, dedicated, hardworking, nurturing person I know—the very best mom. I feel her love in everything I do.

I think I'm a lot like my Hamii. She had a dry sense of humor, and she was shy and reserved yet also tough and discerning. She needed her alone time for reading or watching Korean soap operas, and she was clear about when she liked something and when she really didn't. She used to tease me and call me spoiled, as did my mom and Adolfo. I was "the spoiled child." I truly feel spoiled with their love and all that they made possible for me. In part, their joke—both the warmth and the bite behind it—prompted me to think about what spoiling can do. I readily offer up this book to them, as proof of how they spoiled me.

INTRODUCTION

RIPE FOR SPOILING

An arm reaches out, not helpless so much as irritated, pissed. Hand-carved from wood, the arm cranes awkwardly to the side, giving in at the elbow. It bends at the wrist, hand twisting, palm exposed, fingers flexed. The contorted limb gesticulates from Cato Ouyang's sculpture, *Kicked Madonna (Crystal)* (2022), peeking out from a light blue pleated skirt misfitted around an amorphous mass of epoxy clay, hydrocal, gypsum, papier-mâché, and beeswax. Oyster shells are fastened to the curves of the sculpture's surface like brooches, and a bleached white pelvic bone of a mustang juts out from the top, all shrouded in a tangle of brown horsehair. Streams of gnarled fabric in shades of white and cream are tucked and enfolded in the skirt, trailing behind like wisps of ocean foam, or a torn dress or veil, perhaps offering evidence of a bride's violation, escape, or both.

To encounter Ouyang's *Kicked Madonna* is to feel Ouyang's touch. It is a touch that spoils. As Ouyang carves and chips away at wood, cuts and tears fabric, plasters and pastes objects, they make work with disfiguring details and disjointed associations that elude linear narratives of violence and ruin, harm and healing. Has *Kicked Madonna* been abandoned and left to decompose, or has it been laid to rest? Does it writhe in pain, crawling toward refuge, or has it made peace with its place, accepting its lot? Does the arm extend in need of our assistance or push us away? Here is a figure that struggles to cohere, or derives pleasure in offending us with its obscure form. A body abstracted, bent out of shape, becomes a suggestion, or a trap. We might want to endow the work with personhood, with intention and motive, interiority and feeling, which I find myself doing now. We might want to rescue or resuscitate it, to find its missing limbs, its castaway bones. But Ouyang does not turn an object into a subject, nor a thing into a body. They do not return a wounded part to a mended whole.

With *Kicked Madonna*, everything seems in an odd place, wedged in, protruding, or punctured. The work sits in wrongness, unamenable to the possibility of its own repair while nevertheless inviting the possibility of its beauty, its own satisfaction gleaned from its hostile form.[1] In confronting and constructing the forms that violence, pain, and injury make, Ouyang approaches their practice as one of indulgent betrayal: a betrayal of those who encounter their work and wish to feel whole and healed in the process, as well as a betrayal of themself, as the artist who risks getting corrupted by their own work and taken in by its suffering.[2] *Kicked Madonna* spoils itself, as well as Ouyang and us, by asserting its hostile form. It lures us in with the suspicion that there is a body to be found, only to then rob us of clear aesthetic judgment, disturbing a sense of integrity, bodily or otherwise, in its degradation and ruin.

In her poem "In Excelsis," Anne Sexton writes of "confronting the ocean," hoping that she might walk into it "like a dream."[3] She stands at the shore with Barbara Schwartz, her therapist during the last nine months of her life, leading up to her death by suicide in 1974. It is a scene where the therapeutic converges with the sublime. Of the ocean, Sexton writes,

> Its mouth is open very wide,
> and it has dug up its green,
> throwing it, throwing it at the shore.
> You say it is angry.
> I say it is like a kicked Madonna.
> Its womb collapses, drunk with its fever.
> We breathe in its fury.[4]

Like the ocean, from which it derives its name, Ouyang's sculpture has been spoiled by its raging appetite. *Kicked Madonna* is intoxicated with itself, caving inward with the pull of the tide and fuming outward with the crest of a wave. It devours itself, then spits itself back out again: a miracle and perversion of conception received on the shore, as a waterlogged, wrecked form. Its shreds of dress and veil cover the sacred, devotional figure of the Madonna as a "still unravish'd bride" remade into the profane.[5] As a damaged, feminized object—thrown, kicked, collapsed, furious—Ouyang's sculpture recalls unknowable harms through spoiled acts of ravishment, ornamentation, and assemblage that create by way of destruction.

Spoiled attends to the ways contemporary Asian American artists challenge the expectation that their work should provide ameliorative sites of repair. Rather than reject repair, they make use of its destructive capacities and the damage it risks and invites. The artists in this book take up what I call the spoiled: the racialized, gendered Asiatic body, and all that it consumes, imposes, expels, and destroys in its vulnerability and volatility, indulgently and with desire, but also under conditions of constraint. The spoiled is the gratuitous excess and derivative waste produced through embodied processes of Asian racialization that make the Asiatic body legible as such.[6] More broadly, the spoiled aggravates categorizable identities and recognizable subject positions in the preoccupation with the body's sensation, matter, and form. Through the spoiled, the artists here insist on the deidealized, deforming aspects of Asian racialization that critically irritate cathartic, affirming representations of Asian American subjectivity and social life, which promise one can and will arrive at a self that feels whole by way of claims to a legibly minor, resistant, radical Asian American subjecthood.

When something is spoiled, it has become rotten or contaminated, fallen out of use and into disrepair, near worthless. At the same time, spoils can be valuable materials ruthlessly and enviously seized by force, as evidence of an unfair trade or power imbalance, in the wake of extractive violence or received in return for an opportunistic favor. When someone is spoiled, they, too, have gone bad. They might be a person with what Erving Goffman called a "spoiled identity": a result of the failure to fulfill one's allotted social role due to the stigma of one's "undesired differentness."[7] Such spoilage can be a repository of bad feelings, bred from the experience of disqualification and exclusion.[8] On the other hand, someone spoiled might not be interested in what is appropriate to their social role. They might realize that the social roles they have been expected to play were already spoiled in the first place.

The spoiled, perceived as stigma, is vulgar and abrasive. Like Roald Dahl's Veruca Salt, screaming about what she wants *now*, and like the band that adopted her name, turning the character's obnoxious entitlement into unruly irreverence, the spoiled is girly, bratty, needy.[9] To be spoiled is to rebuff the virtues of self-correction and self-control, to taunt a politics of respectability that would moralize and pathologize racialized, gendered sexuality and loud, flashy expressions or enactments of sex and desire.[10] The spoiled is encapsulated in the figure of the polymorphously perverse girl, seeking pleasure and gratification from inappropriate or unlikely places, without regard for convention or restraint.[11] A "bad egg" with a temper, a "snarl-toothed Seether," she takes and consumes in willful, belligerent play, imperiling those around her—and herself.[12]

To confront the spoiled is to realize that one's own body and self are susceptible to spoilage. To spoil and be spoiled entails forms of indulgence that cannot secure a subject's autonomy and sense of self.[13] Yet such spoilage does not inevitably lead to self-injury and self-destruction, to the annihilation of the self and its removal from the social, shattered, turned away, or cast out. This is because the spoiled covets too much of who and what surrounds it. It wants to stay in the midst of things, not disappear in them. Given this, the spoiled devours but it also leaks; it cannot hold all that it wants to consume and contain. The spoiled can get pretty filthy, capable of delighting in the mess it has made.[14]

The spoiled can get so full of itself that it is always poised to seduce and ready to brag. Like funk, which L. H. Stallings theorizes as nonvisual sensation, mood, and embodied movement within Black sexual cultures, the spoiled takes pleasure in telling stories about itself—producing fictions of the self in lieu of truths—"as a con and joke" made at the expense of so-called civilized sensorial regimes.[15] These spoiled stories get around, taking on an erotic and social life of their own. In the vein of good gossip, the spoiled never lacks for embellishment, drama, and exaggeration. As a concept, elbowing its way into different disciplines and fields of study, the spoiled compromises its own reputation, associating itself with too many different people, places, and things. The spoiled assists in constructing deidealizing theories of the social; specifically, it illuminates the fact that hostility is not antagonistic to the social but an integral part of it and the kinds of relations we seek and desire within it.[16]

The spoiled names what comes from outside the body and the self and is taken inward, like the consumption of a decadent meal or the demand for and ready acceptance of gifts. It also names what comes from inside the body and the self and gets transmitted outward, like a temper tantrum, or spit, blood, sweat, and vomit. This ambiguity around the origins of the spoiled—the question of whether it comes from within or without—is one of its most defining qualities. The spoiled refuses to offer a clear delineation of where it begins and ends, only of the psychic, social, and bodily boundaries it overwhelms. The spoiled works against the consolidation of the subject and the identities the subject tries to fit into. It clutters tidy, liberal fantasies of autonomy, sovereignty, and self-possession. As an impediment to utility and productivity, to a clear sense of moral rightness and moderation, the spoiled consists of awkward mishandlings, bulky proportions, and overambitious appetites.

In this book, I encounter a range of aesthetic practices of spoilage by contemporary Asian American artists who poke and prod at the limits of our desire for processes of restoration and repair, at the limits of our relations with others. They prefer to stay in instead of go out; they are too into themselves to be sociable; they use people and speak as another; they turn cold, giving up or letting themselves go to waste; and they inflict injuries to see what forms of relation emerge from open wounds. These artists do not assert mastery and dominance in an aesthetic or relational register; they do not aspire to omnipotence. In the vein of what Avgi Saketopoulou calls "exigent sadism," they take pleasure in their harsh, sometimes ruthless aesthetic practices of spoilage, but they put themselves in harm's way too, letting what they create transform them in ways beyond their control.[17]

The work of these artists does not offer relatable, comfortingly linear narratives of healing and repair that culminate in formations of Asian American subjecthood adherent to liberal ideals of autonomous, contained, discrete individuality. They have relinquished this subject position for themselves. For them, the damage of spoilage is intrinsic to processes of repair that Asian Americans seek in their aesthetic encounters, political commitments, and social and psychic lives. They know that in spoiling and being spoiled, they might get dragged down into the havoc they have wrought, not unscathed but there for whatever comes, belly up, hand out.

On Wonder

In 2022, the gallery Jeffrey Deitch showed some of Ouyang's work in a group exhibition called *Wonder Women*.[18] Presented at the gallery's New York and Los Angeles locations, the exhibition consisted of paintings, sculptures, and installations centering the figure of the Asian American woman as a site of wonder, whether as a mythological, heroic being not of this world or as the protagonist of her own story in the ordinary world we know. Walking through the exhibition on its opening day in Los Angeles, I saw Asian American women transformed into fantastical creatures like mermaids or depicted through self-portraiture as introspective subjects in their day-to-day lives.

The exhibition's title is inspired by Genny Lim's poem "Wonder Woman," published in Cherríe Moraga and Gloria Anzaldúa's 1981 anthology of women of color feminist writers, *This Bridge Called My Back*. "Sometimes I stare longingly at women who I will never know," Lim writes.[19] She sees "Chinese grandmothers," "Japanese women tourists," "Young wives," "Lesbian women," "Smiling debutantes," "Giddy teenage girls," and "Widows."[20] "I look in their eyes and wonder if / They share my dreams," she muses.[21] She wants to know if she can see parts of herself in them, in the same way that she can "see reflections on bits of glass on sidewalks."[22] Across differences in race, ethnicity, class, sexuality, and geography, Lim asks, "Why must woman stand divided? / Building the walls that tear them down?"[23] Her singular "woman" is tasked with holding a multiplicity that the word cannot carry. By way of its plenitude, the *Wonder Women* exhibition aimed to carry out the wishes of the poem's singular "Wonder Woman," resulting in a tension between the production and affirmation of the Asian American woman's figure and that figure's impossibility and negation.

Perhaps this is why I was initially wary of the exhibition.[24] It seemed to align with the ways that, as Vivian Huang writes, "invisibility has become such a common grammar of Asian America that visibility has become the telos of Asian American public life."[25] If Asian Americans are always understood as not-yet-visible subjects, who must become visible as a political necessity and inevitability, then such subjects are simultaneously subject to what Huang calls the "trope of violent disappearance."[26] The force of this trope pressed itself upon the reception and exigency of the exhibition. By the time of its opening, Donald Trump had made repeated references to the "Chinese virus" and "kung-flu virus," six Asian women had been murdered in shootings at three Atlanta spas in March 2021, and security footage of the harassment and violence of Asian women and elders in New York City and other US cities had led to nationwide calls to "Stop AAPI Hate." As the exhibition's curator, Kathy Huang, states in *Wonder Women*'s press release, "The increasing violence against Asian Americans, particularly against Asian women and the elderly, emphasizes the need to tell our own stories. Figuration allows the artists to present themselves, their communities, and their histories on their own terms."[27] The representation of Asian American women felt necessary to the moment, providing an urgent site of agency, resistance, and care for figures subject to violent disappearance. In the exhibition, there was no singular, definitive style in which the figures of Asian American women appear. Lim's "Wonder Woman" became more than one, as a way of making amends for whom the term "Asian American woman" might otherwise overlook or exclude. Altogether, these figures, as sites of inclusion and empowerment, became a collective means of recovery, where a subject can reclaim her own image and means of self-representation.

Wonder Women, then, seemed to position "Asian American woman" as a positive term of recognition, inclusion, and celebration. This is a familiar move, and one that somewhat frustratingly overlooks the fact that, as Laura Hyun Yi Kang reminds us, "Asian American woman" is not a preexisting identity to be made whole but a "political and syntactical formulation" that emerged at the intersections of feminist, antiracist, and anti-imperialist social movements in the late 1960s and '70s.[28] Yet what I found while walking through the exhibition was not the restoration of the figure of the Asian American woman but its destruction by way of spoilage, which is also to say that for me, it produced an experience of *being spoiled* with too much. What I saw was not the ideal of an abundance of representation so much as that ideal's ruin in excess. I encountered figures estranged and defamiliarized, figures bristling against the cozy coherence of the term "Asian American woman." Wonder did strike, perhaps just not in the way the exhibition had intended. As I experienced it, wonder—the feeling evoked by contact with the curious, awe-inspiring, not easily grasped—served to short-circuit the idealization of "Asian American women," sullying forms and figures of knowledge riding on the presumption of the term's knowability. I felt wonder in encountering what Mila Zuo describes as an "overperform[ed] narcissistic self-love" that comes with a near crushing commitment to undo the self it promises to restore and represent in the first place.[29] *Wonder Women* overwhelmed the recognizability of figures corralled under its name. There, in the gallery, the wondrous spoiled me.

Ouyang's work touches on the forms that pain makes, yet it does not resolve or "work through" trauma, nor does it express resignation in trauma's face. Ouyang attaches themself to the memory of painful experience in ways that read as more sadistic than masochistic; they probe their pain for what it holds and creates when worn down and built back up into something new. As Saketopoulou might put it, Ouyang recalls the ways people have violated them, disappointed them, or let them down, and makes these experiences "circulate": spreading them around, letting them spoil whatever or whoever lies within their reach.[30] Their work ensures that the difficulty of pain—felt and inflicted on another—is not passed over, that pain is not rendered into something from which one can be rescued or cured.[31]

Importantly, the hostility that pervades Ouyang's work is not a form of punishment the artist brings down on themself or another. It is not a means of exercising their power over others via ressentiment and its claims to a higher moral ground. Instead, this hostility brings both artist and viewer down into the matter of who and what hurts and irreversibly changes us, dislodging an impermeable sense of self. We cannot always know what we might be capable of in the face of what harms us. This is another source of wonder: the ways that difficult, painful experiences can spoil us, not inspiring resilience and tolerance so much as necessitating the manifestation of new relations, new forms. These new manifestations speak to how we are sometimes damaged in our encounters with difference that lies both in and outside of ourselves.

In the *Wonder Women* exhibition, I noticed another kind of wonder, too, one attached to repeated intimations of Asian American women's sleepy, dreamy interior worlds we could not see. In Livien Yin's *Dreaming Host* (2022), an oil painting of soft lavenders, yellows, greens, and blues, a woman rests with her eyes closed, head tilted to the side, with fingers interlaced. The image is based on the sleeping "Chinese Beauty" shown at the 1893 World's Columbian Exposition, but it is also a likeness of Yin's friend.[32] Tidawhitney Lek's oil, acrylic, and pastel painting *Napping* (2022) shows a woman sleeping on her side on a living room couch, hands cradling her head and knees tucked in, surrounded by the deep purples and yellows of dusk peeking through a front door left ajar. These scenes appear interested in the affordances of rest and respite, located in the solitude of private psychic or physical space. They suggest that to move through the exhaustion of everyday life, exposed to the danger and damage of an antagonistic world, is wondrous in and of itself. Relief from such onslaught becomes a form of resistance and refusal, a means of survival and care.

Though not representative of the exhibition writ large, these works caught my eye because they seemed to express a political desire for a kind of therapeutic aesthetic encounter that resounds within contemporary Asian American culture. Healing, care, and repair have emerged as throughlines in recent discussions of Asian American mental health, wellness, and disability. Scholars, writers, and activists have asked: How do Asian Americans care for themselves and their communities, in the midst or in the afterlives of war, immigration, intergenerational conflict, and a global pandemic, or in the face of illness, ableism, and the enduring figure of the model minority? What practices of healing and care can Asian Americans foster, especially when, as the model minority, they are often assumed to be high-functioning and self-sufficient?

A few avenues of thought have been particularly helpful in apprehending these questions. One is a psychoanalytic approach taken by scholar David Eng and psychotherapist Shinhee Han in response to widespread complacency around Asian American mental health struggles, and specifically the struggles of Asian American students on college campuses. In their collaborative work, Eng and Han identify "racial melancholia" and "racial dissociation" as psychic processes through which Asian Americans and other people of color are simultaneously assimilated into and excluded from social and political life under neoliberalism, wherein past and ongoing racial violences are repressed in service to the celebratory affirmation of difference.[33] Eng and Han, along with other Asian Americanists and critical race and ethnic studies scholars working with psychoanalytic theory, insist on the dynamic particularity—as opposed to the static universality—of the racialized, gendered psychoanalytic subject, articulating psychic processes not as individual and pathological, but collective and structural.[34]

Another approach to questions of care in Asian American life has taken disability as its starting point. In this vein, Mimi Khúc has developed what she calls a "pedagogy of unwellness," which takes into account that "we are all differentially unwell," and as such, "need differential care at all times."[35] Khúc's pedagogy rejects the idea that we can or should transcend what hurts us, instead offering to teach the reader how to live outside the violent ideology of cure that maintains an impossible ideal of a nondisabled original state of being.[36] Along similar lines, James Kyung-Jin Lee proposes a "pedagogy of woundedness" to conceive of nonableist modes of "Asian American embodiment beyond the model minority" that take into account failure, disability, illness, and death.[37] Lee attunes us to our vulnerability and dependency, in both our living and dying.

During the COVID-19 pandemic, rising anti-Asian discrimination and violence, as well as the need for mutual aid and support for essential workers—doctors and nurses, but also in-home caretakers, grocers, cooks, and delivery workers—intensified considerations of care within Asian communities. In the spring of 2020, for instance, a group of writers, scholars, and activists created A/P/A Voices: A COVID-19 Public Memory Project, building an oral history archive and developing a collective writing practice committed to "dwelling in unwellness . . . from a place of unending rupture, anxiety, and depression, as well as anger and urgency."[38] To dwell in unwellness enacts the "refusal to 'adjust' and 'return' to business-as-usual."[39] The emerging body of work on Asian American unwellness and woundedness refuses what it identifies as a racist, ableist idealization of the Asian American body and mind. It refuses the expectation that Asian American subjects can stand on their own, without support, without the acceptance that, as Johanna Hedva writes, "we can't tell how we will die—and that we're already doing it all the time."[40]

I write with an indebtedness to these scholars' and writers' refusals of unobtainable ideals of health and wellness, insofar as these ideals shore up the image of the good, productive, assimilated model minority and citizen subject.[41] Alongside Khúc, Lee, and the members of A/P/A Voices, I stay with the rage, sorrow, frustration, and exhaustion that shapes the ways we live with our pain and the pain of others, with the fact of our own finitude. What they describe is not so unlike the hostility I consider here, especially given their refusal of wellness and repair. Where *Spoiled* differs, and resonates more with the work of Eng and Han, is in its engagement with psychoanalytic frameworks, which begin from the premise that there are always parts of the self that it cannot consciously know and communicate to itself or to others. In contrast, projects on unwellness work with the notion that the self has a privileged, transparent knowledge of its own unwellness, and can use this knowledge to fuel a cathartic, empowering shift from injury to affirmation. I want to spoil the idealized self that lives in this account—or rather, I hope to show how such a self is already spoiled, in ways that we cannot always recognize or clearly convey, whether to ourselves or to others. As Eng and Han remind us, "Psychoanalysis thus alerts us to the fact that our agency is compromised and our will is limited from the beginning, that we are pregiven to and dependent on others."[42] The spoiled is the material, psychic, affective trace of such compromise and limitation. It is the stuff of unwellness, yet by its very nature it cannot be conscripted into giving us a full, adequate account of the self as such, as whole.

To clarify the limits and stakes of this critique, I want to underscore the material urgency of concerns around Asian American mental health and wellness, and the dire importance of establishing liberatory, sustained models of care. The questions I am raising lie elsewhere, taking issue with the fact that Asian American art and culture is valued and prioritized when and if it is deemed to be healing—in other words, when it is experienced as ameliorative and affirming. The spoiled teaches us that what we hope might heal can also hurt us, leading to conflict, shock, pain, and disappointment. In the poem "Wonder Woman," the spoiled shows up in Lim's wonder at the women around her, at how they cannot fit together as a whole despite her desire for wholeness. The women she recognizes and hopes to care for, including herself, are broken up, like shards of glass on the sidewalk. Perhaps Lim broke them herself in dividing and naming difference with each line she wrote. What Lim sees in her poem, and what the poem offers its reader, are partial, fractured images of the self and others—images that can also cut, especially if one is not paying attention, not treading carefully. Lim does not suture the cut of difference; she does not try to salvage the glass on the ground. Instead, she remains in wonder of how it shatters.

The Shorn Parts of Repair

> What survives once the model of reparative relation is forced to share space with all sorts of negativity or when it starts to open onto a negativity of its own?
> —Lauren Berlant and Lee Edelman, *Sex, or the Unbearable* (2013)

Wonder can be the source of dreams and, in waking life, what Barbara Johnson calls "the surprise of otherness"—"that moment when a new form of ignorance is suddenly activated as an imperative."[43] In Lek's *Napping*, and in some of her other paintings of domestic scenes, this surprise of otherness takes the form of a hand with brown or green skin and long pink nails. Hands encroach upon their setting and upon us as the viewer, creeping from behind a couch or on the other side of a door to turn a lock, hovering inside a closet, or peeking out from a pan on a stove. Who does the hand belong to? We cannot know. These hands interrupt otherwise realist depictions of the everyday, and like the hand in Ouyang's *Kicked Madonna*, they hold themselves out in distress, desire, or both. As a surprise, they bring to the fore "an imperative that changes the very nature of what I think I know," which is also what I think I know of my capacity to respond, and what I think I have to give to, or hide from, an outstretched hand.[44] The surprise of otherness comes from someone else's hand, but also from one's self in the moment of encountering it.

As Eve Sedgwick writes, surprise is anathema to practices of paranoid reading driven by a "hermeneutics of suspicion."[45] This critical style plumbs the hidden depths of the world with a "terrible alertness" that anticipates the discovery and exposure of a secret truth.[46] In a paranoid reading, there can be no surprises. Everything must be known in advance; wonder is not welcomed. In her famous essay "Paranoid Reading and Reparative Reading, Or, You're So Paranoid, You Probably Think This Essay Is about You," Sedgwick takes issue with the ways paranoid reading became the dominant mode for critiquing structural violence. Writing in the mid-1990s during the AIDS epidemic, in the midst of devastating loss and state negligence, Sedgwick questions the usefulness of critiquing and responding to such violence from a paranoid position, which assumes that unveiling the truth of oppression, pain, or suffering—whether one's own or another's—is the same as transforming it. She suggests that we take seriously a reparative mode of reading the world and its objects. Reparative reading practices are inclined toward surprise, receptive to the wonder of the unknowable from unlikely if not outright inhospitable objects remade into forms of sustenance and care. For Sedgwick, paranoid and reparative reading practices are dynamic and nonhierarchical in relation to each other, and are necessary to each other's functioning.[47]

Sedgwick's argument draws on Melanie Klein's distinction between paranoid/schizoid and depressive positions. Unlike Freudian "stages" that impose linear narratives of development, one can oscillate between these positions, just as one can oscillate between paranoid and reparative modes of reading. Klein's paranoid position is aligned with negative affects like "hatred, envy, and anxiety," which one simultaneously disavows and directs toward idealized objects that one "defensively projects into, carves out of, and ingests from the world around one."[48] But in realizing the damage one can cause, even if only in phantasy, one can experience feelings of guilt, and the paranoid position can give way to the depressive position. From the depressive position arises the wish to "make good" the damage inflicted in phantasy, to repair such destruction by assembling an object's fragmented parts into a deidealized, complex, nonoriginary whole within one's psychic, interior world.[49] This process of repair attempts to reinstate the whole object by integrating its good and bad qualities—accepting what is loved with what is hated, what is desired with what is scorned. "Once assembled to one's specifications," Sedgwick continues, "the more satisfying object is available both to be identified with and to offer one nourishment and comfort in turn."[50]

As many have pointed out, the title of Sedgwick's essay that directly addresses "you" as the reader is a callout as much as it is an invitation.[51] Sedgwick elicits the paranoia she critiques, and to make her argument, she separates, not without hostility, the reparative from the paranoid. Such a separation belies the necessity of destruction and negativity to the reparative, drawing attention not only to what must be amassed for repair but also to what must be cut out. The ongoing process of repair, then, is "additive and accretive," but in its relation to the aggression of paranoia and the destructiveness of hate, it is subtractive and corrosive, too.[52] For if the reinstatement of an object must bring together separated, divided parts into a whole, then some parts must also be, to use Eng and Han's phrasing, "shorn away."[53] These shorn parts, discarded for the sake of repair, constitute the spoiled work of the artists discussed in this book, as materials that recall the destructive, violent aspects of reinstating and integrating an object. The spoiled is *of* processes of repair, just not what is repaired itself.

For Klein, the process of repair can also be called love, and love does not always feel good. If the reparative offers a language for thinking about love as that which can temper the forces of the death drive, it is a deidealized love that comes with dissatisfaction, failure, and anger. Scholars have shed light on such deidealization by way of the reparative's destruction, aggression, and hostility both in Klein's work and in Sedgwick's reading of it.[54] Elizabeth Wilson reminds us that the reparative can lead to further destruction, precisely in the attempt to make good on the damage one has caused. One cannot fully know what one is capable of doing to a loved object, or what that loved object is capable of doing to oneself. One always has the potential to harm who and what one loves, even while trying to care for them. The reparative, Wilson writes, requires "the recognition that sadistic attacks are inevitable, that they can originate from me, and that while their viciousness can be down-regulated, such attacks cannot be eradicated."[55] In their varying practices, the artists here explore their own capacity to attack what they love, not to unconditionally open the floodgates of cruelty and make excuses for bad behavior, nor to cultivate a toughened response to pain. They want to learn how this capacity for hostility and harm shapes the forms of relation they, and we, desire and pursue.

The spoiled does not shy away from more recent critiques of the reparative as a political and psychoanalytic concept, and the basis of a reading practice. The spoiled offers a means of addressing how repair, and the love it makes possible, is shaped by what it has destroyed, and also made. In Eng's reading of Klein—who, as he notes, was writing on love and repair in the wake of World War I, a period of broad disillusionment with European civilization on the brink of fascism—he argues that the reparative enables "the continuous psychic and political consolidation of a European liberal human subject embedded in a long history of colonial relations."[56] Through the reparative, objects are affectively divided between those of love and hate, of "good *liberal*" objects worth repairing, and "bad *colonial* objects" that are not.[57] For Patricia Stuelke, the reparative, particularly by way of Sedgwick's readings of Klein, has become an ahistorical mode of critique that enables neoliberal forms of governance by accepting an "earnest commitment to making room for pleasure and amelioration" as a substitute for structural change.[58] "The widespread commitment to the reparative," she writes, "can sometimes seem to stave off the difficult work of imagining possible worlds that break definitively with this one; instead, allegiance to the methods people use to survive things as they are becomes a form of solidarity."[59] Through the reparative, "feeling good" becomes the grounds for forms of solidarity, as if tantamount to collective resistance and liberation.[60] In part, the problem with contemporary iterations of the reparative is the role that affect plays in securing rather than undoing the boundedness of the liberal subject. Through the reparative, the liberal subject is one whose guilt ensures that they feel the right way about the right things with the right people, and feel that that is enough.

This book stays with the destructive capacities of repair, attending to, but not resolving, the affective division between good and bad objects. As the shorn parts of loved and hated objects, the spoiled reminds us of what can neither be fully recuperated nor forgotten—what cannot be assessed for means of redress but cannot be dismissed as unworthy of it either. In his critique of reparation, Eng turns to forgiveness, relaying Jacques Derrida's belief that "the only thing truly worth forgiving is the unforgivable"—what lies beyond the pale, the near insurmountable, and what, for the "I" in the position of offering forgiveness, comes at an unknowable cost.[61] Forgiveness is not world-making so much as world-shattering, a gesture, unbidden, that disrupts business as usual, any sense of scale or proportion. Forgiveness, Eng writes, "cannot be tendered through an economy of equivalence, reciprocity, or commensurability."[62] While a focus on the reparative is oriented around the one who has inflicted injury on another, an engagement with forgiveness is aligned with the one who has experienced injury at the hands of another. The spoiled cannot be said to take either side in all this, nor, I think, is Eng proposing that we do so. But the spoiled, produced by repair's destruction, does bring us—if not drag us—to moments when we encounter such nonequivalence, nonreciprocity, and incommensurability. These are moments when we are met with harm and injury—our own and another's for which we might be responsible—and presented with the question of what to do next given that there is no clear way to calculate what can earn and warrant repair or forgiveness.

If processes of repair are acts of love that mitigate love's more negative, unwieldy qualities, such processes can also involve a feeling like envy. Klein defines envy as the impulse to possess a desirable object that someone else has and to "spoil it" by putting the "bad parts of the self" into it, thereby destroying it.[63] Envy is a hindrance to repair, as a feeling that can overpower guilt. It is for this reason that I am interested in envy and its modes of destruction: they hover in the vicinity of the capacity for love, ready to spoil it. To spoil an object—to enviously desire it and destroy it—is to bestow one's unwanted parts upon it as excessive, uninvited gifts, thus ruining the object for everyone. Generally, envy is discouraged and dismissed. It is, as Sianne Ngai writes, a catty, "petty," feminized feeling, morally devalued, reduced to a subject's insecurity around what they lack ("penis envy") and ressentiment.[64] Alternatively, Ngai suggests that we view envy as the expression of "an ability to recognize, and antagonistically respond to, potentially real and institutionalized forms of inequality."[65] I keep in mind how envy's destructive impulse prompts the kinds of spoilage moving throughout this book. It is a hostile feeling which, by upsetting processes of repair, draws attention to the unequal, asymmetrical division of good and bad objects, between what must be repaired and what must be forgiven. Spoilage cannot ensure repair and it does not and cannot ask for forgiveness. I look to the damage that circles within repair's orbit by handling its shorn parts. Here, artists spoil an object, enviously indulging it with all their "bad parts," and arguably, I do the same. We do so without asking for forgiveness, without the assurance and consolation of repair.

Feeling Asian and the Affects That Fit

In "United," Cathy Park Hong's opening essay in *Minor Feelings*, she describes an "imaginary" facial tic that emerged as a symptom of her depression.[66] She was sure that a tic in her right eyelid, which first appeared seven years prior as a result of a neuromuscular condition, had returned. But her husband told her he did not see it. "It was my mind threatening mutiny," she writes. "I was turning paranoid, obsessive."[67] Hong decided to seek out a therapist, specifically a Korean American one. "She'd look at me and just *know* where I was coming from," Hong was convinced.[68] After she met with one such therapist for an initial consultation, she felt "remarkably cleansed."[69]

A couple of days later, however, the therapist left Hong a voicemail saying she would not be able to take her on as a patient. Hong called the therapist repeatedly, wanting to know why, and—after a final, angry confrontation over the phone—Hong found herself grappling with what had felt unsayable. Was she turned down for the same reason she sought out this therapist in the first place? Was she sent away because she was a Korean American woman, just like her? What did it mean that Hong's appeal for recognition was met with rejection? Hong's paranoia was confirmed. Her tic might have been imagined, but what it symptomatized was not. Like other Asians, and like her tic, she lacked "presence," even for those with whom she shared a likeness.[70]

For Hong, this noncathartic failure of the therapeutic scene pointed to a set of dynamics surrounding "the self-hating Asian," a well-worn figure akin to the subject of "racist love."[71] Hong's feelings of rejection stung because she imagined this therapist would offer relief from what we could identify as the symptoms of racial melancholia.[72] Hong writes,

> Your only defense is to be hard on yourself, which becomes compulsive, and therefore a comfort, to peck yourself to death. You don't like how you look, how you sound. You think your Asian features are undefined, like God started pinching out your features and then abandoned you. You hate that there are as many Asians in the room. *Who let in all the Asians?* you rant in your head. Instead of solidarity, you feel that you are *less than* around other Asians, the boundaries of yourself no longer distinct but congealed into a horde.[73]

Anger and hatred—manifesting as acts of self-harm like pecks, imagined from on high as God's pinch—turn in on the self. Hong chips and hacks away at the self to become smaller, at the same time that she fears feeling "lesser than" and disappearing into a horde. She wants to feel singular, different from other Asians, at the same time that she does not want to feel alienated from those around her, Asian or not. For Hong, this encapsulates the condition of being Asian American, in light of the fact that, generally, Asian Americanness remains hard to define. "The paint on the Asian American label has not dried," she explains. "The term is unwieldy, cumbersome, perched awkwardly upon my being," like a facial tic no one else can see, or the scene of a nonreciprocal therapeutic encounter.[74] What pulls at Hong's right eye, what pecks and pinches, are what she calls "minor feelings." Drawing from Ngai's work on "ugly feelings," Hong describes "minor feelings" as "the racialized range of emotions that are negative, dysphoric, and therefore untelegenic, built from the sediments of everyday racial experience and the irritant of having one's perception of reality constantly questioned or dismissed."[75] These feelings emerge when what one experiences as their reality, psychically and materially, is scrutinized, questioned, and disproven, over and over again. Minor feelings run against the grain of what and how someone is supposed to feel.

While Ngai characterizes ugly feelings as noncathartic and nontherapeutic in their duration, it seems that Hong's book became quite cathartic and therapeutic, particularly for Asian American readers. Many of these readers looked to Hong for advice as if she were a therapist like the one Hong herself had pursued, rather than a poet and writer. In Clio Chang's profile of Hong in *New York Magazine*, Chang shares a series of questions readers have asked Hong since the book's release, like "What should I say to someone who says, 'Where do you come from'?" or "My mother is super-toxic . . . I don't know how to make her understand my identity as a queer person. What do you think I should do?"[76] These questions speak to the desire for art to fix and repair, and the assumption that through an aesthetic encounter, the writer and reader, the artist and audience, can be healed and made whole.

In this context, the therapeutic becomes synonymous with what feels soothing, comforting, and good, with what can lead to the right answers regarding how to have affirming, nontoxic relationships. This narrow view does not account for how therapeutic encounters can feel exhausting and bad, provoking our hostility and aggression. One need only recall the times when, upon leaving a therapist's office, one feels spent, used up, unsure of what happens next. In this book, I take issue with flattened, impoverished understandings of the therapeutic in the contemporary popular imagination, more than with actual therapeutic practices and treatments. I contend that the artists in this book do the same. Like me, they are suspicious—in a somewhat paranoid fashion—of the tranquilizing therapeutic properties attributed to "feeling Asian," and the kinds of self-possession and wholeness these feelings presume as its telos.[77]

Minor Feelings came out in 2020, and in the following years, the book became a touchstone for readers seeking to know more about Asian America—about how Asian Americans felt in the face of how others feel about them, and about the history of anti-Asian racism in the United States more broadly.[78] Many Asian Americans who read the book felt a recognition in knowing someone else felt the same way they did, and gave it a name. As Min Hyoung Song told Chang in their profile of Hong, "the affect fit."[79] Hong's writing gave others what her potential therapist could not give her. To claim "minor feelings" as one's own became healing and empowering, a means of taking back those parts of one's life that had until that point been ignored and disavowed. What had previously felt like it did not quite fit—the label, "Asian American"—now slipped on like a glove.

This is to say that while Asian Americans continue to interrogate what "Asian American" is—whether as a political identity or social demographic—it seems that Asian Americans do know what it *feels* like. In contemporary Asian American popular culture, some people and things, through their affective resonance and attunements to the world, feel Asian. To feel Asian forges relations intergenerationally and transnationally, through and across the space and time of diaspora and the differing waves of immigration and historical processes of Asian racialization. These feelings hold out the possibility that the ongoing debates around the need to properly account for the heterogeneity of "Asian American" might be resolved, not surpassed so much as held in productive tension, in difference.

To experience, express, and identify Asian feelings has become a meaningful part of contemporary Asian American culture that lets "Asian American" as a category stay diffuse, as an incoherence remade into possibility, imbued with potentiality. As Wen Liu points out, this is what makes "these excessive feelings" so efficacious: they "largely constitute the unresolved identity of Asian Americanness. They create emotional, prediscursive bonds that are hard to enunciate but can only be felt, coming together in what are understood as Asian American experiences across ethnicity and culture."[80] Liu critiques the ways that "feeling Asian American" affords "a sense of a collectivized history of racial injury, despite its categorical internal demographic and ideological heterogeneities."[81] I share this critique, except while Liu understands Hong's minor feelings to confront the "affective excess [that] challenges the authenticity and political legitimacy of one's racial injury," to my mind, Hong's work has legitimated such injury, now legible as the accumulative, banal, and everyday of minor feelings, whether in the form of a facial tic or unanswered phone calls. Hong has expanded our language regarding such feelings, and it is precisely because such minor feelings are noncathartic and minor that healing and repair become necessary, as always yet to come, just on the horizon.

Recent discussions of feeling Asian are indebted to José Esteban Muñoz's theorizations of feeling brown, as a nonidentitarian attunement to minoritarian difference, to ways of feeling different in excess of the emotionally barren whiteness of a dominant national affect and liberal forms of recognition and inclusion. When one feels brown, one can feel down—such affective difference does not only feel good.[82] Muñoz thinks alongside W. E. B. Du Bois's famous query: "How does it feel to be a problem?"[83] For Muñoz, the bad feelings of the minoritized subject are structural, shaped by exclusion from social life and material conditions that can become the grounds for minoritarian recognition, survival, and social belonging. More broadly, scholars working at the convergence of affect theory and feminist and queer theory have produced a complex vocabulary to describe the ways that feelings like depression, "feeling down," "feeling backward," and feeling out of time and place are not individual and private, confined to one's interiority, or reducible to evidence of a minoritized subject's trauma and lack.[84] Feeling Asian, like feeling brown, fits into and promises to sharpen this critical perspective.

At the same time, it seems like the critical, collectively developed perspective afforded by feeling Asian has become diluted and oversaturated all at once. It has range. To feel Asian is to never feel settled, always indeterminate: to feel Asian is to feel desire and pleasure, to feel sad, angry, and burned out, like a model minority or a perpetual foreigner. Akin to what Lauren Berlant describes as women's culture, feeling Asian has come to base itself on "the cliché and the convention" of "insider knowledge" that constitutes an "intimate public."[85] Feeling Asian, like the public intimacy of women's culture, is an "achievement" of something special: "it flourishes as a porous, affective scene of identification among strangers that promises a certain experience of belonging and provides a complex of consolation, confirmation, discipline, and discussion about how to live as an *x*"—in this case, how to live as an Asian American.[86] That is, if you know, you know, but if you do not know, you could, because feeling Asian has become relatable, as well as marketable.

I do not aim to evacuate Asian feelings of meaning or difference, but it would be a mistake to overlook how mobile and flexible they have become. Asians are "crying in H Mart," "turning red" with anger and desire, brushing up against a longing for past lives within the diaspora, and giving in to road rage.[87] As stated in the marketing copy for *Feeling Asian*, a podcast created by comedians

Youngmi Mayer and Brian Park that ran from 2019 to 2022, "feeling Asian" affords "a healthy and compassionate space for Asians, Asian Americans, and Asians in America to be themselves without feeling as if their time is a fleeting moment."[88] For Mayer and Park, feeling Asian provides "a catharsis that is, well, pretty Asian!"[89] The release of the 2022 film *Everything Everywhere All at Once*—wherein the relationships between a Chinese immigrant mother, her husband, and their queer daughter are resolved across and within the multiverse—prompted a batch of articles explaining how the film had healed its actors' and viewers' intergenerational trauma.[90] The film fueled conversations around how art "hold[s] space for trauma and offer[s] catharsis."[91] The film's quixotic multiverse offered what Michael Dango might call a "style [that] provides a fantasy of reparation," insofar as it made it possible for its audience to momentarily displace the crisis of the contemporary moment, and the crisis of Asian America, through narratives of redemption, coming out, and familial acceptance.[92] Whatever Asians feel, they are feeling Asian while doing it, and when recognized as such, it is deemed healing, not just for Asians but for other people, too.

Within the bounds of this discourse, feeling Asian might sometimes feel bad, but it can also feel restorative, as if by feeling bad, one is becoming one's true(r) self. What has previously felt inaccessible about oneself, to oneself, can now be freed and made freeing by one's ability to feel a particular way, which is to say, Asian. While the turn to racialized affect has made important interventions into nonidentitarian theorizations of difference and of minoritarian aesthetics, it has also ironically brought about a set of aesthetic expectations for healing that enable and affirm new claims to identity. These expectations run counter to Muñoz's articulations of feeling brown, wherein brownness does not affirm identity but negates it. "Brownness," he argues, "is a value through negation."[93] This negation is projected from a racist public sphere that turns brownness into a problem, but it also reflects the ways that Latinx, as an identity, has become a problem for those it is supposed to represent, across lines of racial, ethnic, class, national, and language difference. Feeling brown entails "owning the negation": owning the ways feeling brown does not fix or compensate for these problems, whether they come from a racist public sphere or from those with whom one feels in common (or not).[94] Feeling brown is a mode of recognition and belonging made possible by what it cannot resolve. We would do well to remember this when encountering Asian American cultural production with the hopes of feeling seen and healed. Rather than affirm an identity, we might own its negation instead.

Hong defines minor feelings as affective modes imperceptible to the therapeutic encounter, and yet what feels minor has now veered into the major. To enter into the difficulty of a therapeutic scene comes with the affective expectation of purification and release, and to read what hurts is to enter into a painful encounter for the sake of being healed. But even in *Minor Feelings*, Hong comes up against her own hostility—moments of psychic obstruction, resistance, and difficulty—directed inward toward herself as well as outward toward others in her line of fire.[95] These instances of aggression are not solely projections, the symptoms of a self-hating Asian in need of healing. To take a cue from D. W. Winnicott's writing on aggression, such "symptoms" can also function as a means of coming to know the world as nonretaliatory, external to oneself and beyond one's control.[96] Aggression does not dissolve distinctions between what is the self and what is not. It shapes them. Aggression presents the opportunity to figure out what we want "feeling Asian" to do in our relations with other people, with objects external to the self. It pushes us to consider what we construct *and* destroy in our affective claims to and about Asian Americanness, through the racial injuries that have come to define it as such, as well as through the processes of repair that we hope might heal them and let us feel better.

It cannot be assumed that feeling Asian is in and of itself liberatory and resistant, paving the way for a good, healing relation to the self as Asian American. I do not negate the importance of certain kinds of recognition and relation (and pleasure) that feeling Asian affords. Yet I remain cautious and skeptical of the idea that feeling Asian is an act of self-healing, and hold back from idealizing the appearance of this feeling, in its various guises, within Asian American cultural production. In doing so, I align myself with scholars such as Kelly Chung, Vivian Huang, Christina León, Lilian Mengesha, Lakshmi Padmanabhan, Tina Post, and Xine Yao, whose rich theorizations of inaction, inscrutability, refusal, opacity, the deadpan, and disaffection within performance, literature, art, and film show how such suspicion and wariness harbor neither a disavowal of feeling (Asian) nor a rejection of the social.[97] For these scholars, and for myself, what is otherwise deemed a negative turn away from relation offers a means of critiquing the demands placed on minoritized subjects to make themselves sympathetic, expressive, and transparent through the authenticity of biographical detail, proper displays of affect, and productive, legible forms of sociality.

A therapeutic encounter might provoke our aggression; it might be quite "irksome."[98] This is not because we are doomed to feel terrible forever or because therapy does not work (that would be sad news for us all), but because the therapeutic encounter, whether in culture or in the clinic, cannot ensure that we will come to feel "remarkably cleansed," as if this were the primary motive of our lives, the stories we tell, and our construction, destruction, and division of objects we love and hate. Asian feelings should not be the only aim, desire, and capacity of and for Asian American cultural production. The artists in this book do not hold out for such feelings as a cleanse or a cure; they know that processes of repair, like learning, and like analysis, are wayward and "interminable."[99]

The Bitter Therapeutics of Asian America, in the Classroom and Elsewhere

This book proceeds from the assertion that the desire for "narrative plenitude," for more Asian American stories and representations, has spoiled.[100] In the post-1965 era of Asian racialization, in the midst of increased visibility and representation in popular culture and the institutionalization of the field of Asian American studies, we—Asian Americanist scholars, Asian American writers, critics, and artists—have spoiled and been spoiled by this desire. I do not mean we have had too much representation and that we should stop wanting more. I mean that we have put too much emphasis on the pursuit of representation—not only, per a familiar critique, as that which can afford us the cozy comforts of "feel-good entertainment," but also as that which can account for the ambivalence the term "Asian American" has provoked since its emergence in the late 1960s and '70s, whether as the grounds of a social movement, an identity, a field of study, or all of the above.[101]

Implicit in the call for plenitude is the belief that it could, in some way, make up for—or make good—a formation of "Asian American" that has been lost or fallen apart. There is a hope that a plenitude of representation, and the feelings it inspires, might restore or recover a minor form or sense of Asian Americanness, irreducible to DEI initiatives and the institutions that manage them, and immune to the model minority pursuit of capital.[102] But what if the restoration and recovery of "Asian American" as an ideal—as the good, right, and minor—is not possible? How has "Asian American" become damaged, not just at the hands of others, but also because of our own repeated attempts to repair it, protect it, and preserve it?

Negative affects and uneasy feelings stick to the term "Asian American," in Asian American studies and more generally in the US cultural and political imaginary. Asian Americanness is marked by what Kandice Chuh calls a "constitutive ambivalence," which she rightly describes as by now "axiomatic."[103] Such ambivalence can be attributed to the ways that those whom the term includes shifted and grew after 1965 with the Immigration and Nationality Act, contributing to what the Pew Research Center described in 2012 as the "Rise of

Asian Americans": "the highest-income, best-educated and fastest-growing racial group in the United States."[104] As Chuh and many other Asian Americanist scholars remind us, declaring that Asian Americans are on the "rise" as the model minority overlooks how globalization, wars between the United States and Asian nations, and post-1965 immigration policies prioritizing familial relationships and educated or skilled migrants have contributed to the uneven growth and transformation of the Asian American population.[105]

The model minority is not a role afforded to all Asian Americans. Yet those who can (quite literally) afford it "have enthusiastically identified *as* the model minority," as "active agents of racial capitalism and the U.S. nation," Chuh writes.[106] This has unsettled a version of Asian American studies organized around Asian American subjects as historically minor and marginalized; it has made Asian American studies ambivalent about its own project. To point this out is not to make any claim about historical or contemporary Asian American experiences of racial discrimination and violence. Rather, with Chuh, I am contending with the contradictions that allow and compel some Asian Americans to strategically "identif[y] as a racial minority in order to further majoritarian ends"—by claiming, for instance, that affirmative action policies are discriminatory toward Asian American students.[107] Under these circumstances, we would do well to realize that our critical, political investments in a particular notion of Asian Americanness—one fixedly oriented toward the minor and marginalized—have, over time, spoiled.

In efforts to position Asian American studies decidedly not on the side of the complicit, assimilated model minority, Asian Americanist scholars have turned to the model minority's ostensible opposite, which Viet Thanh Nguyen, Susan Koshy, and Christopher Lee refer to as, respectively, "the bad subject," "the resistant Asian American subject," and the "ideal critical subject."[108] These "bad," "resistant," and "critical" Asian American subjects have allowed Asian American studies to pursue forms and feelings of "Asian American" that are liberatory, antiassimilative, and anti-imperialist. Like Nguyen, Koshy, and Lee, I am skeptical of the extent to which the substitution of one subject for another can preserve—or unspoil—Asian American studies, let alone the politics of one racial group as a whole. The spoiled consists of what has been disowned, cut, and cast out in reparative processes of alteration, if not quite substitution. It does not offer up a better Asian American subject to be represented in politics and popular culture or centered in Asian American studies. Instead, the spoiled is that which has been disposed of in efforts to locate and construct this idealized subject.[109] In continuing to think with Chuh, the spoiled is the stuff of "subject-less discourse," but insofar as it betrays the desire for Asian American subjecthood—by which I mean that it discloses that desire to then double cross it.[110]

I propose that we take up the spoils of Asian Americanness and processes of Asian racialization to grapple with what about "Asian American" has deviated from our idealizations of the term's formation and then been shorn away. We might have a better idea of what we want "Asian American" to do for us in the present once we acknowledge that the term must continue to bear our negativity, our capacity for aggression and destruction, especially in our attempts to repair it. I am not asking if we have done irreversible damage to the ideals of love, solidarity, and collectivity that "Asian American" has been asked to hold. Damage has already been done. My question is: Now what? What happens when we start from the supposition that in the pursuit of our ideals, we risk ruining them—and ourselves and others—in the process? In other words, what else becomes possible when we acknowledge that what we wreck cannot be fixed, and instead takes other different, hostile forms? To handle the spoiled is to confront the misalignments, frustrations, and annoyances that come from repeated, by now familiar, confrontations with the impasses that "Asian American" creates, as an identitarian category and the grounds of a field.

I hope my approach to thinking with the artists in this book makes clear how the cruel notion of rightness—of the right subject or right object of study—is itself deserving of our hostility and destruction. These artists are not exemplary figures who consistently identify themselves or their work as Asian American; they are not selected because they encapsulate what is happening within contemporary Asian American art. They are not ideal subjects of Asian America, they are spoiled ones. Their work is not always "about" Asian Americanness in ways that assume a transparent relation between form and identitarian categories of difference, but they do intrude upon that relation and tamper with it.[111] Susette Min writes that the naming of Asian American art as a means of institutional recognition and formal inclusion "threatens to fix Asian American art as a site of reconciliation and containment, a filter and point of entry for select artists to enter into the art market or an exhaustive repository that absorbs those artists who are on the threshold of fading into obscurity."[112] These artists do not reject the naming of their work as "Asian American," nor do they dissociate themselves from an Asian American identity and the communities forged through it. Instead, they critically navigate the ways that naming oneself and one's art as such can affect the curation, acquisition, circulation, and interpretation of one's work within various institutional spaces. They know that in the era of neoliberal multiculturalism, representations of "feeling Asian" have led to greater Asian American visibility, and that this has affected how the art world, the publishing and music industries, and the academy encounter and engage with their work. This is not an individual issue of an artist "selling out" or compromising their principles, but a structural one that speaks to the ways artists of color are habitually required to promote their work by identifying themselves, in some way, within it and alongside it.

I understand these artists' work in the context of the broader history of Asian American art—not to neatly lump all of the artists together as descendants of a singular lineage but to trace the ways their work either follows or interrupts previous aesthetic expectations, political demands, and institutional constraints that have shaped the emergence of what can be loosely be called Asian American art. Members of the Asian American community arts movement in the late 1960s and '70s viewed their art as a form of radical resistance from the margins of mainstream culture that shed light on the history and lived experience of Asian American communities in pursuit of recognition and social change.[113] The artists who followed—particularly the Generation X cohort that Min Hyoung Song calls "the children of 1965"—were typically understood to be less burdened than their predecessors by the need to represent a collective Asian American identity, thus having more freedom to experiment in their practice.[114] In the wake of 1965, and during the 1990s, which saw a surge in the production and celebration of Asian American fiction, these artists showed their work in community spaces, but they also began to receive wider recognition once their work entered gallery and museum spaces, particularly in the context of race- or ethnic-specific group exhibitions.[115] For this generation of artists, success has resulted in tenured faculty positions at universities, bringing the art world and the academy together, such that the structural precarities of one promise to offset the structural precarities of the other.

The younger millennial generation of artists who are the main (but not only) focus of this book have also interfaced with institutions. While making their work, they navigate their entanglement with institutional spaces like museums, galleries, art schools with prestigious MFA programs, and universities with Asian American studies initiatives, institutes, programs, or departments. Often, they are students under the guidance and mentorship of artists from previous generations—a relationship that is formalized and partially shaped by the institutions both of them move through. The former generation came to know their work as Asian American once they had come into contact with institutions.[116] Alternately, these artists, from early on in their careers, have had to learn to move through the terms and conditions of their visibility and inclusion within these spaces, which often come with the expectation that to some extent, they will become familiar with Asian American studies scholarship as that which shapes the ways their work will be read, and how it will be received. Given the growing presence of Asian American studies on college campuses across the United States, this means finding their way through a field that, as Mark Chiang reminds us, has become a site of cultural capital and thus a source of authenticity, legibility, and stability for scholars and artists alike.[117]

These variations of (post-)post-1965 generational differences are not meant to be prescriptive or diagnostic, let alone accusatory. No generation is better than another, or capable of better, more politically radical or meaningful art. However, it is worth noting that a younger generation of Asian Americans (of which, to be clear, I am a part) has come to know itself as Asian American via the marked presence of Asian American representation in popular culture, the institutionalization of Asian American art and Asian American studies, and what the term "Asian American" has become. These artists and I are spoiled insofar as we have come of age in a moment when "narrative plenitude" has presented itself as a possibility and could, in turn, become a source of our embarrassment, if not ire. I write this book from this position, which is to say, *after* the acknowledgment of Asian American ambivalence, after the damage has been done and the question of what happens next remains as open as an oozing wound, as indefinite as the term of a tantrum.

Alongside Eng and Han's case studies of Asian American students is the hope that Asian American studies can offer a Winnicottian "holding environment" able to address and alleviate pain by reflecting the growing population of Asian American students on US college campuses.[118] This perspective has been instrumental to the fight for Asian American studies programs, course offerings, and faculty at universities throughout the United States.[119] Nor is it unfounded: students do look to courses in Asian American studies in search of a vital kind of recognition and readiness to learn, as I did, and this does speak to the necessity of Asian American studies in the classroom. Yet it is often overlooked that, as Eng and Han write, a holding environment does not just validate and maintain one's sense of self but also facilitates the emergence of a self that can "tolerate paradoxes—an ability to listen, to play, and to (be)hold multiple narratives not only for their similarities but also their contradictions."[120] It is these paradoxes and contradictions that have been glossed over and consolidated into a singular narrative of healing the self and making it whole, present not only in the classroom but also in popular culture.

Courses in Asian American studies, as well as ethnic studies, gender and sexuality studies, and queer studies, are a vital resource for students. As a student,

I eagerly threw myself into class readings and discussions, ready to learn something new, sometimes in relation to myself, and I would not begrudge that experience to others. But that experience was not wholly one of validation—it was not all warm and fuzzy feelings. It also held moments of antagonism and defensiveness, of being jolted out of my ideas about the world and my place in it. In these moments, the classroom can and does provoke hostility and aggression, and we should not merely attribute this to irresolvable generational differences and sensitivities. We should take it as a sign that sometimes the recognition afforded in the classroom cannot always feel good in the way we anticipate and imagine. The classroom, including the Asian American studies classroom, cannot and should not guarantee that we will feel grounded and affirmed, because sometimes we will walk away unmoored, but—crucially and hopefully—with the feeling that there is more to learn.

Trying to uphold this impossible guarantee, both in and outside the classroom, often relies on autobiography and its confessional modes as sources of catharsis and relief. As Michel Foucault tells us, confession is not a practice of freedom, but a coercive effect of power that "Western man" as a "confessing animal" believes can uncover the truth of the self, as a secret to set free.[121] While Foucault primarily considers the function of confession within older forms of disciplinary society and its institutions, contemporary forms of autobiography—often made legible through identitarian categories—have altered the confessional models he examines and the selves produced therein. As Rey Chow writes, confession is experiencing a "prolific, mediatized afterlife" in which twenty-first-century subjects readily and gladly offer their selves to a broad public on the internet and elsewhere.[122] "If giving an account of oneself (to the authorities) in Foucault's narrative is synonymous with self-devaluation and self-destruction," Chow writes, "in late capitalist society giving an account of oneself (in public) promises rather a way *out of* self-devaluation and self-destruction."[123] The confessing self becomes a "*complainant*" ready to share the secrets of their injury, in the hope it will be recognized by another. This recognition, if achieved, opens up "a passage to freedom" that we could also think of as healing, insofar as the complainant can now reclaim and empower themself.[124] Crucially, as Chow makes clear, the complainant's presentation of grievance—their act of "voicing bitterness"—is an entrepreneurial endeavor that takes the guise of a therapeutic one.[125] The process draws value from experiences of devaluation by repackaging them into neoliberal narratives of self-growth as self-optimization.

Chow's exemplary complainants are two women: Princess Diana and Oprah. The complainant who makes it her business to give an account of her injury in order to heal is a woman who utters, as Berlant calls it, the "female complaint."[126] While Chow speaks of confession as voicing bitterness, Berlant notes that "in the contemporary world of U.S. women's culture the bitter vigilance of the intimately disappointed takes up a lot of space."[127] Bitterness becomes the spoiled sensation of femininity—watchful and self-referential, vengeful and envious—made to submit to a hostile world. For Berlant, the intimate public of women's culture is not grounded in the individual confession of the self, but in the presumption of a shared, collective experience of disappointment. Ultimately, though, Chow's theory of confession and Berlant's understanding of the intimate public's shared story describe two dimensions of the same therapeutic encounter in which the sharing of grievance produces a healing site of belonging. Together, they speak to the therapeutic properties of feeling Asian within Asian American culture, where the intimacies granted by the comforts of narrative and genre convention are cathartic and, as such, good (unfinished) business.

The burden of the therapeutic—as curative and lucrative—has been placed on fields like Asian American studies, as well as critical race and ethnic studies and gender and sexuality studies, which are, at times, included within the university as a corrective to bias, a form of sensitivity training, or a contingency plan that will make the university more diverse, equitable, and inclusive. These fields, as Chow writes, are meant to rehearse a "*reparative* logic whereby some kinds of knowledge carry the service function of delivering (or at least bringing us closer to) social justice and whose presence supposedly attests to a neoliberal academy's compassion, atonement, and capacity for 'self-culpabilization.'"[128] Here, the reparative adheres to a moralizing narrative about becoming better and feeling better, too. By the conventions of this narrative, a field like Asian American studies should shore up and reflect a clear image of the Asian American subject, and proffer a narrative of the university and its progress.

The pursuit of an ideal can guide us to the classroom. However, as Muñoz writes, the task of the teacher of minoritarian knowledge might be to "playfully call attention to the sense of abandonment that shadows that endeavor."[129] Pedagogy is founded on the "failure and incompleteness" of the teacher who must remain accountable to the student in light of a spoiled ideal.[130] The artists here develop a pedagogy that can spill out in bitterness, yet in doing so, they teach us that we can and should desire more from our encounters with Asian American studies and Asian American culture than cathartic confession.

Irritable Bodies, Deidealized and Deformed

To take up the spoiled involves handling the matter of the Asiatic body, which in the United States has been predominantly perceived as and associated with the ethnically Chinese body. This body is viewed as ornamental and inorganic, like Afong Moy, the "Chinese Lady" exhibited throughout the United States in the early nineteenth century.[131] It is diseased and contagious, like the figures of the predatory Chinese bachelor and Chinese prostitute that threatened to seep out of the depraved, unhygienic opium dens of Chinatowns in the nineteenth and twentieth centuries.[132] It is a viral body, imagined as the carrier of COVID-19 and other public health threats that make their way into the United States and infect its healthy citizen subjects. It is a body impervious to pain; it is inscrutable, submissive, alien, and robotic with nimble parts, like the cheap migrant laborers arriving throughout the nineteenth and twentieth centuries, the communist spy during the Cold War, but also the self-sufficient model minority of the latter half of the twentieth century into the present.[133] It is also the provenance of the perverse, the femininized, the queer, the emasculated, the bottom, where, as Richard Fung writes, "Asian and anus are conflated," or where the Asiatic body becomes a hyper(hetero)sexualized fetish object of white fantasy and indulgence.[134]

The artists here take up these various iterations of the Asiatic body—bound to East Asianness and Chineseness—to see what can be made with these lasting wounds. They fume and seethe within the aesthetic, political, material incoherence between bodies and things, subjects and objects. They do not rescue the Asiatic body from the harms of history on behalf of an Asian American subject in need of healing. They are invested in what forms injury makes for a subject marked by difference. Such investments were on display in the *Wonder Women* exhibition, where the proliferation of the Asian American woman's figure became something that felt (more than it actually looked) vulgar, excessive, and wasteful rather than respectable, modest, and useful. Perhaps, then, the figures in Yin's *Dreaming Host* and Lek's *Napping* are not just portraits of rest as resistance and self-care, but also portraits of irritable figures full, taut, and glutted. They are not quite comfortable and content, so much as overdone, bursting at the seams, with hostility brewing just underneath a seemingly serene surface.

I am guided by this affective, embodied sense of irritation. What has drawn me to write about the artists in this book is not how they refuse a good Asian American politics or the moral authority of cathartic autobiographical narratives of healing and repair, but how they *irritate* them. Irritation is an inflammatory, durational feeling where the boundaries of the body start to blur, when physical and psychic states become difficult to separate from each other. It can feel like a fragile, edgy temper, but also like a skin rash or sunburn. The irritability of the spoiled belies the self's affectability. When someone or something is irritated, it cannot masquerade as unbothered. Something on the surface of the body or in one's disposition gives it away. As Ngai writes, to be irritable is to be perceived as rash and careless, either as too sensitive or not sensitive enough.[135] Following this (il)logic, the chapters of this book attend to what is irritating about its objects of study. Indeed, they, or I, might irritate you.

Guided by the sensation of irritation, I am in keeping with the methods of queer studies scholars working on aesthetic form who—as Kadji Amin, Amber Musser, and Roy Pérez write—place "unlikely" objects in relation "to think together concepts and works of art that might appear inconsonant according to the strictures of historical period, genre, medium, or perceived cultural context, but whose relevance and discursive imbrication become visible through the activity of the queer critic."[136] Amin, Musser, and Pérez speak to many of us who have long followed Sedgwick's suggestion that "ideally life, loves, and ideas might then sit freely, for a while, on the palm of the open hand."[137] The image Sedgwick offers is a tactile one. For her, touching people and things, from friends to textiles, attune us to "the middle ranges of agency," where we make sense of our relations through who and what resists or softens, gives or takes.[138] Such queer methods are in line with Sedgwick's articulations of reparative reading, wherein "life, loves, and ideas" are incommensurable: there are no equivalences, no symmetrical relations. Instead, there are "strange affinities" between varying forms of difference.[139] In my chapters, performance, music, poetry, literature, film, and visual art are placed beside each other to incite aggravating moments of friction and heat, as well as frigidity and coldness. People and things repel each other, bump up against each other, rub each other the wrong way, bringing out the other's hostility as an invitation and challenge to respond, to engage, even if it is annoying and tedious to do so. I am aware of how I, as the author, am present throughout the text, as spoiled as the objects with which I engage. My hand that holds the objects in this book, like the hand of Ouyang's *Kicked Madonna* and the hand in Lek's paintings, cannot be trusted to always stay open. At times, it might want to hold onto its objects too closely, so much so that it may destroy them. My readings inhabit that moment between the open hand and a closed fist.

Although irritation is felt in and on one's own body, it is structural, fleshing out relations of power and producing "theories in the flesh."[140] Irritation is a resource for theorizing, able to signal and hold varying embodied psychic contradictions and material differences that neither cede to abstract universalist theories of personhood nor guarantee narratives of repair in the face of power. For Ngai, irritability presents the problem of an excess or deficiency of anger, particularly in the face of racist violence. Like envy, it is disproportionate to the social scene where it emerges. As a misfitting feeling, irritation makes possible a critique of how minoritized subjects are expected to respond and react to the harm they endure. "In other words," Ngai writes, "it is irritation's radical inadequacy—its stubborn 'offishness' or incommensurateness with respect to objects . . . —that calls attention to a symbolic violence in the principle of commensurability itself, when there is an underlying assumption that an appropriate emotional response to racist violence exists, and that the burden lies on the racialized subject to produce that appropriate response legibly, unambiguously, and immediately."[141] Irritation troubles the notion that in the face of racist violence, there is a right response commensurable to the hurt, pain, and damage inflicted. This does not mean that there is no escape or relief from violence. Rather, the "offishness" of irritation makes palpable how racist violence is followed by another kind of violence, borne from the expectation that there could possibly be an appropriate and proportionate response to such violence—as if there were a way to measure the pain, harm, and injury caused, and that once things are even, such violence will be absolved, forgotten, or irrelevant. We might say that by valorizing Asian American cultural objects for being soothing, as opposed to irritating, we slide into the assumption that they provide that right response to injury, thus enabling adequate processes of redress and repair. Therefore, throughout these chapters, I remain committed to the incommensurability of the irritable and how it chafes, nags, tugs, and rubs raw.

To spoil is to deidealize and deform. These two processes organize the progression of chapters in this book. Through these processes, the spoiled inflames the line between the sensible and the nonsensible—between the sensus communis of a dominant social order as described by Jacques Rancière,[142] and what Chuh calls "illiberal, uncommon sensibilities" disavowed and excluded from that social order, barred from the realm of reason or good taste, proprietary to the idealized, universal, modern liberal subject.[143] The first two chapters focus on deidealizations of the Asian American subject's relatability, healing, and care. In the wake of this deidealization, the subject of the remaining two chapters is not one of preservation but of deformation; here, form does not disappear or become formless, but it does shift into something unsettling and aggressively unfamiliar. Taking all four chapters together, the rest of this book proceeds from the figure, as seen in the work included in the *Wonder Women* exhibition, then moves to its gradual disfigurement and decomposition that necessitate a different kind of reading, another kind of relating.

Deidealization is the process of relinquishing one's fantasies of control and omnipotence. For Kadji Amin, "deidealization is not the wholesale destruction of cherished ideals, but a form of the reparative that acknowledges messiness and damage."[144] Amin critiques, in particular, the valorization of deviance in queer studies and argues for "spoilage of the ideal": the ideal objects of study, but also the frictionless relations and politics we want these same objects to activate and afford.[145] The artists here take up forms of hostility in order to account for the nonideal violence, harm, and vulnerability of "living with damage in a damaged world."[146] They spoil our ideals and our desire for a good politics, as well as for a contained, affirmed sense of self. After all, as Heather Love notes, some ideals are "ripe for spoiling."[147]

The first chapter, "Staying In," engages with the work of poet and writer Ocean Vuong, singer-songwriter Mitski, and the earlier works of artist Patty Chang, which direct us toward autoerotic forms of asociality through the act of staying in. Staying in spoils the ideality of sociality and world-making often espoused in scholarship on the intimacies of queer performance and the publics they make possible. By disidentifying with the stereotype of the awkward Asian American recluse, Vuong's, Mitski's, and Chang's acts of staying in redraw the boundaries of what constitutes desirable, legible forms of sociality. Rather than reduce these acts to relatable lessons on self-care, I argue that the notable earnestness of their work discloses an awkward truth: the need to relate to other people in spite of oneself can be perversely embarrassing.

In the second chapter, "Using Quotations," artist Wu Tsang pushes relatability to the extreme in her performance practice of "full body quotation," wherein she recites the speech others, as an embodied practice of taking and giving. By turning the words of others into material for her own performance, Tsang's work betrays idealized notions of reciprocity and equivalent exchange. Such notions are often invoked not only with respect to our relationships with other people, but also to our scholarship and aesthetic practices—and Tsang's determination to flout them has provoked discussion, if not outright accusations, of appropriation. Without denying or dismissing such charges, I understand Tsang's practice of full body quotation to mine the uneasy, destructive dynamics of encounter, of using people and being open to being used by them too, through the transmission and contamination of quotation.

While the first two chapters deidealize the self-possessed Asian American subject, the next two are guided by the dispossessed, by the contaminated or contaminating Asiatic body—not removed from the social but in the wake of trying to stay committed to it. I follow Brent Hayes Edwards's reading of Georges Bataille, who defines "*informe*" as that which undoes binary oppositions between categories and classifications of difference, like form and formlessness, or form and matter.[148] *Informe*, Edwards writes, is the name given to "what is allowed no *right* to form."[149] As such, it can be what Kyla Wazana Tompkins calls "crude."[150] *Informe* "insults what it designates, brings it down, by rudely asserting that everything has a form *but you*," Edwards writes.[151] *Informe* is "vulgar," "crass," "unrefined or uncivilized," "rough, rude, and blunt."[152] It singles you out by calling you out. These remaining chapters pursue such moments of insult.

The third chapter, "Cold Leftovers," moves toward the Asiatic body's undoing as it is consumed, decomposes, lets go, and gives up. I revisit David Henry Hwang's 1988 play *M. Butterfly* as a canonical object of study that, while seeming to have gone cold over time, offers a materialization of Asiatic femininity via skin cold to the touch. Alongside the play, scholar and filmmaker Mila Zuo's 2016 short film *Carnal Orient* depicts Asiatic femininity as food unfit for consumption, the spoils of cold leftovers. Meanwhile, in her installation, performance, and video work with gelatin, artist Alison Kuo sacrifices herself to the goopy substance, making herself fit for consumption through its touch, thereby giving herself up to waste.

In the last chapter, "Injured Enough," artists TJ Shin and Jes Fan experiment with what the Asiatic body creates in its injury. Shin and Fan damage objects and nonhuman forms of life rendered analogous to the Asiatic body through processes of contamination, cutting, casting, and injection. They do not try to evoke sympathy by showing the Asiatic body in pain; instead, they make use of the fact that the recognizability of Asian American injury depends on such injury's analogous relation and comparability to the injury of racialized others. Their work thus interrogates what is understood in Asian American studies and in Asian American politics as a dependence on others, a dependence that is at times spoiled because of how it can lead to a neediness that encroaches upon others.

This book begins with bitterness, and it ends with the sweetness of Julie Tolentino's durational performance *HONEY*. Over the course of several hours, Tolentino eats honey fed to her by her collaborator and lover, Stosh Fila, also known as Pigpen. The performance waffles between a scene of nourishment and one of spoilage, between what the body needs, what the body wants, and what the body can endure. The performance presents a scene of love constituted by the harm of honey, a material excess that envelops Tolentino's body, capacity, appetite, and desire. Between Tolentino and Pigpen, the threshold of care is traced and transgressed by the drip of honey into Tolentino's mouth.

Throughout this book, the spoiled does not refuse repair. The spoiled loosens fixations on affirmation and wholeness—it is concerned with what processes of repair can damage and leave behind. The spoiled is the hard, bitter pill to swallow (or chew or choke on). In a moment of spoilage, we must ask: What becomes possible in our relation to another once we know that we are capable not only of experiencing harm at the hands of another, but also of causing such harm ourselves? What might be destructive about our desires for repair, healing, and care, and what does such destruction make and leave for us to find? This book invites you to scavenge among the spoils of such destruction. These spoils are what I hold in my hand, now extended out to you.

1. STAYING IN
THE AUTOEROTICISM OF ASIAN AMERICAN ASOCIALITY, IN EARNEST

Nobody fucks me like me.—Mitski, "Lonesome Love" (2018)

I taste my mouth the most & what a blessing.—Ocean Vuong, "Beautiful Short Loser" (2022)

On a weekend night, prompted by a text message from a friend, or unprompted on any other night of the week, you might ask the question, "Should I stay in or go out?" and sometimes, you decide it is better to stay in. The seemingly antisocial act of staying in, whether for a night or a weekend, can reconstellate one's relation to others, from the momentary position of being alone, as *a*social. In the music video for her song "Your Best American Girl" (2016), singer-songwriter Mitski Miyawaki, known as just Mitski, stays in, in a particular way.[1] The video cuts back and forth between Mitski and the white all-American boy she serenades. The boy coyly looks into the camera, pale skin glowing. Under his gaze, Mitski smiles. As the boy winks and waves, Mitski responds with a timid wave of her own. The exchange is interrupted when a white woman—an all-American girl—comes into view. She glares as she territorially drapes her arms around the boy. The boy turns to her, leaning in and holding her chin for a kiss, as Mitski looks on with a fading smile. "Don't wait for me / I can't come," Mitski sings, as she mirrors their gestures, turning to face her hand alone.

When the song's chorus rumbles in, overwhelming the verse preceding it, Mitski's other hand shoots into the air before trailing down her hair and face to cradle her chin, which she guides to kiss the open palm of her hand. The couple greedily kiss each other's faces and bodies. Mitski nibbles her own wrist, licks her palm, kisses and sucks her fingers, grabs and holds her body close. The couple shares their saliva, strung between their lips and tongues, while Mitski shares her saliva with her skin. Although Mitski sings that she cannot come—not with this all-American boy—she comes in other ways. There are other pleasures to be had, now that no one is looking. In the chorus, Mitski admits, "You're an all-American boy / I guess I couldn't help trying to be your best American girl."[2] Initially she tries, but Mitski is not his girl, and there is no all-American boy she wants to claim. "Your" best American girl becomes "my," which is to say, mine. The boy she addresses was never in the picture; he never entered the same frame as her. By the second verse, when she sings, "You're the one / you're all I ever wanted / I think I'll regret this," she addresses herself, as her own object of desire, in spite of herself.

In "Your Best American Girl," Mitski's body reaches toward the touch of her hand with frustrated longing. In the video, she becomes the solo artist and singer-songwriter who insists on collapsing distinctions between self-disclosure and self-involvement. Mitski conflates the structure of a solo performance with the solitary experience of being an Asian American woman singer-songwriter in the indie music scene of the 2010s, where the confessional voices of white masculinized, misunderstood genius, and of white feminized, vulnerable artistry, took precedence over that of a supposedly timid, quiet Asian American woman.[3] For Mitski, to be an Asian American woman is to not be the best or all that American, and to be an Asian American singer-songwriter is to confound what a singer-songwriter promises to reveal in her singularity. Mitski cultivates a relation to her aloneness, ill-fitted to fantasies of meaningful intimacy tethered to the white heterosexual couple form. For Mitski, staying in is not a way of coping with what she lacks so much as it is a way of keeping what she already has to herself.

Staying in, keeping to one's self, could be read as selfish. It could also be claimed as a form of self-care. To my mind, staying in is self-care at its limit, at the limit of what we deem necessary as opposed to gratuitous, a little dramatic and extreme. Staying in draws attention to what can feel spoiled about practices of self-care: one might take up a lot of time and space, annoy someone, piss someone off, cancel plans, and generally be an unreliable flake. Staying in has us confront how self-care disrupts the social, especially when practices of self-care become an inconvenience for other people. Staying in is not just about the nurturance of the self for the sake of protection and preservation. Along with staying in comes the hostility surging from within the unclear distinctions between affirmation and assertion, between taking care of oneself and only thinking about oneself.

This chapter considers the greedy, hungry, destructive qualities of staying in, evident in the way Mitski devours herself, revealing the aggression of an appetite that yields what I sense as an embarrassing kind of autoeroticism verging on autocannibalism. In "Your Best American Girl," Mitski pulls down one of her sleeves to expose more of her skin, she frowns with focus while stroking her hair, moving it away from her face. These are earnest gestures of self-love, but they are also near stifling gestures that threaten to overwhelm the bounds of the subject with its desire for itself. The earnestness of Mitksi's performance that can make us self-conscious—embarrassed to watch—is integral to the autoerotic act of staying in.

For poet and writer Ocean Vuong, staying in also involves an earnest relation to his hand and playing alone. In his poem "Ode to Masturbation" (2016), masturbation is a solo act: a performance of the self as an ode to the self. An ode, which Anahid Nersessian describes as "sweet talk," is about whom the ode is for, but it also says something about the person who wrote it.[4] In Vuong's ode, both are one and the same. During a reading given in 2016, Vuong tells his audience that his ode to masturbation is for others, too. He says, "I often think of other bodies and what it means for other bodies to empower themselves, and sometimes the only control that we have is the control and the power of self-pleasure and self-joy, which is inexhaustible."[5] He pauses, then adds, "And is free."[6] He smiles and waits as his audience laughs, snaps, and cheers for him, for themselves, and their shared proclivities. In Vuong's ode, a private preoccupation with masturbation becomes a way of relating to others, where his body and "other bodies" collide via the "self-pleasure" and "self-joy" that are sometimes all "we" have. In the same way that Mitski's possessive pronouns bleed into one another, with "your" lips becoming "my" hand, Vuong's "other bodies" slide into a "we," who steadily guide his and our hand.

To be in awe of "the control and the power of self-pleasure and self-joy" that comes with something as ordinary as masturbation, and to express that awe in the form of an ode, can feel sort of embarrassing, at least for me (who is definitively neither a singer-songwriter nor a poet). This is not because masturbation is embarrassing, but because such hushed reverence for masturbation, and by association for one's self, is expressed so earnestly.[7] I do not mean Vuong is gravely serious and without humor. He knows that what he is saying is funny, and he welcomes the rowdy response from the audience. Vuong is sincere in the way he lays his reverence on too thick, because to do something in earnest is to do something, like masturbate, like read a poem, with a strong commitment in and to excess. Like Mitski's encounter with her hand, Vuong's relation to his hand, as "all you have / to hold / yourself to this / world" can feel like an affront to more modest sensibilities.[8] When your hand, in the act of masturbation, is all you have to hold yourself to the world, the self and the world converge: the self swells and inflates to worldly proportions, while the world gets a little smaller in order to fit into the palm of your hand.[9] This might offer a humble—reparative—means of inhabiting and finding pleasure within an inhospitable world. Yet endowing your hand with such "control and . . . power" permits a playfully narcissistic way of inhabiting a world, too, instating the self as the world through writing as an autoerotic act, where the need for satisfaction derived from your own body (and writing) becomes indistinguishable from the need for nourishment.[10]

If, for Sigmund Freud, the childish behavior of thumb-sucking exemplifies the autoerotic act, Mitski's kissing of her hand and the sucking of her fingers can be autoerotic, too.[11] However, rather than interpret these autoerotic acts as pathological attempts at fortifying one's childish fantasies of omnipotence, I approach Mitski's and Vuong's autoerotic acts, as well as those in the earlier works of the artist Patty Chang, as attempts at loving one's self, which, in their embarrassing earnestness, interrupt the consolidation of the self—both theirs and ours.[12] Autoeroticism, as the manifestation of narcissism, is not solely a self-absorption that isolates the self and excludes others. This is not because a narcissist would not have it so, but because such isolating self-absorption is not entirely possible. Narcissism's hostility comes out of the obstructed expression of what Adam Phillips by way of Serge Viderman describes as the "the tyranny of [the narcissist's] need for other people."[13] The tyranny of that need, in Mitski's and Vuong's work, is the tyranny of earnestness.

Calling Mitski's, Vuong's, and Chang's work narcissistic could sound like I am making an accusation or a negative judgment. It could also sound like I am saying narcissism is something to reclaim and embrace. I do neither, holding back from the ways that narcissism, as Phillips writes, "is always keenly moralized," determining which kinds of self-love are deemed acceptable and which are not—"what we should value, what forms of exchange we should aspire to . . . what, ideally, we should be giving our attention to."[14] I take seriously—which is to say, earnestly—how narcissism presents a problem for such moralizing tendencies as well as for what we imagine to be ideal types of exchange, and the dictates of sociability therein, which would demand a self that is modest, and in moderation, with the right appetite for one's self and others.

Staying in is not a withdrawal from a world. It is the spoiling of our idealizations of the world and of world-making practices through the attempt to overtake it with one's desire. From the hand of Cato Ouyang's *Kicked Madonna*, I follow the hands of Mitski, Vuong, and Chang to trace the act of staying in as a mode of Asian American asociality. Staying in is not a lonely thing to do. One can stay in at home, but one can also stay in at a show, at a party, or on social media. One can be surrounded by acquaintances or a lover, and still stay in. Staying in is a means of navigating the liberal mandate impressed upon minoritized subjects to make themselves relatable. It gives form to fraught feelings that show themselves around and in social life and the compulsory forms of sociability that go along with them, particularly for Asian American subjects, who have been racially figured as a problem for and of sociality. Akin to the queer female diasporic subject who, as Gayatri Gopinath writes, transforms and expands how we define queer diaspora by "staying put," the asocial Asian American subject enriches our understanding of what is needed from our relations with others in the deidealized world we inhabit by staying in.[15] To stay in redraws the boundaries of what constitutes the social by enacting spoiled ways of turning toward oneself that incline the self differently toward others, however antagonistically.[16]

Staying in affords a critique of relatability and compulsory sociability. I say this without overlooking how Mitski's and Vuong's work invites collective identification from their audience, readers, and fans. In addition to having a following, Mitski and Vuong have received recognition and praise. Vuong's 2019 novel, *On Earth We're Briefly Gorgeous*, was a finalist for the PEN/Faulkner Award for Fiction and was longlisted for the National Book Award for Fiction. Meanwhile, Mitski has had a growing, devoted base of fans since she started self-releasing albums in 2012, and since then her songs have gone viral on the short-video app TikTok, leading to millions of streams of her songs on audio streaming platforms. Mitski's and Vuong's popularity seems due, in part, to their perceived relatability. The embarrassing blow dealt to a viewer when watching Mitski's video for "Your Best American Girl" comes from how familiar and personal that rejection from a white boy feels. The audience's delight in Vuong's ode comes from recognizing what it means to spend "free" time alone, and ultimately, those who might bristle against such candor, I suspect, still know and partake in what Vuong is talking about.

As a singer-songwriter and a poet, and more broadly as artists of color, Mitski and Vuong are expected to assert their authenticity through the disclosure of biographical detail, prioritizing lived experience and personal history.[17] Like others, I am wary of the wielding of authenticity, or what Som-Mai Nguyen calls "blunt-force ethnic credibility."[18] For this reason, I turn away from these artists' biographies, even when they appear throughout their work, as it does for Vuong, whose writing touches on his memories of growing up as queer, as Vietnamese American, and as a refugee, as well as his relationships with his mother and father.[19] I do not disregard the importance of the personal in Mitski's and Vuong's work, but I do want to consider how their autoerotic gestures are modes of relating to the self that are distinct from giving a transparent account of the self. Their work can confuse the authority and authenticity of biography, rendering personal history an at times tedious, restrictive subject. While Mitski and Vuong might be expected to reveal something true and deep within themselves, I take note of how they disclose the self through suspended narratives of non-encounters with others: with flirtation's failure or with the act of masturbation, both of which leave them with their own hand. These non-encounters are not a consolation but an indulgence, sometimes preferred.

During the COVID-19 lockdown of 2020, staying in became a collective practice for the sake of public health. Staying in prevented the spread of disease, and held out the promise that in the future our social worlds could be the same as they once were. By staying in, there was the promise and hope that things could get back to normal, closer to the world we already knew and missed. In contrast to this view, here, staying in does not reassure the reemergence and preservation of the normal. Staying in deidealizes the supposedly normal kinds of socialities we had relied on to make a world, which privileged the able-bodied at the expense of the disabled and immunocompromised, and assumed that self-care is for the purposes of rehabilitating the self to return to productivity and business as usual. I keep this in mind to argue that staying in is not a therapeutic, ascetic, or moralizing kind of restraint and self-correction in service to routine and sameness, but the embarrassing self-extravagance of an autoerotic gesture, like getting off alone, which, for the most part, one must do in earnest, in ways that can interrupt the flow of the day and yet are a vital part of getting through it.

Relatability and Repair

Staying in puts pressure on notions of relatability, which minoritized subjects, whether as artists, writers, teachers, or otherwise, have been expected to express and display for the benefit of others. To deem something like a song or a poem relatable is contingent on the simultaneous evacuation and valorization of difference, and the reduction of difference to identitarian categories made legible in graspable, everyday scenarios. In the era of neoliberal multiculturalism, minoritized subjects bear the burden of representing and standing in for the totality of the community to which they belong.[20] As such, minoritized subjects also bear the burden of relatability. To be relatable, one must not only be legible and knowable but also accessible, and likably so. Relatability, in the contemporary moment, has become an omnipresent neologism described as a "modern peculiarity" and a "scourge."[21] In the *New York Times*, Ben Zimmer traces the use of "relate," as in, "to understand, to empathize with, to feel a connection with," to the late 1940s, particularly in literature on social work and childhood education.[22] To be relatable meant in some way to be teachable. The term "relatable" continued to appear in the second half of the twentieth century primarily in the context of education; however, in the mid-1990s, it was used in reference to the television industry, with the growing popularity of the talk show genre and its modes of confession.[23] Hosts, and sometimes their guests, had to tell a good story, and often a good story was relatable. From there, relatability spread "like an interspecies contagion."[24]

Brian Glavey points out that in its usage, relatability "often appears not as a description of an object but merely as a reflection of a subject."[25] For Marjorie Garber, it aligns with popular culture's fixation on memoir. "What is relatable is personal experience, especially when painted with a tinge of pathos and framed with a gilded border of self-help," she writes.[26] The relatable is endowed with therapeutic effects: one's reflection in the object elucidates and therefore potentially betters oneself. Yet relatability might not incite change but instead invite stasis. For, as Rebecca Mead suggests, to call an object relatable expresses the expectation that "the work itself be somehow accommodating to, or reflective of, the experience of the reader or viewer."[27] Relatability privileges the passivity of the reader or viewer in an aesthetic encounter. It becomes the responsibility of the object to accommodate whoever encounters it, waiting for themselves to be recognized—to "feel seen." What kind of relation is assumed, forged, and sought after by way of what and who is relatable? Between reader or viewer and their object? For Laura Salisbury, it is a reciprocal one, where the object encountered is wholly "present, available," immediate and transparent in its meaning and feeling, cut off from the kinds of slow, reflective work foundational to critical thinking and reading.[28] Relatability operates according to idealized symmetrical relations, to a fantasy of engagement and encounter without imbalance, discomfort, or difference.[29]

Critics and scholars began writing more frequently about relatability in the 2010s, as a common yet vague aesthetic category for evaluating and engaging with television, film, art, and literature.[30] Some find relatability deserving of our attention because it speaks to subjects underrepresented within the canon, who rarely have the opportunity to see themselves in what they view, read, or listen to in the first place.[31] For others, it is a problem precisely because it either affirms what one thinks they know about oneself—"like a selfie: a flattering confirmation of an individual's solipsism"—or presupposes and asserts its own universality to which everyone can, and therefore should, relate.[32] Difference is simultaneously harnessed and tamped down in these battling iterations of relatability. Who relatability accommodates, who is bestowed the quality of relatability, is granted visibility and legibility, but also an interiority and affective capacity others can and should feel, too. Alternatively, those who are deemed unrelatable might have an interiority or affective capacity not worth knowing at all, thus interpreted as someone else's problem, not adequately or convincingly conveyed as relevant to oneself. In this way, relatability plays an essential role in the instances of "feeling Asian" that I have described in this book's introduction, in the sense that "Asianness" becomes a feeling with which Asians and others can relate, insofar as it relates to themselves.

Relatability has presented challenges for professors teaching their students. When Garber considers the question of how to make William Shakespeare relatable to students in her classes, she takes issue with how the question assumes that Shakespeare should be made easier or simpler, catering to a student who is otherwise focused on another, perhaps more lucrative, discipline or field of study, such as those in the sciences.[33] One does not read Shakespeare for what it says about oneself. For "it's not even all about Hamlet," she writes, "much less all about *you*."[34] The classroom also becomes the anecdotal site for scholars who want to put pressure on critiques of relatability. These scholars want to consider how relatability is an aesthetic and ethical category that informs a contemporary reading practice attuned to the nuances of our encounters with cultural objects. Glavey opens his essay "Having a Coke with You Is Even More Fun Than Ideology Critique" with an anecdote about an English course he taught on "the poetics of oversharing."[35] In one class, he assigned midcentury New York School poet Frank O'Hara's poem "Homosexuality"; however, in a discussion post, one of his students introduced the rest of her peers to another O'Hara poem, "Having a Coke with You." Glavey writes, "The consensus of their posts was resounding: . . . the Coke poem's celebration of infatuation and fun was irrepressibly *relatable*."[36] Similarly, in his essay on the relatability of Kazuo Ishiguro's *Never Let Me Go* (2005), Thom Dancer offers his recollection of reading Ishiguro's novel in a graduate course, where he, along with his peers, discussed their different ways of relating to the novel, filtered through their own personal experience.[37] In both instances, from the point of view of a professor or a student, an examination of what relatability offers is borne from the question of how to relate to others and to one's self in a pedagogical encounter. Although what counts as relatable might not be about Hamlet, or a singular, particular "you," it might, Glavey points out, be about you, your friends, or your peers, and what you read or talk about together.

What one relates to becomes another way of relating to others. Such relatability can be about the cultivation of taste and cultural capital, but Glavey notes that it also shapes queer modes of reparative reading, of finding one's relation to cultural objects even when and if they are not made for oneself that in turn make other socialities possible. Relatability becomes the site of a "reparative sociability" among those who, together, are in on an "open secret."[38] Relatability in a minoritarian context becomes a reparative quality that lets us covertly make certain objects whole via our own reading practice that decides an object is for us and our people, whoever they may be. I do not disregard this reparative reading of relatability. Many are drawn to Mitski and Vuong for the reparative sociability their perceived relatability affords. It is akin to what Karen Tongson by way of Jennifer Terry describes as "remote intimacy"—asynchronous forms of "communion" via "shared consumption."[39] However, if we tend to the reparative's destructive qualities, relatability's forms of sociability are not just the reciprocal, symmetrical sharing out of what is felt and loved in common. For while relatability can be the grounds of commonality, there is something possessive, divisive, and competitive about it, too, in the same way that the remoteness of "remote intimacy" is constituted by separation and difference, about a secret you do not always know you share with others and might guard accordingly. Only some, and not all, can be in on a secret, however open it is, otherwise it would no longer be a secret. This makes relatability a quality that is alluring, special, and a little bit smug all at once: the idea that you know something that others do not, and that because others do not know it, you get to be the one who decides to tell them, or not.

You are the one with the secret to spoil, to tell, nevertheless beholden to others who are in on it, too.

For Frank O'Hara, "having a Coke with you" was not like having a Coke with just anyone or everyone. It was "more fun than going to San Sebastian, Irún, Hendaye, Biarritz, Bayonne / or being sick to my stomach on the Travesera de Gracia in Barcelona"; it was with "you" whose face was better than "all the portraits in the world" ("except possibly for *The Polish Rider* occasionally") and who stood as proof that the impressionist painters "never got the right person to stand near the tree when the sun sank."[40] Other people "were all cheated of some marvelous experience / which is not going to go wasted on me," and this, O'Hara writes, is "why I'm telling you about it."[41] Part of what makes the poem so relatable is the wanting to tell us, as the addressee of the poem, the secret of this "marvelous experience." Vuong relates by holding his hand to the world; O'Hara relates by sharing a Coke with us and "you." In both instances, the experience of the "I" of the poem takes over with its effusive address, with all that it furnishes upon a lover. Even if O'Hara is speaking to us, as his lover, who has shared all these experiences with him, we as the reader are only hearing about this experience now, in reading the poem (but also again and again, as we read and reread). It is as if we are hearing a story about us that we should not have missed, but since we did, we might feel a little envious for having not been clued in sooner. We are let in on the secret while also sort of left out of it given the belatedness of O'Hara's telling, or, rather, his relating.

It is this aspect of relatability—relating through the risk of overwhelming another with a sweeping sense of the self in love—that Mitski and Vuong draw out through the autoerotic act of staying in. The modes of relatability they move through, and how their fans relate to them, are not just about the reflection and consolidation of a self or a collective, but instead about the collapsing of "your" and "my," "you" and "I" that cannot stay singular and contained. Relatability is a leaky category, which is why whatever is relatable can really get around. Consider how Vuong's and Mitski's work, like O'Hara's, has circulated online. Their songs and poems appear as a few lines of lyrics or poetry shared on the social media site X (formerly Twitter) or on the blogging website Tumblr. Their readings and live performances are recorded with someone's phone and then uploaded to TikTok. Mitski's songs are sung, sometimes with no accompaniment, by TikTok users sitting alone in their bedrooms, accompanied with the hashtag #mitskiistherapy.

This might feel like sharing a Coke with someone, as a democratizing utopian gesture rooted in the quotidian, but as I suggest, it might also feel like being left out and excluded, but being told about it anyway, after the fact.[42] This was certainly the case for me, when I found out that Mitski had become popular to a younger audience on TikTok by way of trends that I had missed. This is the antagonism of relation embedded within relatability's promise of repair: the possibility that in being told, in having something related to me, it has indeed, been wasted on me. Through the relatability of staying in—which is to say, through an act that others can relate to and practice themselves—Mitski and Vuong flirt with the kinds of passivity attributed to the relatable cultural object, or in this case, to themselves as cultural figures. When we watch Mitski and Vuong perform, we are given the sense that what we consume is what they, in their spoiled performances of the self, have consumed first, which we then get to have related to us—wasted on us—later.

Patty Chang's Appetite

> ... (the original version of the question do you want to have sex with me? would be the question do I want to eat you or spit you out?). For something (or someone) to be loveable it must be already inside one, or we must want it to be inside.
> —Leo Bersani and Adam Phillips, *Intimacies* (2008)

How might Asian American artists indulge in relatability's association with the solipsism of the selfie, in a way that spoils notions of self-care with a narcissistic self-love? In artist Patty Chang's work from the late 1990s and early 2000s, she experimented with video alongside body-based feminist performance art, through the emergent identity politics of the time.[43] Chang is from a different generation than most of the artists in this book. I include her here because I want to place Mitski's and Vuong's autoerotic acts in a lineage of performance art, rather than solely indie music and lyric poetry. Alongside Chang, I am able to approach Mitski's and Vuong's attention bestowed on the body, and particularly their own bodies, in the autoerotic act of staying in.

In her performance and video work *Fountain* (1999), Chang intrudes on her own image, thirsty for it. In the video, Chang's face appears in a close-up, upright and partially in profile. With a furrowed brow, she gazes intently into her reflection that stares back at her. Her reflection ripples and wavers from her breath as she draws closer, closes her eyes, puckers her lips, and drinks herself. Chang first performed *Fountain* at her solo show with the same name at the Jack Tilton Gallery in New York in 1999, before recording a shorter video of the performance in her studio. For the initial performance, she wore a gray suit, knelt on the floor, and drank water on a mirror's surface for thirty to forty-five minutes at a time. As she drank, a stationary camera, tilted at a forty-five-degree angle, streamed the performance, which played on a monitor outside the gallery and on a screen behind her. Those who were in the gallery to witness the performance, who might not be able to see her face as she bows down to the floor, only need look behind her to see her face at a cropped, upright angle. The intimacy of a face's expression bowed down, tucked away from view, is made visible, exposed. What is otherwise a horizontal position of supposition and deference is repositioned into an emboldened, vertical stance of confrontation and attempted (self-)possession.

Chang drinks her fill of herself, gulping up water, pulling back to lick her lips, swallow, and catch her breath before leaning in for more. As she continues to drink, the mirror's surface peeks through the water. The sound of Chang's slurps is satisfying, but strained. She works with mouth and throat to suck more water from the mirror's surface. As she drinks, she does not look pleased or content with her reflection, just concentrated, fixated. Her gaze wields an envy for her image infused with a "fleshy mixture of self-production, insatiability, joy, and pain" that Amber Musser calls "brown jouissance," which is destructive yet vulnerable in its openness, raw and laid bare to wanting.[44] Chang's desire for her own image is a perverse kind of love, wherein to keep the self through the self's image is to also spoil it. Chang's performance makes the attempt to *stay in* one's own image, so much so that this attempt is consumptive, more so than caring. Preservation and destruction become intertwined endeavors bound to sabotage each other. What she wishes to possess of herself cannot wholly be taken in. Water escapes, and a part of her image goes along with it.

In a 2003 interview with Eve Oishi, Chang muses, "A body with integrity is hard to find. Perhaps I am trying to take my damaged, divided, and immoral body, and making [*sic*] it as whole as possible."[45] Where one's body ends and begins, where it is one's own and where it begins to leak, impinge, and give itself away, is hard to know. For Chang, maybe this is beside the point. Given her remarks, it would seem that Chang's work speaks to a desire for repair. However, I am drawn to the way she articulates the difficulty of bodily integrity and "making" the body "as whole as possible." How whole is possible? The durational aspects of Chang's work propose this question and arrive not at wholeness but, instead, at the damage she causes in attempting to attain it.

In her video work *Melons (At a Loss)* (1998), Chang tells a fantastical story about the death of her aunt and the inheritance of a poisonous plate. While she shares this story, she balances a plate on her head, takes a knife to cut open a cantaloupe stuffed into her bra, and scoops out the cantaloupe's flesh. She gouges the melon with her fingers to take out its seeds, placing them on the plate on her head. She begins to eat the melon's flesh, scooping into the melon and chewing as she speaks, using her fingers and a spoon. Chang's story keeps intact the memory of her aunt who had passed away due to breast cancer, at the same time that she simulates the destruction of her own breast as melon. What Chang destroys of herself becomes her source of nourishment, as well as poison, for in listening to the story, one might wonder if the plate that rests on her head is the same poisonous plate to which her story alludes. Like with *Fountain*, Chang takes herself in, but through the staging of autocannibalism, where the violence she enacts on herself is for the sake of her own sustenance, and that of her aunt's memory, too. What might otherwise seem like the closed circuit of touching and eating oneself—as "inexhaustible" and "free," to use Vuong's words—is susceptible to the contaminating presence of memory and fantasy, of her aunt's body and poisonous plate. Chang speaks while her mouth is full of melon, breast, and story, and in gnashing them up with her teeth, her body cannot separate itself from her aunt's. Whose breast is it? Who is being eaten? Who is being preserved and cared for and who is being destroyed and hurt?

In Chang's two-channel video installation *In Love* (2002), two monitors are positioned side by side on a wall. One monitor shows her slowly passing a raw onion back and forth between her mouth and the mouth of her mother, as they eat it together. The other monitor shows Chang doing the same with her father. In both, the sharing of an onion looks like the sharing of a long, leaky kiss, as they blink away tears and jut out their jaws, arranging their teeth and tongues to balance the onion between them. In one moment, Chang's mother holds up her hand to the side of Chang's face, as either a tender gesture of intimacy or an attempt to hold the onion in place. The two monitors play the footage in reverse, so that for the duration of both videos, the onion does not disappear, but gradually asserts the crisp, stinging layers of its form that their mouths work around.

When Oishi first saw Chang's *In Love* at the Guggenheim Museum, she noticed the "audible expressions of discomfort and unease" from other viewers.[46] In Musser's reading of the work, she argues that this discomfort and unease speak to the sensual excess of the shared act, materialized through the automaticity of the tears that might be brought about by the onion's fumes, or by the feelings that come with embracing one's parents. The inability to decide between the two possibilities holds the "opacity of perversion."[47] While Musser reads the opacity of Chang's work as it pushes up against the incest taboo, I read the work for how the act of sharing an onion becomes a secret shared in the space between mouths and onion, harboring a relation that pokes fun at Freud's notion that "the attitude of affectionate parents towards their children . . . is a revival and reproduction of their own narcissism."[48] The way Chang and her parents share an onion might not be so different from how O'Hara has a Coke with you, but also from how Chang drinks herself, insofar as these are all enactments of love that never stray far from the self, as it relates.

With *In Love*, what feels perverse about the relationship between parent and child is the possibility of narcissism, alongside the possibility of incest. Sharing an onion with one's child can be akin to sharing an onion with one's self, which is also to say that the act of loving one's child can become indistinguishable from the act of loving one's self. This is not a critique of reproductive futurity (although it is a little funny to think about) so much as it is a proposal to think of how, particularly in Chang's work, narcissism exceeds the bounds of the self, spilling over like one's tears that melt into the tears of another. This is not an impersonal form of narcissism or an "unlimited intimacy" given that the self is not shattered, wholly devoid and evacuated of difference.[49] Yet it is a kind of narcissism felt in loving the other because of how the other reflects—in however a distorted, wavering way—the self that risks destroying and consuming itself and the other. If Chang drinks up her entire image, she might not be able to see herself anymore; if and when the onion is ever completely eaten—which never happens given the video's loop—Chang and her parents will no longer be connected. Similarly, if Vuong lets go of the world with his hand, he will lose himself, and if Mitski does not have her hand, she has no one. As Leo Bersani and Adam Phillips suggest, then, "Narcissistic desire becomes the medium for recognition rather than the obstacle."[50]

In Love was inspired by Marina Abramovic's video performance *The Onion* (1996), where she eats an onion as she lists a series of things and actions that tire her, from waiting to decision-making.[51] Upon watching this piece, Chang tells Oishi, "I felt it was so sad to be having this experience alone. Sharing an awful experience with another person binds you together."[52] She proceeded to make *Untitled (For Abramovic Love Cocteau)* (2000), wherein she eats an onion with a friend, before deciding that she wanted to share what she describes as "this awful yet exquisitely touching act" with her parents, "the least likely people I would want to do it with."[53] For Chang, to eat an onion alone is not enough. If narcissism is the frustrating reminder that one needs other people, *In Love* expresses that need through Chang's act of loving herself made inseparable from the act of loving her parents, founded on an experience, which, because it is "awful" and done with "the least likely people," constitutes a bond that spoils itself in the process.

When watching *In Love*, an onion is made whole by the video's end. However, because the onion has been passed back and forth between multiple mouths, the act, as well as its object, has been spoiled, shredded with teeth and tainted with spit. To be *in love* is the act of sharing an experience with another that can begin and end in tears. *Melons* does not end in tears but in a mess, for when Chang has finished telling her aunt's story, she triumphantly lifts the plate from her head and smashes the plate down to the ground with a crash, as the melon remains gouged out, dripping, and exposed on her chest. The onion, melon, and plate remain at the end of these works as the spoils of Chang's "damaged, divided, and immoral body" in the face of her destructive attempts to make it whole. Chang expresses the diffuse desire to spoil and be spoiled: to enfold her body into space and time where her actions cannot contain her body or what it consumes and expels, whether that be her tears, her parents' tears, their spit, the juices and pith of a melon, or water on a mirror. The self intrudes on its relations with others, which is to say, intrusion becomes a constitutive part of how the self relates.

In *Melons*, Chang's fictionalized account of what happened in the wake of her aunt's death plays with the value and virtue placed on personal narrative. Turning in toward the self, as narcissistic, becomes simultaneous with the self's erosion and contamination in its need for who and what lies outside of itself. Chang does something similar in *Fountain*, which directly draws on the Greek myth of Narcissus, who died of starvation and thirst in utter devotion to his own image. For Freud, there is one type of narcissism that marks an instinct of self-preservation, present in all subjects during their development. Even so, the story of Narcissus remains a cautionary tale, for Freud wrote that in order for the self to have a nonpathological relation to the world, this particular instinct had to eventually be relinquished.[54] One must be willing to give up a cherished relation to the self—or else one's instincts lead not only to the harm of others but also to the harm of oneself.

To love oneself too much, like Narcissus, is to deprive oneself of the nourishment given by the surrounding world. But to this, Chang asks: If Narcissus gazed at his own reflection, did Narcissus also try to consume it? Self-sustenance and self-deprivation, self-preservation and self-destruction, become two sides of Chang's reflection, gravitating toward each other to confront the asymmetry and division within something like relatability, which assumes that what a relatable image, text, or object relates is a reflection of ourselves. In *Fountain*, Chang disproves relatability's equivalence as affirming and a means of arriving at wholeness. After all, the act of consuming her image took a toll on her body. As she tells Oishi, "It was painful, and I thought I was going to puke."[55] Elsewhere, she recalls, "I did [*Fountain*] for an extended period and almost died from drinking so much water."[56] The tense silence that fills the pause between each drink pull us toward her throat as she works to swallow and keep the water down, all while horizontal, caved in on her own bodily organs. Her body's exertion exposes the work it takes to stay in, and the possibility of relating to others while doing it.

Chang's openness to herself means she must keep drinking, and she must keep talking and eating, even if it makes her sick, even if she might choke or trip over her words while trying to chew. Her strained body threatens to spoil itself with its own image, trying to hold in too much of itself, prying itself open, making ill use of itself in the desire for itself. The desire for oneself that provokes the charge of narcissism might alienate other people, as an affront to a presupposed collective "we" or sense of belonging to a world. This is why I like thinking of Chang's work alongside Mitski's and Vuong's: their acts of staying in, across medium, genre, and time, excessively interrogate the need for other people and for belonging via autoerotic acts, and in doing so they not only critique and disrupt the kinds of compulsory sociability their need for others might engender, but also deidealize the worlds they are purportedly making and building in their work.

Deidealizing a World, After You

Staying in prompts a critique of the ways that Asian Americans are viewed as a hindrance to productive forms of sociality. It also puts pressure on how Asian American studies has idealized particular forms of sociality that promise to recall and revive the field's roots in the Asian American movement and student protests on college campus in the late 1960s and '70s. Staying in is not a turning away from this history, but it does have us attend to other forms of sociality that do not culminate into a legible movement—or the making of a world. Along these lines, staying in could also be viewed as an obstruction to the socialities and intimacies that queer worlds hold, as refuge from a phobic majoritarian public sphere.

To stay in might spoil all the fun. Whether because one is sick, generally exhausted, wants to avoid an ex, does not want to go to *that* one party, or just does not feel like it, staying in is seen as separate from the kinds of utopian queer socialities that center going out, that privilege the ephemeral world at the club, at a bar, anywhere that is out, not in. As Kadji Amin aptly observes, there is a tendency in queer studies to idealize certain cultural objects as productively transgressive sites for queer social worlds. This has become the privileged task of queer scholarship: mining and valorizing deviant aspects of queer culture and its objects as evidence of social forms imbued with queer world-making possibility. Amin writes,

> Our sex, because outlawed, is hotter; our love, because uninstitutionalized, is truer; our families, because freely chosen, are uniquely supportive and antihierarchical; our political movements, because unbound by narrow social identities, are coalitional and capable of fighting oppression on all fronts. In short, because we are forced to invent relations outside of tired old blueprints, our socialities are not only better, more authentic, and more pleasurable; they also actualize real-life alternatives to existing relations of oppression. This idealism, which neatly inverts the denigration of queer bonds, has been one of the powerful redemptive impulses of Queer Studies.[57]

The sting of this passage, for me, quite frankly and not without embarrassment, is relatable. It aggressively tells on me, as someone who has sought out this redemptive impulse, both in life and scholarship, and who has, in the process, been caught in what Lauren Berlant calls the temporal genre of the "impasse," where the socialities of and in the (queer) good life become a cruel attachment, a source of pressure more than relief.[58] Queer studies pursues an idealized notion of world-making within social forms, in ways that overlook how queer studies must engage with what cannot be idealized, valorized, or, repaired about queerness and about itself as a field. I think Asian American studies could afford to do the same. While some moments within queer sociality and intimacy feel good, others do not, and staying in mediates the contentious, underlying shift between the two, rather than rejecting one or the other, or propping up one at the expense of the other. Staying in, then, is not some better form of relating that is more right, more queer. As a critical stance against the compulsion to be sociable, staying in is not against going out into the world, or coming out to it, for that matter. It urges us to come to terms with the possibility that investments in certain formations of the social, particularly in Asian American studies and queer studies, are not always guaranteed to repair or make a world, and might sidestep or damage the one we are in instead.

Sometimes—in the midst of fascism, of genocide—it seems like none of us should or can afford to stay in. Staying in can be too passive and complicit, apolitical and apathetic, a turn away from social life and the kinds of collective transformation it makes possible. I do not dismiss the cost of staying in. I do not deny that it can be a luxury. When staying in, one risks giving something up, missing out, or losing something. I am not interested in trying to answer for the perceived negativity of staying in by debating whether one is a better or worse political subject for going out or not. For me, such negativity speaks more to the difficulty of getting through the present moment, which, in its turbulent duration, its "crisis ordinariness," wears down our attachments to idealizations of the social, troubling the presumed vitality and redemptive qualities of social life.[59]

Of course, we should not give up on the social, we should not retreat, certainly not for good. We should, however, deidealize it. Staying in prompts this deidealization in the moment when the world and the relations it holds out to us have expired. Such expiration is not what brings us to "the end of the world" so often invoked in our contemporary moment. Alternatively, expiration is that which, as Hentyle Yapp writes, "restarts the impulse to relate."[60] Relationality comes after itself, from a deidealization of a world whose possibility might otherwise be conceived of in utopian terms. Staying in marks the moment of a world's expiration—"*the moment of an ideal's deflation*," Amin writes—from which one must be willing to go back out again, at the world's limit, in the face of our own loving, frustrated attachments to it.[61]

After relationality, there is "after you," a polite utterance of accommodation, of making room for someone else to pass you by. Asian Americans become recognizable, legible subjects, "after you." They have been rendered as accommodating to the nation-state, whether as the ideal worker for cheap, flexible labor or as the upwardly mobile model minority.[62] To approach the production of Asian American subjectivity through such accommodating terms addresses how Asian Americans subjects are perceived as capable and willing to fit in, as "hospitable thresholds," discreet and ready to be used by another as a "solution" to problems within a preexisting social world.[63]

At the same time that Asian Americans are expected to accommodate and uphold the social, they are not particularly soluble in it. To be "after you" is to enter into a particular social scene—whether a party, a dinner, a classroom—a little late, when everyone else has already settled in and gotten their bearings. Given the belated arrival, one is expected to be unobtrusive and tactful so as not to disrupt what is already taking place. However, to stay in the time of "after you" can also be a little disruptive and rude, like walking into a meeting late—the last one there. To say "after you," is not just the acknowledgment that someone precedes you but also the act of letting them go on ahead, and not because one is passive or helpless but because one has decided to stay back, stay in. The relief of relinquishment and the hostility of the lag blur into each other.

While Asian Americans occupy a nebulous position within social life, Asian American studies—in ways not wholly dissimilar from how Amin writes about queer studies—holds a tense place in the university, too. Given the field's history and its ongoing development and emergence, particularly at East Coast universities, distant from California and its histories of student protests for ethnic studies, there is the question of how to preserve and uplift the radical roots of Asian American studies while also making appeals for its legitimacy and relevancy in the university—for its relatability and relevancy as an area of study. The field finds itself torn between accommodation and resistance, between making bids for recognition and being critical of having to make such bids in the first place. Generally, we understand the importance of being "in but not of" the university, but what being "in but not of" means for Asian American studies remains an open, uncomfortable question, especially when taking into consideration Asian American anxieties around the contemporary production of Asian as a racial category that veers into the major, more so than the marginalized status of the minor—*in* rather than out.[64]

Asian American studies must wrestle with its positions "on the side of institutionalization that takes it as an established fact," as Robyn Wiegman puts it.[65] To find ourselves on this side is to grapple with how Asian American studies has moved through the academy while having a complicated, dissatisfactory relationship to it.[66] Asian American studies is a resonant site for interrogating fantasies of political efficacy and equivalence that rely on legible forms of sociality, their formations of subjecthood, and the institutionalized minoritarian forms of knowledge often attached to them. From this side of institutionalization, staying in "after you" can ground a mode of Asian Americanist critique capable of addressing what happens from the other side of an identity's recognition and a field's institutionalization. To stay in "after you" is to insist on the tension and ensnarement of the lag between resistance and complicity, inside and outside, the social and the antisocial, as the spaces where Asian American asociality and its modes of critique reside.

"Not Well-Rounded," or Going to Shows Alone

Throughout her US tour for her fourth album, *Puberty 2* (2016), Mitski answered a series of posts on the social media platform formerly called Twitter. These posts were from fans who planned on attending her shows. In addition to fans looking for an extra ticket to a sold-out show, there were fans who had already bought a ticket for themselves and were looking for someone who would give them a ride, or someone who would want to go with them. Mitski would repost these requests for a date, a ride, or an extra ticket, connecting fans with one another when she could. In addition to sharing these posts, she would reply to fans, letting them know they always had another option: they could go to her shows alone.

One fan's post turned to Mitski for advice, asking, "How do u feel about going to shows by yourself? For example, I wanna go see you in Jacksonville, but my friends are lame."[67] In response, Mitski wrote, "I prefer to go alone, I can come+go as I please+b in my own head instead of think abt whether my friends' having fun."[68] In a separate post, she writes, "You can go to shows alone! you can go alone talk to no one feel the music then go home. abolish the notion of going to shows to be seen."[69] For Mitski, live performance and the scenes around it are not always sites of recognition from which collectivity inevitably springs, nor should they be. Mitski does not urge her fans to put themselves out there for the sake of making friends, she does not guarantee that you will always make a meaningful connection at her shows. She advocates for a way of being at a show or performance that takes the form of staying in, of keeping to one's self to "b in my own head."

Mitski's insistence on her fan's interiority and invisibility at her show is enabled by her own exteriority and visibility on stage. What she offers her fans through her shows and music is a scene where people can come together, but also an unseen space where someone can step inside and hide if they really want to. Going to shows alone does away with the expectation that you will always find your people in the crowd, or that the show might become a revelatory experience that sheds light on some part of one's self. Sometimes neither will happen. At Mitski's shows, you can be alone without friends, either because they cannot or do not want to go. Notice how Mitski's fan's wording in her post conveys that even though she might be irritated with her friends for not wanting to go, she ultimately has accepted that her friends will not do something they do not want to do. Those friends, who perhaps are not fans of Mitski, got to stay in, too. Going to shows alone lets you be on your own "instead of think abt whether [your] friends' having fun," which is another way of caring for your own time as well as that of your friends. The fan's question to Mitski and the slight she directs to her friends express an awareness of the limits of friendship that is playfully antagonistic yet determined by what her friends want or do not want. On the other side of staying in, then, is the accommodation of your

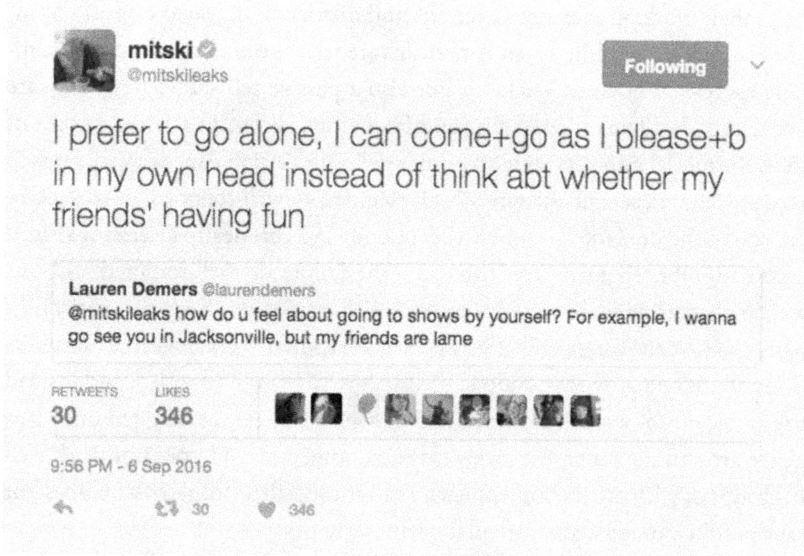

FIGURE 1.1. Mitski Miyawaki, Twitter post, September 6, 2016, 9:56 p.m. Screenshot by the author.

friends who do not always want or need to enter into the same room or scene with you.

Mitski's cultivation of her "impersona" on stage is made of mixed signals.[70] This becomes evident in the differences between Mitski's way of communicating with fans online and her earlier live performances that revolved around her music as well as her quiet, hesitant unwillingness to engage too much with the crowd. When I saw her play at the Bowery Ballroom in New York City in 2016 for her album *Puberty 2*, Mitski rarely spoke in between songs, or else she briefly mentioned the astrological forecast. She told us there was a strawberry moon. She told us to look outside at the sky, and also told us what it might mean for her mood and ours. In a review for a show she played in Denver, Colorado, also in 2016, a music critic called the performance "distant," and wrote, "Audience interactions were not the smoothest—at one point, Mitski deflected an enthusiastic fan's declaration of love by saying she had earplugs in."[71] Her in-ear monitors prioritize her own voice in her head so that she can better hear herself on stage, drowning out the voices of others. Disappointed, the critic stated, "Even the few smiles Mitski let slip all night seemed like they were for herself."[72] For the critic, the performance was lacking, but it seems that for Mitski, it was not, as she took pleasure in her music in a way that others could neither hear nor know.

In their work on racial melancholia and dissociation, David Eng and Shinhee Han state that while Asian Americans are seen as economically or academically successful in their "enclosed but also a passive self-sufficiency," they are not seen as "well-rounded."[73] Eng and Han write, "From an academic point of view, the model minority stereotype also delineates Asian American students as academically successful but rarely 'well-rounded'—'well-rounded' in tacit comparison to the unmarked (white) student body. . . . This nearly successful assimilation attempts to cover over the gap—the failure of 'well-roundedness'—as well as that unavoidable ambivalence resulting from this tacit comparison in which the Asian American student is seen as lacking."[74] I stay with the implications of not being "well-rounded." This failure to be well-rounded, and instead too imbalanced, insular, separate, and generally off, can be mapped onto language around the loner, the awkward nerd, someone who does not work well in groups or with others, someone who cannot socialize properly, who does not take part in enough extracurricular group activities.

To not be well-rounded means to not be that social: to be alone, to not be personable,[75] to not be an adaptable, cooperative team player. On the other side of this, to be well-rounded is to be white. The well-roundedness of whiteness is passably self-sufficient, but not so much so that it closes itself off to the world. Whiteness produces itself by way of having the whole world available to it. What of whiteness's accessibility to and of the world is couched in discourses on proper sociality and sociability, by way of a term like "well-rounded"? Seemingly, to not be well-rounded is to be closed off from the world, to have a passive relation to it, both willfully and unwillfully in one's own interiority as stunted and unchanging. Given whiteness's orientation to the world, Asian Americans' relation to it figured through maladjusted forms of asociality is not a failure, but a critique of how understandings of the social and the relational are based on individuated, autonomous formations of the subject that do not and cannot hold.

The now-defunct 2010 Tumblr blog called "Asians Sleeping in the Library" offers another means of approaching the Asian American student as the figure of academic success and social failure.[76] Started by a white student at Birmingham University, the blog collected photos of Asian students sleeping alone in various odd, awkward positions in college libraries. The blog's description stated, "Asians sleeping in the library: they're better at life and they get better grades than you for a reason. Pictures of Asian students from universities sleeping in the library and lecture halls."[77] The images were meant to be humorous, depicting the lengths Asian students would go to for the good grade. The blog's joke rested on the disjuncture between Asians being "better at life," while also failing at it in their exhaustion. The blog was swiftly met with criticism and subsequently taken down.

When looking through the archived images from the blog, I wonder if this is what the failure of well-roundedness looks like: sleeping solitary figures curled up with their sweaters or laptops used as pillows, with office chairs arranged into loose, enclosed structures built for some semblance of discretion, whether for a quick nap or a whole night's rest. These images are uncomfortable because they are taken without the sleeping subject's consent, but also because they are an unglamorous portrait of the Asian student as the model minority. For some visitors of the blog, as well as its creator, they represent the excessive, torturous lengths Asian students will go to overachieve. I want to interpret these images differently. While these sleeping figures have been caught and called out in public, they do not let you in on their dreamy, sleepy interior life.[78] They are intruded upon, but they also intrude upon public space, as figures who, in their postures of not-well-roundedness, inhabit the limits of sociality in space. While being "better at life" might be a jab at the limits of what being the model minority affords, and at what cost, these images show us something messier, more provisional and makeshift, where crashing at the library gives way to one's success in at least having figured out how to build a bed out of a desk and a chair.

When I began working as a teaching assistant in graduate school, I attended an orientation where we were told that as teachers, the university and our classroom is a site for socializing students. I am reminded of this as I look at these images from this now nonexistent blog. Our job, as the university saw it, was to train students to become adults who would take initiative with their studies that would then reflect on the way they live their life as an adult. They would learn to be a good peer, and therefore a good colleague. They would become people who contribute to society in the right way. The students sleeping in the library taught another lesson. They show how the failure of well-roundedness, of being properly social and socialized, comes to constitute the problem of Asian Americanness. However, they also show that such failure need not solely be a sign of exclusion, but also that which provides an excuse from having to engage in compulsory forms of sociability—from having to go to a bad college party, or elsewhere. One might be excused from having to participate, and instead, pursue the pleasures of going solo, or going to a show alone. The asociality implied in the designation of not being well-rounded expresses a divestment from and deidealizations of forms of likable, relatable sociability that refuse and are refused by Asian American subjects.

After / In the Style Of

I love me after you.—Mitski, "I Love Me After You" (2023)

From the position of the not well-rounded, I return to the moment "after you" that Vuong inhabits in his poem "Someday I'll Love Ocean Vuong" included in his collection *Night Sky with Exit Wounds* (2016). The first version of the poem published in 2015, in *The New Yorker*, begins with a dedication that is also a citation. It reads, "After Frank O'Hara / After Roger Reeves."[79] The horizon of "someday" is grasped through the work of other poets: from O'Hara and Reeves, a contemporary poet. The title of Vuong's poem comes from the last lines in O'Hara's 1953 poem, "Katy": "Some day I'll love Frank O'Hara. / I think I'll be alone for a little while."[80] These last lines are also cited by Reeves in his poem "Someday I'll Love Roger Reeves."[81] In these poems and their relation to each other, the possibilities for loving yourself emerge once you come after another. Recalling Glavey's reading of O'Hara's "Having a Coke with You," we might understand Vuong's and Reeves's dedications as a way of relating to O'Hara, as a poet who came before them, as people who, together, relate to the same things, which is also to each other.

In "Katy," O'Hara begins, "They say I mope too much / but really I'm loudly dancing."[82] He explains, "I dance, / I am never quiet, I mean silent."[83] These lines moving underneath and before Vuong's own add breath and body to Vuong's poem. Staying in, within the lyric, is not the same as being lonely, silent, quiet, or still. What appears to be mopey and self-indulgent, caught up in the switch between "quiet" and "silent," in the quick self-corrective, "I mean," is the not-well-rounded space of asociality, wherein the poet finds himself alone for a little while. "After you" doubles as a temporal marker and as poetic form. For Vuong, to come after O'Hara and Reeves is to be in their style. While Vuong writes of a self-love just out of reach, the shape of it starts to peek through with the reminder that he is not the only one who makes this promise to himself. His pleasure taken from and in himself comes with the pleasure that others already have experienced for themselves, by themselves.

In "Someday I'll Love Ocean Vuong," Vuong addresses himself with the assurances, "don't be afraid" and "don't worry."[84] These are fears and worries of being left behind and alone with memories of his childhood and loved ones—of his mother, his father, or a lover. But it is from the position of being left alone that he writes this poem. Its lines fill the space left by another's leaving and guide him toward what is ahead—"Just call it *horizon*."[85] To "just" say it is a horizon renders it into a regular, ordinary one, without the promise of utopia or an otherwise. The poem ends:

. . . Ocean. Ocean—
get up. The most beautiful part of your body
is where it's headed. & remember,
loneliness is still time spent
with the world. Here's
the room with everyone in it.
Your dead friends passing
through you like wind
through a wind chime. Here's a desk
with the gimp leg & a brick
to make it last. Yes, here's a room
so warm & blood-close,
I swear, you will wake—
& mistake these walls
for skin.[86]

The prodding repetition of self-address—"Ocean. Ocean—/ get up"—nudges Vuong in the direction of where he and his body are going, following a path of "afters," one after another, which move beside O'Hara and Reeves yet lead him back to where he started: his own body, its "most beautiful part," perhaps his own hand, again. This might read like regression, maybe the kind implied in the childish narcissism of autoerotic acts wherein the self still turns inward to the self for nourishment, and nowhere else. This is the tug of the after, as he follows O'Hara and Reeves, not yet arriving at a horizon. This after he tells us that even though he finds himself alone back where he and we began, he insists that what might appear to be loneliness, what might go by its name, still pulls him toward a world made compact like a "room with everyone in it."

His loneliness in his writing, like his hand in his ode, makes for an earnest display of self-devotion. The room becomes his body's most beautiful part; his body is built into a home "so warm & blood-close." Like a hand that holds itself to the world, the poem, given the warmth of a body, holds itself as a home. The body in and of the poem is Vuong's own, but also that of "you." Everyone is in the same room where Vuong's skin and your/ours are mistaken for one another. It is a way of relating that feels as off-balance as "lop-sided furniture," which is just sturdy enough to build a temporary resting place, to write, to study, to stay in. Once again, Vuong writes of a self who overtakes the world of the poem and everyone else living in it. He does so with a sincerity that can make one blush or cringe—responses attributed to the sign of feeling embarrassed.[87] The pleasure he takes in loving himself, someday, becomes our own, and while I do not refute the ways his work dips into sentimentality, I want to take seriously how such pleasure, in earnest, also feels like a confrontation or onerous encounter, insofar as we feel overwhelmed by Vuong's own feeling and body, and thus, become all the more attuned to how we might feel differently, rather than the same.[88]

In Mitski's "Your Best American Girl," a listener might also sense a fear or worry of being left behind or left out. For while this all-American boy is the "big spoon," and "the sun," Mitski can only wish to be his "little spoon," and is "not the moon . . . not even a star," but someone down below, on earth, looking up into the sky at what she cannot reach. But like those in Vuong's poem, body, and room, she is not trapped and neither are we: she can look up at the sky, even if she cannot be a constellation in it. When she sings, "Don't wait for me / I can't come," she is not accepting or resigning herself to her own isolation. The issue is not that she cannot come because she is on her own. Rather, by insisting "don't wait for me," and by remaining after you, she is saying that she cannot come because this boy—now this couple—is in the way. If they pay her no mind, she can exit, avoid the setup she finds herself in, even when the setup is her own music video. Although Mitski sings, "I have nothing ahead of me," it is she who at the end of the video walks off the set and opens the doors to leave, while the white couple stays behind, trapped in their own embrace and bound up in an American flag.

Throwing a Temper Tantrum

In 2019, Mitski announced on her social media accounts that one of her shows for her album *Be the Cowboy* (2018), in New York City's Central Park, would be her "last show indefinitely."[89] With the success of *Be the Cowboy*, she had a newfound visibility and recognition that left her feeling exposed and exhausted. Soon after her announcement, she deleted all her social media accounts, and for the next few years there were no more messages to fans. However, in 2021, she reactivated her social media accounts to announce the release of her new single "Working for the Knife," and to promote her 2022 album *Laurel Hell*. Her social media posts were straightforward dispatches about the album, merchandise, music videos, press, and tour dates. Unless posts began, "From Mitski:" they were not written by her. Otherwise, as if for transparency's sake, she posted videos of herself sitting at a piano and speaking directly to the camera. All her old social media posts, like those I have quoted, have been deleted, and now circulate as screenshot images on social media fan accounts, or else in our own personal archives stored on our laptops.

With the announcement of Mitski's album and its single, it was reported that the album was made to fulfill a contractual obligation with her record label, Dead Oceans. She owed them one last album. "Working for the Knife" expresses her resistance, as if she were dragging her feet, not keeping up with the pace of production. One can hear it in the way her singing and the song's instrumentals—its dark, cold synthesizers and percussion—chug along with the clang of factory equipment that courses throughout the track. "I always thought the choice was mine / And I was right, but I chose wrong" she sings, with a sigh, "I start the day lying and end with the truth / that I'm dying for the knife."[90] In the single's music video, Mitski approaches and enters The Egg, a performing arts venue in Albany, New York. Once she is inside the venue, and "Working for the Knife" begins to play, she takes on the stilted gestures and frozen expressions of a puppet, before they melt away. By the song's end, Mitski has made her way to the venue's stage. She collapses to the sound of applause echoing throughout the empty space. Soon the applause is overtaken by the sound of Mitski's breath, as she gets up, not to take a bow but to rock back and forth on her hands and knees. She stands up, with back arched and head thrown back, hands clutching her chest. She starts to breathe faster. She lies back down on the stage and starts shaking and pumping her arms and legs, slamming her hands and arms on the floor; she stands back up and jumps, swinging her arms in the air; she thrashes from side to side. Finally, she falls to the floor and lies on her back, panting with a small smile.

Before Mitski had announced her hiatus in 2019, movement and choreography had come to play a significant role in her work. Her music videos and live performances had evolved, no longer tethered to a standing microphone and a guitar in hand. For "Working for the Knife," some of her other music videos, and her 2018–19 tour for *Be the Cowboy*, Mitski worked with artist, choreographer, and movement director Monica Mirabile. During her 2022 tour for *Laurel Hell* and her music video for her single "The Only Heartbreaker," Mitski collaborated with artist, choreography, and movement director Jas Lin. Even though Mitski's live shows have changed, to watch her perform still feels like watching what should otherwise stay private, perhaps because of the earnestness of each gesture, whether crawling on all fours and panting with her tongue out like a dog, or miming as if she were holding pools of moonlight in her hands. Here, I return to the self-conscious feeling of embarrassment in the beginning of this chapter because, for me, watching Mitski's performances, in her commitment to a pose or movement, can feel embarrassing.

While I, or others, might feel embarrassed by Mitski's and Vuong's performances, this does not mean we feel embarrassed *for* Mitski and Vuong. I suggest that Mitski's and Vuong's performances cultivate a feeling of embarrassment to bring unavoidable attention to the social context at hand. For Erving Goffman, embarrassment can be felt for and by one person or a group of people in an encounter. Embarrassment is social and contagious, felt in the company of other people when someone, which could be yourself, fails to present an "acceptable self," coherent and appropriate to an encounter.[91] Goffman uses the metaphor of mechanics to describe how the person who is embarrassed and embarrassing "cannot for the time being" properly respond within a social interaction that would allow that interaction to run smoothly, like a machine.[92]

Akin to the sense of being "after you," of following the clang in "Working for the Knife," Mitski's performance inhabits the improper response time that renders a social situation improper. When someone is embarrassed or embarrassing, it is because they have presented a version of the self that is deemed incoherent and discreditable by those around them. In short, they have found themselves beyond the bounds of compulsory sociability. "He and his flustered actions block the line of activity the others have been pursuing," Goffman writes, "He is present with them, but he is not 'in play.' The others may be forced to stop and turn their attention to the impediment; the topic of conversation is neglected, and energies are redirected."[93] The embarrassed/embarrassing person spoils social interactions and what they are expected to uphold: the social norms and values of poise, composure, and tact that sustain the appropriate, productive workings of sociality. This person impedes the progress of the social encounter, causing conversation to slow down if not break down completely. We might say that the embarrassed/embarrassing person, whether they like it or not, has managed to make a situation all about them.

Embarrassment weakens boundaries between people, between the self and other, between individual and encounter, hence why the embarrassed/embarrassing person and everyone else around them might feel they are expected to try to keep the social encounter intact, to conceal the disruption that has taken place. Since embarrassment manages to implicate everyone involved, it alters our awareness of our social roles in relation to one another—how we are all expected to be "in play," which is to say, sociable, with others around us. So when I say that Vuong's introduction or poem, or Mitski's performances, can feel embarrassing, I mean that in their earnestness, which is also a commitment to making it all about them, they risk theirs and our own embarrassment so that, in "the time being," like "after you," we become more aware of what we think we should be producing and getting out of our social interactions with others. Once we become aware of what has broken down, rather than reconstruct and preserve the social interaction at hand according to what is acceptable and coherent, we might do differently. We might, for instance, throw a temper tantrum.

Jas Lin describes their choreography for Mitski as an "adult tantrum."[94] Likewise, Mitski's movements on stage at the end of "Working for the Knife," choreographed by Mirabile, could be read as the enactment of a tantrum. Although a tantrum is an outward display of feeling, there is something interior and compact in its fury, inaccessible to those who witness it with unease. As a loud burst and fit of anger, a tantrum is always somewhere it is not supposed to be. A tantrum is inappropriate, immature, and unwelcome. It provokes embarrassment, as well as the judgment, shock, and discomfort of whoever sees it, especially if it happens in public, around strangers. When we see someone having a tantrum, we leave or at the very least look the other way, though we might also be tempted, with embarrassment, to stare. When we see a tantrum, whether from a child or an adult, we wonder if this person is acting out and blowing things out of proportion, or if this is someone who is in distress, in pain and in need of assistance. From within the moment of a tantrum, the embarrassed/embarrassing person, Goffman writes, "answers to a new set of rhythms, characteristic of deep emotional experience, and can hardly give even a faint impression that he is at one with the others in interaction. In short, he abdicates his role as someone who sustains encounters."[95] Mitski and Vuong stage a social encounter to then spoil its terms, abdicating themselves from it, letting it be sustained on its own.

Mitski's tantrums are not about the catharsis or redemption of the self, but an aggressive redirection of energy that carries the embarrassment of the unacceptable self to spit it out in public. Once it is in front of us, we are responsible for the encounter as much as Mitski is, in the same way that when we are present for a tantrum, we have been pulled into the orbit of the scene, even if we desperately want to remove ourselves from it. We have agreed to the norms that have discredited the tantrum or autoerotic act as embarrassing. But, as Goffman also points out, "the discreditor is just as guilty as the person he discredits—sometimes more so, for, if he has been posing as a tactful man, in destroying another's image he destroys his own."[96] Embarrassment, like narcissism, mirrors and overwhelms the image we hold of ourselves, as well as the roles we have been determined to play in the company of the others. As a feeling, it threatens to overtake us, and in doing so, it gives us an image of ourselves that feels like it does not fit.

Everything Is Embarrassing

What draws me to Mitski's and Vuong's work is what also makes them appealing to a broader audience. To put it bluntly, what, for me, had initially made Mitski's and Vuong's work push against the constraints and conventions of relatability has, in recent years, made them quite relatable. This is embarrassing for me, not them. What had initially made them my ideal objects of study, has by the same turn spoiled them as such. Mitski's albums after *Puberty 2*—which, at the time of this writing, include *Be the Cowboy* (2018), *Laurel Hell* (2022), and *The Land Is Inhospitable and So Are We* (2023)—and Ocean Vuong's novel *On Earth We're Briefly Gorgeous* (2019); his second poetry collection, *Time Is a Mother* (2022); and his second novel, *The Emperor of Gladness* (2025), have received a mix of critical acclaim and criticism. Mitski and Vuong are praised and loved as well as dismissed for being too preoccupied with sadness and suffering, too tender and soft in ways that encapsulate how discussions of boundaries, care, and emotional labor have gone too far, particularly for younger generations of fans.[97]

This chapter is not an attempt to defend Mitski and Vuong as the right objects of study, whom I restore through my readings. Yet clearly, I do not reject them or leave them behind. Mitski's and Vuong's deidealized place within this book and in popular culture requires my own tact in the face of what might feel embarrassing within the healing socialities and world-making practices a book is imagined to illuminate, if not enact.[98] What can feel so off-putting is Mitski's and Vuong's candidness in the face of this—an openness that risks the wrong kind of relating from critics and fans, which includes biting, sarcastic takedowns, as well as intense, aggressive forms of adoration.

During her 2022 tour for *Laurel Hell*, Mitski asked fans, in one of her cordial social media posts, to take less video on their phones during her shows. Some fans responded that recording moments like these were important to their mental health.[99] As music critic Lindsay Zoladz writes, "A kind of therapy-speak stalemate ensued."[100] People either defended these fans in discussions about self-care and accessibility, while others criticized them for being the very reason why Mitski had retreated from the public in the first place. Watching the arguments unfold, seeing how it revolved around accusations of harm and ideas of what it means to care for oneself and one's audience, felt embarrassing. No resolution was reached. People probably took videos with their phones at her shows when they wanted to, others did not, and Mitski's initial post was deleted, as was the post criticizing it.

The risk of relatability had been exposed, and both artist and fans could not continue relating and communicating like they did before. As D. A. Miller writes, "the embarrassing risk of *being too personal*," of indulging in the confessional mode so earnestly online and at live music shows, had befallen "the dismal fate of banality, of *not being personal enough*."[101] Someone relatable is subject to be spoiled, held up and bound to the desires of those who relate to them and who, in turn, are confronted with how their personal attachment to an artist, a poem, or a song is, in fact, not very special and quite banal. Knowing this, when you revisit the familiar question, "Should I stay in or go out?" as Mitski did during her hiatus, you might decide to be in play, to spoil the social, to risk the embarrassment of being both too personal and not personal enough, at least not in the way that others want and expect. This time, you might be ready to go out to that party or show, or on that tour. In that case, after you.

2. USING QUOTATIONS

THE RISK OF SPEAKING AS SOMEONE ELSE

With my work, I'm always asking, "What does it mean to speak for oneself, but on behalf of a group?"—Wu Tsang

Perhaps a synonym for "using people" would be, paradoxically, "trusting people," creating a space of play and risk that does not depend on maintaining intactness and separation.—Barbara Johnson, "Using People" (2008)

When artist Wu Tsang was an MFA student at the University of California, Los Angeles, she conducted research at UCLA's Film and Television Archive on Jennie Livingston's well-known 1990 documentary *Paris Is Burning*, about the Black and Latinx ball culture in New York City from the mid- to late 1980s. Tsang viewed unedited footage cut from the film, mainly consisting of Livingston's interviews with ball participants. The footage includes Livingston's interactions with interviewees, who respond playfully and guardedly, clarifying what they mean or trying to clarify what Livingston means. In the final cut of the film, Livingston stays out of frame and her voice can only be heard a few times, thereby letting the film assert and retain claims to the objectivity of its narrative and representation. The unedited footage promises to expose Livingston's presence, investments, and intentions around the film. Perhaps most notably, the footage shows how those whom Livingston interviewed—in particular, Octavia St. Laurent, a Black trans woman, and Venus Xtravaganza, a Latina trans woman, who were both significantly featured in the film—gave an account of themselves by tactfully answering her questions, despite what Livingston wanted and what the documentary film expected of its subjects.

If the final cut of *Paris Is Burning* obscured the context of the conversations between Livingston and those she interviewed, how could Tsang draw attention to this context, specifically for the purposes of featuring the film's trans women of color, not as passive subjects but as active theorists of the self, negotiating the terms of the exchange taking place? Such efforts might be seen as reparative, a means of making right a past wrong with a less damaging artistic practice that restores the agency of St. Laurent and Xtravaganza in the archive. Rather than aim for redress, Tsang gives an account of another—of those in the film like St. Laurent and Xtravaganza—in a way that makes use of what would otherwise be critiqued as the harmful liberties that a filmmaker and artist like Livingston, and like Tsang, might take. For Tsang, this gets worked out through and on the material, resonant site of her own body. With her body, Tsang invites and intrudes on those she does not speak *for*, but those she speaks *as* by way of quotation. If Livingston, as the filmmaker, left her body out of things, Tsang, as a student in the archive, does not. This does not make for a better kind of representation, just a riskier one, where Tsang's body is on the line.

Here, the student from the previous chapter reappears, except this time they are not staying in. Instead, they are going out. They go out to parties and performances; they go to class and search through the archives, too. Tsang and her collaborators are the students of this chapter, who enact a performance practice she calls "full body quotation." In full body quotation, Tsang samples, inhabits, embodies, and re-cites the speech of others, of friends, acquaintances, and people she encounters. Full body quotation touches on Tsang's training in operatic vocal performance, as well as in lip-synching in drag performance. In this chapter, full body quotation is also a practice akin to the citational practices developed by a student, who, in working on her studies, learns about the stakes of quoting others.

Full body quotation is a mediating practice that puts pressure on idealizations of sociality premised on the symmetry, equivalence, and immediacy of relatability. When Tsang speaks as another through full body quotation, it is as if she were a radio picking up someone else's frequency. By relating, she mediates, tuning in to the voices of people around her in ways that are not always clear, direct, and frictionless because of how these voices move through and between bodies with their own capacities and markers of difference—their own signals and waves. The voices can get a little fuzzy, pushing through static and bad reception, or else they might carry patches of indecipherable speech that have lost their context, subject to interference. So, while Tsang's performances of full body quotation are precise, the material presence of Tsang's racialized, gendered body makes processes of relating contingent on the possibility of interruption, interception, and miscommunication.

In Tsang's video artworks *For how we perceived a life (Take 3)* (2012) and *Shape of the Right Statement* (2008), as well as in her documentary film *Wildness* (2012), Tsang uses full body quotation to make herself into a sonorous medium tethered to its message that is not hers to claim, only hers to cite and quote.[1] She speaks as another in a way that draws attention to the possibility that she might not belong. She tries to insert herself where she cannot fit, and it is the effort of this fitting that we hear. To speak as another could be seen as a hostile act insofar as she imposes herself on another by taking the voice and words of and from another. Distinctions between who is taking or being taken become unclear, and this is the point. Full body quotation does not discount questions of power and difference between the self and other, but instead demands that those questions always be asked, in performance, as well as elsewhere, in the work we do, for instance, as scholars and students.

Tsang's full body quotation entails the careful study of those she quotes—to breath, tone, pacing, and inflection. Her performances are virtuosic, yet Tsang must readily leave herself open to mistakes, slights, and errors, like a student must do when learning about the uses of quotation in their work. She becomes a student who risks spoiling her sources with her own desire to learn what she does not know. In thinking of Tsang in the role of the student, I do not overlook how she is a well-established artist, who shows her work internationally at elite, major art institutions. I view Tsang in this role because of how full body quotation emerges during her time as a student and dramatizes some of the problems that arise around teaching and learning about citation and the use of quotation as ethical, social, relational practices that go on between people who are different from each other.[2] Citation and the use of quotation leave us indebted to those we cite and quote, who, possibly, become indebted to us. I argue that full body quotation, as a mode of performance, leaves Tsang, and us as her audience, indebted, too. Full body quotation requires us to reflect on how we cite, on how we use quotations, and how we use the people we quote.

A quotation can be used without citation. Quotations can live and travel on their own without context. This is what makes quotations subject to misuse. If not used properly and with care, if not accompanied by a citation, quotations can lead us to err and overstep in our relationships with other people. Quotations are the site of our social anxieties around citation, which shape our means of communication in and outside of academia—the way we share our ideas and thoughts with others. Tsang's full body quotation brings us to the uneasy realization that in order to speak as one's self, sometimes we have to speak as another, and we do so by quoting them.

"This Is What I Want"

In *For how we perceived a life (Take 3)* (2012), Tsang's archival research appears as the glimmers of excerpts and turns of phrase. *For how we perceived a life* was shot on sixteen-millimeter film, the same format as *Paris Is Burning*. As opposed to a documentation of a live performance, it is a performance made for film, with the camera playing a character alongside Tsang and the other four performers in the video. If the camera is meant to play a character, it is one with a point of view made accessible to the viewer. One feels like they are timidly peeking into the role of another, as if getting a glance of someone else's phone screen at an angle, looking over their shoulder. This effect comes through in the work's installation: the projector for the film is placed behind a wall and plays the film on a continuous loop through a small hole.[3] One becomes aware of what is projected but voyeuristically and at a remove.

Using the length of a four-hundred-foot roll of film, the video was shot three times in a single take with no editing, with the third take as the final film. What the first or second takes might have been remains unknown and unseen, perhaps stored away in an archive. In knowing this is the third take, one wonders what the other takes might have been like and why they were not used—what made for an unsatisfying performance, in need of being enacted and filmed again? What was repeated, what was tweaked?

The film begins with a beep synchronizing sound and image. The soft click of analog film rolling and the drone of a synthesizer come together, swelling then dissipating into silence. The handheld camera slightly falters, moving through a bare warehouse space dimly lit with free-standing stage lights on gray cement floors, reflecting off brick walls painted white. On the side of the room lies a huddled mass on the ground, partially obscured by a pillar. As the camera slowly approaches, the mass comes into view, revealing the intertwined bodies of Tsang and fellow performers Desiree Burch, Cherrye Davis, Nicholas Gorham, and Mikeah Jennings, all dressed in black. Voices enter from the edges of the film.

"I believe that there's a big future out there," a voice softly murmurs, "A lot of beautiful things, a lot of handsome men, a lot of luxury." Another voice chimes in, "I want a car." A different voice sighs, "I want to be with a man," to which another voice adds, "I love," finishing a sentence spoken by another. Voices overlap each other, all beginning with the declaration, "I want." These voices want "a nice home, away from New York . . . somewhere far where no one knows me." They want "my sex change," "a normal happy life," "to get married in a church in white," "to be a complete woman." These lines, for some, might be familiar, reminiscent of some other context, some other time. The performers primarily speak as Octavia St. Laurent and Venus Xtravaganza, re-citing their words from interviews included in *Paris Is Burning*, but also excerpts edited out of the film's final cut and relegated to the archives Tsang had sifted through.

A few others interviewed in *Paris Is Burning* are also quoted: a photographer directing St. Laurent as she poses for images for her model portfolio, and two young boys spending their evenings on the streets, presumably outside of the Imperial Lodge of Elks in Harlem, where the balls in *Paris Is Burning* were located and filmed. These people remain unidentified and are described as such in Tsang's list of characters that accompanies *For how we perceived a life*. Additionally, performers in Tsang's video speak as Crystal LaBeija, a Black trans woman, pageant queen, and the founder of the House of LaBeija, who appears in Frank Simon's 1968 documentary *The Queen*, to which I will return, as well as Grandfather Hector Xtravaganza, a member of the House of Xtravaganza, from an interview Tsang conducted with him in 2012.

The performers in *For how we perceived a life* speak with voices that are soft and dry, as if close to one's ear to tell a secret. These confiding voices do not resonate within the same space that these performers are in, otherwise they would be washed out by the cavernous space's hard surfaces, reverberating and diminishing into echoes and murmurs. The voices come from another time and place, and yet, given the intimacy conveyed in their audible proximity, they lend an interiority to the group of bodies on the ground. The voices of the performers sit on top of the video, like they might offer objective narration. Yet their voices flowing with and through one another, contained between themselves and drifting mid-sentence without linear sequence, reflects the ways that

Paris Is Burning falls into the documentary tradition of cinéma vérité, as Lucas Hilderbrand notes.[4] As such, there can be no single perspective, no clear trajectory of where a performer's quotation might begin and end, whether from one performer's body to another's. Their voices resonate from within at the same time that they are dubbed from without.

Even though one might be able to place the origins of the dialogue spoken, the voices and the bodies that utter them seem impenetrable, impervious to one's efforts in deciphering who is saying what and which voice belongs to whom. Hilderbrand points out that because *Paris Is Burning* is composed of different footage and interviews filmed over the course of five years, there are many formal and thematic connections, beyond the scope of the title cards, which can be drawn from each viewing of the film.[5] "It is, indeed, a film that can play on heavy rotation," Hilderbrand writes, "as, on repeated viewings, it continues to reveal more."[6] *For how we perceived a life* insists on its own heavy rotation, insofar as heavy rotation is required to study and write about a film, as Hilderbrand does with *Paris Is Burning*. The work invites and demands the keen, obsessive eye of a scholar and a student.

Tsang, Burch, Davis, Gorham, and Jennings lip-synch to recordings of themselves reciting quotations, which are played back in earpieces they wear throughout the performance. In lip-syncing to their voices, they ventriloquize themselves with words first spoken by another. The work does not create a seamless relation between voice and body. Their performances draw attention to quotations constituted by being out of place, as speech not lost or misplaced, so much as relocated and given new context, disassembled then reassembled into different parts. The performers' prerecorded voices are nuzzled in their own ears as voices near and from within, while also afar and from without. The voices heard throughout *For how we perceived a life* give body to quotation and make citation audible. They activate modes of recognition and relating that cannot ensure the consolidation of the self and the stakes it wants to claim, adherent to idealized notions of possession and originality. They perform what feels and sounds derivative, what cannot be claimed for one's self alone.

As the camera draws closer, the performers' bodies move, churning and flexing their parts. Arms reach out and upward with a twist of a torso or wrist. Heads turn, with eyes closed in focus or repose, or open yet downcast. Hands touch the floor, and feet arch and dig into the ground. The camera hovers above the performers as they hold one another, lean against another's shoulder and rest a head on someone's back, encircled in another's arms. There is support in the huddle's constraint that remains unamenable to the comforts of a formal, identifiable structure. For huddles, as Ethan Philbrick writes, are "a relational form of disorderly proximity"—"provisional conglomerations thrown together at a remove and secretive gatherings held quickly in order to plan."[7] As the huddle of performers starts to unfold, the performers continue layering words and phrases, interrupting one another and switching lines, building up into a crescendo of wants: "I want"—"I want so much more"; "I want my name to be a household product." Finally, their voices come together in unison to declare, "I want this, this is what I want, and I'm gonna go for it."

Tsang's body and the bodies of the other performers do not stand in for the subjects they quote, nor do the subjects they quote stand in for them. Full body quotation is, as Tsang explains, "a kind of mimetic channeling of voices that is task-based but appears expressive. The tension is between the voice that you're channeling and the actual embodiment of that voice."[8] As a task, full body quotation is akin to a chore, a rote gesture one might do without thinking too hard about it. Yet to appear expressive, to seem affected, means something in that gesture could be in excess of the task at hand—something can escape from the resonant body. This excess is what Adriana Cavarero calls the "uniqueness" of the voice of another. The uniqueness of one's being is communicated through the voice, which implicates the throat, chest, flesh, and body of the one who emits it. This uniqueness is a singular "deep vitality" irreducible to essence or the idea of a true self. It is no secret to unearth either, for uniqueness takes pleasure in being shared through the voice, as the assertion of the body removed from the masculinist domains of reason, language, and speech.[9] It is relational, not harbored and held but let go and untethered. Uniqueness, in its association with the materiality of voice and body, is feminized as the "secondary, ephemeral, and inessential."[10] In contrast to a universal logos, uniqueness is "epistemologically inappropriate," confounding the ways one might typically come to know oneself and others.[11] Tsang's full body quotation inappropriately spreads around this uniqueness of the subject.

Tsang's attunement to uniqueness is not just about precision and exactitude—of getting the words and voice just right. This attunement is the practice of tapping into the way that the voice, the words spoken, and the forms of difference in excess of both passes through her body. Tsang does not quote another to master their voice and speech, to dominate by way of mimicry. The voice and speech of another presents Tsang with the challenge of becoming affected, expressive, and changed through the "tension . . . between the voice that you're channeling and the actual embodiment of that voice." Full body quotation creates the textured sensation of a voice, a body, or both pushing up against each other, against one's self and another, or straining the back of the throat, the lungs. Between voice and body, in the excess of uniqueness, one hears and feels the difficulty, reluctance, and hostility of being in relation, of spoiling another and being spoiled by them. As Rita Gonzalez writes, "Tsang's innovation of 'full body quotation' does not demand the relinquishing of one's position in relation to the quoted text but establishes the simultaneity and proximity of the subject re-speaking/quoting/delivering with the original author of the text."[12] Tsang makes room in her body for others, as the host that works at the task of being simultaneous and proximal.[13]

In *For how we perceived a life*, the voices and words of interviewees are not raw source material extracted from informants in need of another's narration and framing. Tsang and the other performers' bodies move, speak, and touch one another through an attunement to the interviewees' accounts of the self—particularly to what St. Laurent and Xtravaganza want. The performers' relations to one another are initiated and conditioned by the stories they have been tasked with relating, with the wants they cite that are not their own. The distinction, delay, and difference between the prerecorded voices heard and the performers bodies seen pull at the threads of the video's audiovisual seams, suspending the performers' authority and control over the words they re-cite and lip-synch, holding in tension the ways that the interviewees are not just objects of study and citation but also subjects of knowledge, with quotations and wants.

The Queen's Rage

As Burch, Davis, Gorham, and Tsang lie on the ground together, repeating, like a chant, "I want this, this is what I want, and I'm gonna go for it," their voices begin to overlap with that of Jennings, who rises from the ground. Jennings stands, facing the front of the room to re-cite lines from a now famous scene starring Crystal LaBeija from *The Queen*, which follows the 1967 Miss All-American Camp Beauty Pageant at New York City's Town Hall. In *The Queen*, LaBeija is named the third runner-up, but refuses to accept where she placed in the pageant. Instead, she walks off the stage and exits down the middle aisle. As she leaves, the mistress of ceremonies, Flawless Sabrina, tells her, "This is not the time to show temperament." But LaBeija does not stop, and it is exactly the right time. She refuses to be a good sport, for how can she when the rules seem to have not been fairly applied to her in the first place.[14]

Flawless Sabrina's protégé, a blond white queen named Rachel Harlow, is announced the winner, which fuels LaBeija's frustration and rage at the proceedings. Offstage, LaBeija tells the camera and the organizers of the pageant, the mistress of ceremonies included, that the pageant had been rigged from the start. When she is accused—not very subtly—of "showing her color," she replies, "I have a right to show my color, darling!" She insists that she did not sign any release to be photographed and filmed, and threatens to sue Sabrina if any images of her are released, but then she asks the person filming her to take a photograph of her next to Harlow so that the judges can compare their beauty. As Tavia Nyong'o writes, "This scene is a master class in the perils and possibilities of exposure."[15] In what has been called a "diva tantrum" and an "epic 'read'"—with much admiration, I might add—LaBeija "manages both to solicit the cinematic gaze and to dispute its power."[16] The tantrum, as considered in the previous chapter, is a particular way of inhabiting one's body that might look like the loss of control, and yet, in its spectacular force, it does control a room and a scene, like this one from *The Queen*. Harlow might have been the winner of the pageant, but LaBeija remains the memorable queen. All eyes are on her, including ours, as we encounter *The Queen* decades later, and LaBeija is still quoted, like she is in *For how we perceived a life*.

While Jennings's voice conveys LaBeija's anger that day of the pageant, his face remains deadpan. As Tina Post writes, the deadpan is a performative mode of Black inexpression that is evidence not of the absence of feeling, but rather of the malleability of "a surface quiet that affects its audience through genre, material surroundings, and sensoria."[17] Here, what ripples upon such surface quiet is Jennings's voice speaking as LaBeija. The dissonance between Jennings's vocal performance of dissatisfaction and his embodied performance of stillness and composure marks where LaBeija's quotation ends and where Jennings's act of quoting begins. As Jennings lip-synchs, he slowly turns his head back and forth, surveying the space, while the other performers lie at his feet, sometimes providing the din and aural backdrop to LaBeija's words without interrupting. There are pockets of silence made to feature Jennings's performance, and at other times the words of someone involved in the confrontation after the pageant in *The Queen* are quoted. Context comes and goes, as does the dynamic of dialogue. To quote LaBeija is to isolate her words, highlighting the heft of her critique as it moves through Jennings's body.

Quoting from *The Queen*—a film from the pre-Stonewall era—might seem out of place given *For how we perceived a life*'s primary focus on *Paris Is Burning* and its archival materials and footage. However, the connections and legacy are apparent, particularly with the appearance of the House of LaBeija, and Pepper LaBeija, as Mother of the House, in *Paris Is Burning*. Although *For how we perceived a life* scrambles linear time, what emerges from it and its use of full body quotation is a genealogy of minoritarian performance that revolves around trans women of color like Xtravaganza, St. Laurent, and LaBeija. This genealogy, particularly for scholars working in trans studies and trans of color critique, is fraught because of how trans women of color are idealized and valorized, particularly in queer studies, at the same time that they are subject to exclusion and trans misogynist violence. As Jules Gill-Peterson asserts, trans women always seem to be claimed and spoken for by someone other than themselves, and particularly by queer nontrans people, who are anxious about their proximity to trans women in the first place. How, then, do we make sense of the relations forged through full body quotation between Jennings and LaBeija, between the other performers and St. Laurent and Xtravaganza? I propose that these relations, fraught as they are, are ones of interdependence, which many, queer nontrans people included, have either forgotten or disavowed. This interdependence is not just pleasurable and utopic, as the site of collectivity and care, but also painful and difficult, as the site of harm and hostility. Power moves through these relations that full body quotation tracks, much in the same way that it tends to the uniqueness of the voice that desires to be shared.

Following the 1969 Stonewall Uprising, the gay and lesbian movement "betrayed trans femininity in the early 1970s to secure their respectability as men and women," Gill-Peterson writes.[18] Trans women, and specifically poor trans women of color, who often had to make a living through sex work—like Xtravaganza—were left behind as the movement forged ahead. Due to their nonassimilation into and exclusion from normative, supposedly respectable lifestyles, trans women of color were seen as tragic figures from another time and place, as inevitable victims to trans misogynist violence. These representations, as Gill-Peterson argues, primarily come from nontrans gay and lesbian cultural production, which relegate trans women of color to the past, as figures bound to disappear, without a future and in need of rescue and redemption.

It would seem that such rescue and redemption, in the contemporary moment, would become possible through the queer celebration and restoration of the memory of historical figures like Sylvia Rivera and Marsha P. Johnson. But whom is the celebration and promise of restoration actually for? In keeping with the work of Jay Prosser, Vivian Namaste, and Emma Heaney, Gill-Peterson argues that such reparative gestures are for the advancement of queer theory, nontrans queer people, and their radical politics.[19] "Our politics will be saved by invoking trans women of color and acting in their name," Gill-Peterson writes, "We will rescue them from our betrayal in the 1970s by idealizing them. Or so it seems."[20] But in order to be saviors, trans women of color must also become martyrs. As Heaney writes, trans women are made into allegorical "entrapped" figures for nontrans people's interrogation of and liberation from categories of gender, sex, and sexuality.[21] Trans women of color are made into idealized but also instructive figures, in and through their suffering, as well as in their death.

Gill-Peterson, along with Prosser and Namaste, critique Judith Butler's reading of *Paris Is Burning* in their book, *Bodies That Matter*, as a primary example of this. Butler wrote about *Paris Is Burning* in response to misreadings of *Gender Trouble* that assumed that if gender was performative, gender was then a voluntary performance. Butler also wanted to push back on bell hooks's reading of *Paris Is Burning*, wherein she critiqued the ball participants' desire for and appropriation of ideals of white femininity as that which further subjected them to the terms of their own exclusion.[22] Butler argued that the ball participants' desire for and appropriation of these ideals does not uphold prevailing gender norms, but "repeats in order to remake" and subvert them.[23] This subversion was contingent on "the ambivalence of embodying—and failing to embody—that which one sees."[24] "Then," Butler writes, "a distance will be opened up *between* that hegemonic call to normativizing gender and its critical appropriation."[25]

What happens, though, when someone does not feel ambivalent about who and what she embodies? What happens when someone refuses failure and insists on her desires for and attainment of what she wants, closing in on that distance required for politically productive forms of "critical appropriation"? For Butler, this someone was Venus Xtravaganza, who, during the filming for *Paris Is Burning* in 1988, was murdered, most likely by a client. As Butler saw it, what led to Xtravaganza's death was her desire for the real as opposed to realness—a desire that was improper, nonproductive, and apolitical, removed from what was "critically queer."[26] Xtravaganza—as someone with a community, knowledge, and desires of her own, who knows what she wants—is eclipsed by queer theory's need to teach a lesson. She could not survive because she spoiled her own supposed queer potentiality. In Butler's reading, Xtravaganza becomes queer theory's pedagogical object. For Gill-Peterson, this reliance on trans women of color, and the impulse to make a lesson out of their premature deaths, makes evident an "interdependence with trans women."[27] I am interested in how this interdependency can also be a site of queer theory's spoilage. Queer theory's dependent, at times extractive, relationship to trans women of color obstructs its own desire for repair, for making itself and queer studies more inclusive, more whole. Given this, queer theory, and its articulations of queerness, must work to give an account of the damage it inflicts on itself but also on others, particularly by way of its interdependency.

While Gill-Peterson is wary of how trans women of color are made into a lesson for queer theory, Cameron Awkward-Rich considers what lessons we might learn alongside trans studies' emergence in the 1990s and early 2000s. Trans studies' and trans-affirmative discourse have centered trans people as subjects with the authority to produce knowledge about trans lives and experience, rather than as someone else's object of study. However, Awkward-Rich writes that such authority and affirmation are contingent upon the disavowal of the mad or disabled person, as well as the person of color, and the assertion of sanity, health, and feeling good in service to the representation of trans people as always "well-adjusted, well-supported."[28] Awkward-Rich turns to "trans maladjustment," which can produce the possibility of "a version of trans studies that can acknowledge and think with a more expansive *we*, terrible though it might feel."[29]

Awkward-Rich explains how the term "maladjustment" shifted in its meaning, from a general form of relation—"*misfit between two or more things*"—to the relation between an individual and the social, to a condition within and of the self, "a sense of being (or being evidence of) an incapacity of a person or organism to adapt to life."[30] He understands maladjustment within the context of disability studies' critiques of ableist ideology and its organization of an environment that produces "misfitting bodies as social misfits."[31] Trans maladjustment is not solely symptomatic of oppression, nor reducible to the wrong-body model—expressed as feeling "trapped" in the wrong body put forth by sexologists beginning in the mid-nineteenth century.[32] Trans maladjustment is "integral to trans epistemology and cultural production . . . toward ways of knowing (and not-knowing), of living (and not-living)."[33] It can be pedagogical, providing a lesson that does not expect a queen to graciously accept her loss in a pageant that was biased from the start. In staying with "the terrible we," Awkward-Rich attends to the challenge of speaking as a "we" when that "we" might not like the company it is made to keep, and especially when that "we" might compromise the authority of one's speech, too tainted with rage, taking the maladjusted form of a tantrum or a rant.[34]

How does one, which is also many, go about speaking as a "terrible we"? Full body quotation offers one way. Such a move in *For how we perceived a life* is risky because including St. Laurent, Xtravaganza, and LaBeija in this "we" might make them, as trans women of color, into allegorical figures with symbolic value claimed by other people. Gill-Peterson warns us about taking this risk at the same time that she invites its possibility, especially if everyone within "the terrible we" shares an interdependency with trans women. To be clear, when Gill-Peterson writes of this interdependency, she is not talking about a harmonious, symmetrical kind of relating. As she argues, trans misogyny is a violent reaction to "gender as a system [that] coerces and maintains radical interdependence" with trans women.[35] Trans women are made to bear the brunt of other people's anxiety, anger, and fear around the fact that gender categories are social as well as hierarchical. This renders trans femininity "too sociable," Gill-Peterson writes, "too connected to everyone."[36] Trans misogyny, then, is the "rejection of everyone's interdependence with trans women . . . [that] attempt[s] to refuse a social debt accrued."[37] Interdependency, then, as a form of relation that produces social debt, is the site of harm, as much as it might be a site of care.

By speaking as Xtravaganza, St. Laurent, and LaBeija, the performers in *For how we perceived a life* dramatize this interdependency. They do not make any claims on and for those whom they speak, nor do they aim to perpetuate or incite trans misogynist violence from those who fear their proximity to and interdependency with trans women. However, they do offer the act of quotation as an acknowledgment of a debt owed within that relation of interdependency. The quotations produced in Tsang's performance practice carry this debt, drawing the self in closer proximity to others, implicating the self, making the self complicit with its own utterance as someone else. Such debt, because it is social, cannot be calculated and repaid in full. It is what Stefano Harney and Fred Moten call "bad debt": it generates and fuels one's ongoing commitments to others without end.[38] It remains in circulation, up in the air, and for some, this might cause some stress and discomfort, which is the point.

Full body quotation is not about performing what is most comfortable to and for one's self—it is not about finding the right fit, a relation that demands nothing, no work, and the flawless synchronicity of voice and body. Full body quotation is about performing what is "*misfit between two or more things*."[39] In *For how we perceived a life*, the performers amplify and embody the distinction and difference between themselves and who they are quoting—therein lies the expression of one's debt to another. Misfitting bodies with misfitting speech dramatize the work of learning to relate from within the uneasy proximities that interdependency creates. The performers do not protect themselves and who they are quoting from the possibility of violence and harm. They cannot promise or guarantee that. However, they do express their own capacity to be the source of that violence and harm—this is the risk they take in speaking as someone else.

In *For how we perceived a life*, the desynchronous makes for the maladjusted. Consider the slight hitch between performers' lip-synchs and their prerecorded voices, how one might fall behind or jump ahead of the other. These performers' lip-synchs are not without flaws: there are small hesitations, pulls, tugs, and twitches at the corners of the mouth; lips trip over muted enunciation; breaths are misplaced midsentence revealing the performers' relation to their own voices as one of temporal, embodied interruption, lag, and delay. In these moments, the performers must recall what they studied: how they memorized another's speech, recorded what they memorized, and listened repeatedly to what they had recorded of their own voice in order to rehearse and perform speaking as another. Their study of another becomes inseparable from the study of the self; the viewer, in turn, must study, too, watching and listening closely, in search of where a quotation begins and a body ends. Maladjustment lies between sound and body, between speech and gesture, where the "terrible we" resonates.

Xtravaganza is introduced in *Paris Is Burning* with a particular scene that is not included in *For how we perceived a life*, but is often quoted elsewhere, including hooks's and Butler's readings of the film. Sitting on the corner of her bed near a window and radiator, Xtravaganza looks to the camera and says, "I would like to be a spoiled, rich, white girl" with a small laugh. She jokes at the same time that she knows spoiled, rich, white girls "get what they want, whenever they want it, and they don't really have to struggle with finances and nice things and nice clothes, and they don't have to have that as a problem." For Gill-Peterson, the scene authorizes Xtravaganza as a subject who speaks to what she knows about power, race, gender, sex, and class. Xtravaganza compares her work as an escort to that of a housewife. She, like a housewife wanting a new washer and dryer, knows what she needs to do to get what she wants from a man. "So, in the long run, it all ends up the same way," Xtravaganza explains. Her expression of a wish and a want, of who she would like to be, comes from her assertion that she already knows how she is different, and also not. She knows about interdependency, about how some might try, violently, to distance themselves from her, and in the face of this, she insists on the sociality of trans femininity that Gill-Peterson describes. We might read this scene as a moment where Xtravaganza knows that to speak as herself is to also speak as a "spoiled, rich, white girl" and as the housewife. Xtravaganza authorizes her own speech by imagining that she speaks as another, as someone who is spoiled in the same way she should be.

When in Doubt, Always Cite

Tsang came across *Paris Is Burning* when she was studying film editing with Jonathan Oppenheim, who had edited the film with Livingston.[40] For many, *Paris Is Burning* is often first discovered in the classroom. It was for me. It is a film assigned and taught, guided by a teacher's instruction. From there, the film seeps into conversations with peers outside of class, showing up in group chats and social media, as a GIF, an image, or a line of dialogue performed in front of friends. The film remains a curricular, canonical object that, through its title cards, divulges lessons on drag houses and drag mothers as sources of alternative kinship, on categories of realness, on the art of shade and reading, and the skill of mopping. The film also invites discussions in the classroom around race, gender, sexuality, class, agency, and appropriation. It is taught alongside the conflicts and controversy that followed, particularly taking into account how many of those included in the film struggled financially despite its success, and attempted to file a lawsuit for fair, additional compensation.

In an article written by critic Jesse Green in 1993, it was also revealed that many people in the film—five out of the nine the film featured—had passed away from underlying conditions left untreated as well as from AIDS-related complications.[41] Such disparity sparked necessary debates around who has the right to represent or speak for a community, particularly in documentary filmmaking. When taught, the film is contextualized within the "culture wars" in the United States during the late 1980s and 1990s, in the midst of the AIDS crisis, and as a part of the emergence of what B. Ruby Rich named "New Queer Cinema."[42] It is also an archive of Black, Latinx, trans, and queer New York City nightlife, with footage of the balls but also scenes of sociality and livelihood along the city's West Side piers, in Harlem, and in the private, interior spaces of interviewees' homes. The film has been preserved and restored, re-released with additional footage, making what Tsang discovered as a student available to a wider audience keen to know more, to get a closer look behind the scenes.[43]

When watching *For how we perceived a life*, one becomes aware of the mobility of the lessons *Paris Is Burning* contains, particularly by way of the many quotations used from it. For Gonzalez and Nyong'o, *For how we perceived a life* embodies the forms of media *Paris Is Burning*, its archives, and *The Queen* take in the contemporary moment: cut, edited excerpts of dialogue that interrupt the linear time of documentary film and that frequently circulate online.[44] In recent years, I have found that when I include *Paris Is Burning* on a syllabus, all my students know of the film and have seen clips from it shared on the internet, but a majority have not seen the film in its entirety. While for some teachers this might be something to bemoan, as a sign of the times, shorter attention spans, and young people's irreverence or disinterest in the past, I want to hold back from making those generational judgments. Students sometimes feel like they know St. Laurent and Xtravaganza, as well as other queens featured in the film, like Dorian Corey and Pepper LaBeija, based on what they have seen online, however truncated or brief. They have their own attachments to the people in the film, which exceed the narrative of the documentary genre and are expressed through the memorization and recitation of quotations. Tsang's way of gathering quotations and dispersing them through multiple performers' voices reflects this different kind of encounter, this other kind of lesson outside of a syllabus and a classroom.

"When in doubt, always cite." Often, this what we, as teachers, tell our students in our syllabi and in our classrooms. We tell our students this because otherwise they will be in violation of codes of conduct. Indeed, citation and plagiarism are a matter of conduct—of manners, comportment, and behavior. Citations structure our ways of engaging in intellectual thought and exchange with others, ethically. They are a means of mediating how we relate to each other in writing and elsewhere, as scholars, writers, critics, and students. This is why some teachers include a note about plagiarism in the section of syllabi on policy, but also in a section that outlines a social contract. Citation and the possibility of plagiarism are social matters of the classroom, perhaps even before they are matters of official policy.

In early December 2023, the presidents of the University of Pennsylvania, Harvard University, and the Massachusetts Institute of Technology testified in a congressional hearing convened by House Republicans regarding antisemitism on college campuses. This took place during ongoing protests and demonstrations both on and off college campuses across the United States, organized in solidarity with Palestine and against the genocidal war on Gaza, following the Hamas attacks on Israel in October of that year. In the hearing, Dr. Claudine Gay, the president of Harvard University, evaded questions that tried to conflate antisemitism with anti-Zionism. This led to outrage from certain conservative activists and news outlets, who dug into Dr. Gay's scholarly work and subsequently made allegations of plagiarism against her.[45] The veracity of these allegations was not the point. The point was to call into question Dr. Gay's academic integrity by trying to represent her as a plagiarizer—one of the ultimate violations of academic conventions—so that there would be grounds for her removal as president of the university. Dr. Gay ended up resigning from her position in early 2024. What came up in the midst of the allegations and her resignation were questions about citational practice within academia: What are the standards and ethics built around citational practice? What are we wanting them to uphold, not just in academia, but in our relation to one another as teachers, students, scholars, particularly in a time of academic censorship?

During this time, Namwali Serpell made a series of posts on X (Twitter) that suggested academia is partly at fault for leading us here in the first place. "We treat [citation] as a technical 'rule' to follow, rather than a convention grounded in certain values," she writes, "Why do we say paraphrase is not just swapping words? To prevent students from presenting others' ideas as their own."[46] Serpell, of course, does not condone plagiarism, but she does clarify that she speaks "as someone who knows plagiarism is not the same as copyright infringement—a matter of convention, not law. We ought to discuss with students WHY we've adopted these conventions: what they're meant to prevent and encourage."[47] While academia has made citation and the possibility of plagiarism subject to legal assessment, regulation, and punishment, Serpell reminds us that first and foremost, citation and plagiarism are issues of "convention." They are defined through and in adherence with social codes, values, and norms. Note how Serpell talks about citation and plagiarism in the context of the classroom, as that which we have to address with our students. These are matters not just for the president of an elite university but also for the students we teach as well as for ourselves. We must learn these codes, values, and norms, not because, *or else*, we will be sued (though yes, that is a possibility), but primarily because we want to think, write, and publish in good faith.

"When in doubt, always cite" implies that sometimes there will be moments of doubt. Tsang's full body quotation works within the vicinity of that doubt, not to manipulate it for her own ends—as if to get away with plagiarism—but to consider the sticky subject of what we owe and what we are owed when we cite and quote others, and when others cite and quote us. Our indebtedness to others and others' indebtedness to us is a subject of doubt because ultimately, in our citations, we are not entitled to whom and what we cite. The acts of citing and quoting remind us that we do not own what we share with others. Our relationship to what we cite and quote is doubtful, which is to say that our relationship to our sources—to an archive, canonical films, historical figures—is never a given. When describing how she selected quotations to be included in *For how we perceived a life*, Tsang explains, "I chose material where the performers all had complicated relationships to the sources. The full body quotation technique is a way to perform our ambivalences."[48] Complication, like doubt, creates feelings of ambivalence toward one's sources, and full body quotation is the performance of that ambivalence. Such ambivalence comes from wanting to preserve and care for one's sources in the act of citation while also knowing that one risks altering or destroying them, too. This ambivalence expresses our nonproprietary relationship to our sources, like *The Queen*, *Paris Is Burning*, and its archives. Tsang's practice of full body quotation brings us to the limits of the conventions of citation, and what they promise to cement, stave off, and enact in our relations with others. It addresses our desires to relate to one another through citation, by way of the social life of a quotation.

Black feminist and women of color feminist scholars have written on the ethics of citation in relation to a Westernized white canon founded on their exclusion. As a policy, Sara Ahmed does not cite white men so that she may better use citations to build "feminist shelters."[49] This policy lets her reflect on her citational habits, to reorient her ways of knowing, and provide feminist sites of refuge. Katherine McKittrick understands Ahmed's intentions, acknowledging the ways that citations can uphold but also disrupt white patriarchal scholarly traditions. At the same time, she wonders if such a policy and practice give way to "impossible foreclosures."[50] "Do we unlearn whom we do not cite?" McKittrick asks. "And what of our teaching practice? Do we teach refusal?"[51] Rather than teach refusal, McKittrick proposes that we teach a critical engagement with the citations we want to decenter. Refusal, to an extent, is not a mode of critique so much as it is a mode of erasure, and erasure by way of refusal is not the same as unlearning the traditions that bind us.

A question of citation becomes a question of teaching and learning. Citation remains a pedagogical issue because it is a way of showing one's work, the process of arriving at a thought, an argument, an idea through what one has learned from others. Citations can furnish the self, and it can undermine it too. I have been told on more than one occasion that I cite too much—something most are likely to hear in graduate school and beyond. Citation is necessary to staking one's original claims and making one's interventions at the same time that they involve, as McKittrick writes, "*risking the sovereignty of our own stories.*"[52] They bulk up the self, but can decentralize and dispossess it of itself, too. McKittrick lets us know what this might look like on the page in her book *Dear Science and Other Stories*. It includes footnotes in lieu of endnotes that draw a reader's eye downward, inviting them to pause and think with the work that happens below and aside.[53] Writers have also experimented with citation outside of strictly academic publications. For instance, Maggie Nelson's *The Argonauts* includes quotations without formal in-text citations, but instead, with the names of those quoted sitting in the margins.[54] All these gestures, as Jennifer Nash writes, are expressions of "citational desires," wherein to cite, if done the right way, becomes a site of formal, institutional recognition that also promises to be an ethical act of care, preservation, and reproduction.[55]

Alongside and within the practice of consciousness-raising, scholars of queer and feminist theory and critical race and ethnic studies have emphasized the importance of cultivating a "theory in the flesh" and a "politics of location," of grappling with the occasion of "speaking as a feminist," or what it means to "theorize as a lesbian."[56] Some have addressed the problems that arise when "speaking for others," as a privileged, oppressive gesture desirous of mastery, as well as the possibilities of deconstructing categories of identity by "enacting others," or reflecting on one's own self in relation to others by "speaking nearby."[57] All these discussions grapple with the question of how to relate to another without imposing oneself, how to draw clear lines that distinguish me from you, which should then not be crossed, not without permission. Tsang wades into these debates by way of quotation, which, couched within quotation marks, is something outside of the self that is then folded and taken in, incorporated and used elsewhere for the self's own ends.

Tsang's work has sparked conversations about appropriation, similar to those that swirled around Livingston and her relation to ball culture in the making of *Paris Is Burning*.[58] It is then not a coincidence that Tsang draws from *Paris Is Burning* in her development of full body quotation. Tsang's work shifts these conversations with the insertion of her body into her work as a filmmaker and performer, and through her focus on the form of the quotation itself, which shifts the conversation from appropriation to citation. I am not interested in relitigating whether or not Tsang's work is appropriative. I am interested in understanding how Tsang's use of quotation pulls at the taut lines drawn between the self and other. Full body quotation reaches for the thresholds between self-indulgence and giving, between an invitation and an imposition, in such a way that undermines what Ricardo Montez views as idealized modes of collaboration, which presume "a more egalitarian, polyvocal working relationship" between artists, or between artists their objects.[59] Instead, full body quotation activates relations of complicity, which names "the dynamic uncertainty of intimate and creative exchange" that cannot be mapped onto the fantasies of symmetrical, mutual relation often attributed to idealized notions of collaboration.[60] Tsang's full body quotation, as an encounter with voices from the archive, offer scenes of complicity that bring to the fore the structural imbalances and differences collaboration invites, if not requires. Through the framework of complicity, we learn about one's capacity to use another and one's susceptibility and vulnerability to being used by another.

Generally, we are taught that using people is bad, unethical, and destructive. One should not assert power over others, making them an object for one's own ends. But as Barbara Johnson writes, "What is being denied from the outset is the subject's *lack* of power, its vulnerability and dependence."[61] Johnson does not overlook material violent histories of appropriation that bolster the "imperial subject."[62] At the same time, she wants to hold in question—in doubt—the presumption of that subject's power. To use people is to confront our need for them, and to acknowledge our capacity to inflict damage on them out of that very need. Moreover, using people leads us to the realization that other people have the capacity to survive the damage we do to them, without our help or guilt. This is not the same as saying we can treat people however we like, because no matter what they will recover. To believe that people might not be able to survive our destructive impulses, and that we alone can fix them, renders other people into idealized objects that consolidate our image of ourselves as all-powerful. To understand, on the other hand, that people can survive the damage we might cause, and that we are not the only ones who can repair that damage, is to view other people as real, discrete subjects, separated from the self, and beyond the self's control.

Johnson uses D. W. Winnicott to make her point, or put differently, she cites and quotes his theory of the transitional object. When properly used, transitional objects teach us how to become a subject. Using transitional objects makes room for play, in the space between a subject and object, self and world, "me" and "not-me"—for the range of experience that comes with feeling omnipotent and triumphant in one moment and powerless and frustrated in the next.[63] Such play is generative and creative, provoking feelings of love and hate, of ambivalence, and in doing so, transitional objects become, as Johnson puts it, "a kind of navel of the arts," consisting of "words, patterns, tunes, and mannerisms."[64] Here, I would add, resonant, sonorous bodies, too. Tsang and her collaborator's performances tend to the vulnerability and possible violence of interdependency, and one's capacity for care as well as for destruction. This is how we come to learn that in using people, and in being used, we are also "trusting people": trusting that they can survive our destruction, and that we can survive theirs.[65]

A Pedagogical Scene

As a student at UCLA, Tsang became a part of LA's art scene and queer nightlife. During 2008–10, Tsang, along with friends Asma Maroof, Ashland Mines, and Daniel Pineda, threw a queer dance party every Tuesday at a bar called the Silver Platter, located in the then gentrifying LA neighborhood of Silver Lake. Together, they named the party Wildness, and throughout its run, the Platter became a multifunctional space with live music and experimental performance art. What had initially drawn Tsang to the Platter, though, was all that preceded her and her friends.

Since it first opened in 1963, the Platter had served a predominantly working-class gay, trans, and Latinx clientele. When Tsang discovered the bar through a friend's recommendation, it was run by Gonzalo, his ex-boyfriend Koky, and Koky's boyfriend, Javier. Gonzalo and his sister, Nora, inherited the bar from their brother, Rogelio. When Tsang came across the bar, Gonzalo, Koky, and Javier had kept the bar going, witnessing how it had changed over the years, from serving primarily gay men to becoming what Nicol, the bar's host, describes as "a living room" for the trans community. With the success of Wildness, as well as with the gentrification and development of the surrounding area, all who gathered at the Platter—Gonzalo, Koky, and Javier included—were witness to how the Platter changed again.

Tsang's 2012 film, *Wildness*, is an experimental documentary film about the party, the Platter, and the people in the bar's shifting orbit. It is narrated by Tsang, who speaks as herself in English, and the voice of Mariana Marroquin, who speaks as the Platter in Spanish, with dialogue cowritten by Tsang and Roya Rastegar. In the film, Marroquin's voice is the first we hear. Over footage of Silver Lake shot from a moving car, the Platter, through Marroquin, ruminates on the possibility of its disappearance. The Platter asks, "What will become of me? How can I explain my legacy?"[66] The question lingers as the sun sets over the neighborhood, illuminated by LA's pollution-pink sky.

The film cuts to a view of the street at night, no longer from a car but from the sidewalk, following a figure walking alone at night. Marroquin, as the Platter, speaks, delivering her lines with relish. "I'm a beacon, guiding my young out of the darkness," she croons, "This story is one of those journeys. Told through my youngest: Wu. And the Wildness they brought to me." The figure the film follows is Tsang, who approaches the street corner where the Platter resides. Tsang looks up, and as the film cuts to the Platter's glowing neon sign pulsing like a heartbeat, there is a moment of recognition between Tsang and the Platter. The camera looks down, from the vantage point of the Platter's sign, and Tsang looks up, as if to return its gaze. She then directs her eyes straight ahead and enters the Platter.

In an interview, Tsang explains, "[*Wildness* is] about my character being this younger, more naive version of me that comes to the bar with a need, and the bar is this elder parent figure who helps me and is tough with me when it needs to be."[67] In this scene, the Platter and Tsang's introduction to one another is staged as an encounter between an elder and their "youngest"—between a mother and child, but also between a teacher and student. Throughout the film, the Platter has much to teach Tsang. It hopes that Tsang will learn how to tell the Platter's "legacy," which, through the film, has been passed down to others. There are moments of affection between Tsang and the Platter, mixed with moments of frustration, sarcasm, and annoyance—mostly on the part of the Platter. At the same time, the Platter's voice conveys patience, with a prickly wit and soft regard. The Platter's tone is one of a teacher, or a parent, waiting for you to figure out the lesson yourself, always ready to provide some leading questions, not without a few chiding remarks. What Tsang and Rastegar have written imagines the Platter and Tsang entering into a complicit, uneven relation, wherein each has something the other wants and needs. Tsang wants to belong, and the Platter is a place where she can, for the time being; the Platter needs more time, and Tsang has time to give.

What Tsang also gives to the Platter is a voice, which, given that the Platter cannot actually speak, might be understood as an imposition, as projection. Marroquin speaks as the Platter, while Tsang and Rastegar risk speaking *for* it. Such projection, on the part of Tsang, is the expression of a want and need, more so than the disavowal of her lack. Although the Platter cannot speak as an "I" without Tsang and Rastegar's dialogue, and without Marroquin's voice, the same can be said for Tsang. Her "I" can only be uttered and heard once she has felt that the Platter has addressed her and invited her in from the street corner. The question is not if the Platter is actually speaking as itself—of course, it is not. Tsang needs to imagine the Platter can speak so that she can give an account of herself. To give an account of herself in the film requires giving an account of the Platter. Without the Platter, there is no story to tell—Tsang needs the Platter's guidance to learn her lesson.

This lesson ends up being one about the limits of belonging, community, and care, about the turbulence of what José Esteban Muñoz called the "brown commons," constituted by "a choreography of singularities that touch and contact but do not meld."[68] Tsang says that while the party's popularity led to the bar's visibility, she wanted to protect the Platter as a "safe space," which she worries she might have spoiled.[69] She also wanted to give back to the bar's community to preserve what it had been, and who it had been for, before Wildness. As a part of these efforts, in 2009, Tsang and fellow artists Nicolau Vergueiro, Michelle Dizon, and Camilo Ontiveros set up a community center called Imprenta in a rented storefront around the corner from the bar, which offered HIV testing as well as legal services for trans people. For a time, it was all working—the Platter was financially benefiting from the party and Imprenta helped people in the neighborhood. Yet the differences across and between the bar's regulars, the younger (and whiter) queers who came to Wildness, the gentrifying (straighter, richer, and still whiter) crowds that followed, and the transphobic media coverage it drew, jeopardized the Platter as a "safe space." Additionally, when Gonzalez suddenly passed away in 2009, questions arose around his will, in which he had left his portion of the Platter that he owned to Koky. Gonzalez's family, including Nora, did not want to comply, leading to legal disputes, the loss of Koky's and Javier's jobs at the Platter, and a falling out between Nora and Tsang. In solidarity with Koky and Javier, Tsang and the others decided to cancel Wildness until further notice.

In her narration, Tsang explains that she tried to apologize to Nora with a letter translated into Spanish, which went unanswered. In that moment, Tsang discovers that she had "stepped over a line." She was no longer inside the Platter, but outside of it, back on the street corner, on the other side of the line she had been allowed to cross in the beginning of the film. In this particular scene of the film, Tsang breaks from her voice-over narration. Sitting outside the gated, locked door of the Platter in the middle of the day, she looks directly into the camera to say, "I fucked up." "Finally," the Platter chimes in, "Wu realized that [she] too was part of this game. [She] wasn't above the drama, and [she] could hurt people." It is only when Tsang realizes that she is capable of hurting people that she grasps the relationships she had formed in the first place. She becomes aware of how she had cared for and been cared by those around her once she learns that she has become the cause of their pain. At the threshold of the Platter, where she does not know if and when she will be let back in, Tsang understands what it feels like to belong.

By the film's end, resolutions are offered, but only for a few. Tsang narrates that Koky, with the support of lawyers, was able to get his job back (though whether this means he received his portion of the ownership of the bar is unclear). Tsang was also able to make amends with Nora. Javier, however, is shown in the film as still estranged, financially struggling, and angered and hurt by how he was treated and the loss of his job. While Tsang says that Nora and the family (it is unclear if this includes Koky) were open to having Wildness come back on Tuesdays, Tsang and her friends decided the moment had passed. A year later, they could no longer afford Imprenta, so they moved out of the space, and the legal clinic dissolved. Still, however, the Platter remains. In the beginning of the film, the Platter announces that it lives on "borrowed time." This borrowed time is afforded through Tsang's own need, through what she needs to borrow, too—through the way Tsang crosses a threshold, speaks as a bar, steps over a line, and throws a party that will eventually come to an end.

Oversharing the Incommunicable

> Let me clear things up right now by crafting a performative utterance: I love my students.—José Esteban Muñoz, "Teaching, Minoritarian Knowledge, and Love" (2004)

Tsang's performance for video *Shape of the Right Statement* (2008) was shot by artist A. L. Steiner on the stage of the Platter. The camera rests on a close-up of Tsang, who looks squarely into the camera. She wears a nude-colored nylon wig cap and a fitted black top, like a leotard, as if she is dressed for rehearsal. Her pared-down appearance lies in contrast to the visual decadence of the backdrop she stands against: a curtain of silver sequined fabric that adorns the Platter's stage. Without blinking, and with barely any movement, except for the deep inhalations and exhalations that swell and deflate her chest, she recites excerpts of a performance from a YouTube video uploaded in 2007 by the autism-rights activist, writer, and artist Mel Baggs called "In My Language."[70]

The first part of the video is described as being in Baggs's "native language," while the second part is a "translation."[71] In the first part, a voice sings, sliding between notes, as the palm of a hand runs across a computer keyboard; a silver chain twirls in the air as a hand bats at it, propelling its movements; a strip of paper flaps back and forth, mirroring a flag waving from a pole seen outside a window from behind it; a hand's fingers twirl around the knob of a dresser. In the second half of the video, a voice generated by a speaking device begins to speak, accompanied by subtitles in English at the bottom of the screen, as the montage of footage of touching and feeling continues, accompanied by an intermittent hum. With the speaking device, Baggs's nonverbal, nontextual statement is translated into a verbal and textual one. Speaking as Baggs, the voice states, "Ironically, the way that I move when responding to everything around me is described as 'being in a world of my own,' whereas if I interact with a much more limited set of responses and only react to a much more limited part of my surroundings people claim that I am 'opening up to true interaction with the world.'"[72]

Baggs's translated statement is recited in a language that is not their own. What might initially appear to be an antisocial means of "being in a world of my own"—because it is without words, and filled with objects rather than people—is an expansive openness and receptivity to the world not stunted by verbal communication. M. Remi Yergeau writes that autistic people are often given a narrative through diagnosis, given a list of symptoms where "traits and check boxes tell a story" of pathology.[73] And yet, despite all the studies of autism, an autistic person is still rendered "unknowable, as utterly abject and isolated and tragic, as a figure whose actions are construed less like actions and more like neuronally willed middle fingers," which are perceived as involuntary, and therefore proof of impairment and the need for therapeutic treatment.[74]

While the pathologization of autistic people assumes that autism hinders a person's capacity to be social, for Baggs, such pathologization is evidence of a limited, ableist understanding of what constitutes the social. Autistic people do not fail to be social. They shift what the social's conditions of possibility might be, and they do so from an asocial position that could be akin to, for instance, staying in. They have a different story to tell about themselves and a different way of telling it. Yergeau proposes that we engage with these "autistic stories," over and above the language of diagnosis.[75] Baggs's actions and sounds in the video are not symptoms but a means of communication. And yet, to communicate, for Baggs, does not always mean there is symbolic meaning translatable to text or speech. "My language is not about designing words or even visual symbols for people to interpret," Baggs states, "It is about being in a constant conversation with every aspect of my environment. Reacting physically to all parts of my surroundings." The video shows Baggs holding out a finger underneath water running from a faucet, poking, twirling, and stroking its wetness, splash, and flow. "In this part of the video," Baggs explains, "the water doesn't symbolize anything. I am just interacting with the water as the water interacts with me. Far from being purposeless, the way that I move is an ongoing response to what is around me."[76] For Baggs, communication is embodied, something felt, seen, smelled, heard, and tasted. Baggs's language is not for explaining their actions and sounds, but for exercising their capacity and desire to react to their surroundings, to alter and respond to them.

In *Shape of the Right Statement*, Tsang quotes the second part of the video. Tsang's performance is contingent on the limits of her own understanding of Baggs's language, embodying a quotation of a translation provided by a speaking device. Tsang embodies the residue produced and left behind between a language and its translation into another form. What falls out of translation—the gestures, feeling, and sensation—are the parts of communication that remain incommunicable. For this reason, the engagement between Baggs and their environment, Tsang and Baggs, Tsang and the viewer, and Tsang and the Platter, remains open-ended and unfinished. Tsang explains that in *Shape of the Right Statement*, "I was very interested in cross-identification between autism rights and trans/gay rights as being struggles to de-pathologize so-called 'conditions.'"[77] In this performance of full body quotation, cross-identification resides in, and is made possible by, what is deemed incommunicable. Yet, as Baggs shows us, the incommunicable might, in fact, be communicable by other means. It necessitates, as Fred Moten puts it in a conversation with Tsang, a "general communicability that is beyond or outside of any restrictive economy of reduction."[78] While *Shape of the Right Statement* was initially about what Tsang shares, as a trans person, with Baggs, as an autistic person, the work becomes a performance about what else can be communicated and embodied, in excess of diagnosis and identification. Between Tsang's quotations of Baggs's translation and Baggs's own language, the sense of a "general communicability" emerges.

With her full body quotation, Tsang takes on the qualities of the speaking device's computerized voice, with flat, disaffected precision. To imitate this voice requires bodily exertion, heard and seen as Tsang measures and catches her breath to deliver her lines with the right pacing, without racing ahead or falling behind. Her eyebrows slightly raise, her cheekbones twitch, and her jaw clenches. The device used to translate Baggs's language does not need to come up for air, but Tsang does. Her need to fill her lungs to breathe becomes a kernel of difference within her quotation of Baggs's translation. Her bodily needs impinge on the performance, making us more aware of how her body, while sonically attuned to Baggs's translation, visually contrasts with the interactions and reactions to the world that Baggs shares in the first half of their video. While Baggs moves, touches, and converses with many things around them, Tsang is a motionless, solitary figure. Baggs communicates through and with an awareness of their environment, but in *Shape of the Right Statement*, Tsang is framed within a close-up that gives no clear sense of a surrounding—only the shimmer of the Platter's silver backdrop. Baggs's means of communication, delivered through translated quotations, are entangled with context, with a material setting and its objects and elements. Tsang, on the other hand, communicates via Baggs's translation, embodying a quotation without context. Tsang's loss of context within the performance brings to the fore the ways that her relationship to Baggs, from where she speaks, and whom she speaks as, remains questionable, tense, and risky.

However, perhaps someone watching *Shape of the Right Statement* recognizes the Platter. They might perceive Tsang's performance as a response to her familiar environment as it has come to shape her practice. They might want to attribute what happens next to the fact of her location and what it means to her. While Tsang speaks, her eyes start to well with tears that trickle down her face. Like Patty Chang's tears in *In Love* (2001), when watching the video, the origin and cause of Tsang's tears is unclear. They could be a physical response to the exertion of the performance, but they could also be a psychic response, the expression of an emotion rising to the surface. In other words, is this an external or internal expression of the self? As Jennifer Doyle writes, "Tears are suspect. . . . Tears seem to embody both the height of unquestioned emotionality and the depths of emotional manipulation."[79] Given Tsang's expressionless face, her tears beg to be scrutinized, surfacing not as proof of interiority but instead of automaticity, which Amber Musser describes as "sensation without—or at least out of joint with—feeling."[80]

Automaticity, as Musser notes, is a capacity often attributed to robotic, unfeeling Asiatic bodies. Keeping this in mind, the desynchronous relation between body and quotation, between face and tears, means that Tsang's full body quotation always leaves a little room—a gap or discrepancy—wherein a racialized sensation irreducible to legible feeling or emotion escapes, or in this case leaks, as tears falling down Tsang's face. Like water from a running faucet, Tsang's tears might not symbolize anything but an incommunicable relation to one's surroundings. Her tears seep through the body and quotation, through what can be expressed and what cannot be uttered into words. What Tsang attempts to shape, in attempts to get the speech right, can only be an approximation as a result of an ongoing, constant receptivity and reaction to another, to Baggs and their language.

In their critique of the diagnosis and assessment of autism, Yergeau mentions that one of the traits attributed to autism is oversharing: talking too much about one's self in a way that shows one does not know when they should stop and let another person speak.[81] Oversharing is thought to be socially unacceptable not only because it can cause someone to talk for too long, but also because it can be uncomfortable for a person to have to learn so much about someone else, more than what they might want to know. Like crying or having a tantrum in public, oversharing can feel manipulative, a way of seeking attention that brings about secondhand embarrassment or firsthand irritation. In their scholarship, Yergeau wants to play with the possibility of oversharing—to disidentify with the symptom by telling autistic stories that willfully feel out and wear down that which would distinguish communication from behavior.

Oversharing has become something many feel the impulse to do—online or in person, to friends or to strangers. It is an action in excess of diagnosis, at the same time that it is quite banal. For Brian Glavey, oversharing can be a form of "nonmoralizing poetics" distinct from confession.[82] While the latter promises to reveal a singular secret truth of the self, like one's sexuality, the former discloses a fact or story about the self that exists among many. Yergeau and Glavey both view oversharing as that which shifts how we give an account of one's self. Oversharing, when reduced to a symptom, undermines the self that attempts to author a story about one's self. Meanwhile, oversharing as a poetics can overwhelm the self, who might otherwise be reduced to a single story. Either way, oversharing is a means of communicating the incommunicable—speaking as one's self in such a way that cannot help but give away too much, spilling over any clear boundaries of the self. To overshare implies having no filter, no sense of what is or should be in or outside of the self.

When writing about his love for teaching, and specifically for teaching theory, Muñoz begins by oversharing. "I love my students," he writes.[83] For him, as I have also found, to teach theory is to communicate one's love for theory in hopes that others will come to love it, too. Sometimes one must become "more than a bit effusive," Muñoz admits, and one must trust students with something—a text, an object of study—that one loves and that students might, in their learning, misuse.[84] For Muñoz, this performative utterance enacts the love it names, and in the (quite unnatural) nature of performative utterances, it is a commitment to a communicability bound to the failure of "misfires."[85] This failure shapes a "minoritarian pedagogy,"[86] where oversharing is to also gesture, not without some humor and wit, to one's own "failure and incompleteness, as teacher, a subject."[87] To a student, this might feel like being abandoned, left alone without any guidance, but, as Muñoz reminds us, misfires and what they miscommunicate become the grounds of minoritarian knowledge. Baggs's and Tsang's performances express a similar kind of love, even when, and precisely because they gesture to the failure of translation and the impossibility of meaning by way of a receptivity to their surrounds—to its objects, textures, sounds, and voices. In this way, we might call their performances ones of minoritarian pedagogy and of oversharing, too.

Showing Up, or Being a Good Host

In Barbara's Browning's 2017 novel, *The Gift*, the protagonist, a professor and writer named Barbara Anderson, had a reading at a bookstore with Kate Zambreno and Matias Viegener in New York City. The three of them discussed their relationship to writing nonfiction. Specifically, they addressed their approach to writing about people in their lives and the ethical question of whether or not they should be obligated to share what they write about them. Later, Barbara found that some of her students had attended the reading and had written about it on their blogs. "They were nice about our work and what we'd read," Barbara explains, "but expressed a little impatience with all the talk about ethics, which they thought was a sentimental deflection of what really counted: politics."[88]

Was this ethical orientation to one's own writing, and to those who one writes about, a betrayal of one's politics? Was asking for permission too idealistic or naive? Her students felt the writers' ethical standpoint was a hindrance to a radical feminist writing practice that should make no apologies for its transgressions. The audience's comments affected Barbara. "I understood what they meant," she admits, "it's the kind of thing Lauren Berlant often says, and surely I ought to know better, but somehow I couldn't help it."[89] So she decided to write an email to Berlant for "reassurance."[90] Berlant wrote back: "I have also written that ethics to me feels like politics in denial, but that's not always true, because sometimes no matter how politically saturated a relation is, it's just about one person showing up for another."[91] Barbara wonders if Berlant only wrote this to her because they felt sorry for her, but for Barbara, this is reassuring enough. Barbara reached out with a need, and Berlant, understanding that need, showed up by writing back.

Barbara contacts Berlant because she thinks that what she has read on her students' blogs are the same kinds of things Berlant would say. It is as if Barbara's students were speaking as Berlant and vice versa. Barbara turns to Berlant for how they might be able to speak to and speak as Barbara's students, in hopes that Berlant might be able to say more on behalf of her students. By (over)sharing this story, Barbara—the writer of the novel and the novel's protagonist—gets to speak as Berlant, insofar as Berlant, as far as we know, is actually quoted in the book. Like the initial meeting between Tsang and the Platter, this exchange between Browning and Berlant considers what and how language is used to communicate a need and how one uses the other to meet that need—whether by using a bar or pulling a quotation from an email.

Showing up, to be useful, is a lot like being a good host. Tsang knows something about hosting, insofar as she knows how to host a party, but she also knows how to host a quotation by embodying it. In an interview, Thomas J. Lax asks her, "What do you think it is about your body that allows or even wants you to play host?" Tsang answers, "Being ethnically and gender ambiguous, I often 'pass' as a lot of different things. I find that people's assumptions about what I am, become more a reflection of their own identity issues. I guess these first-hand experiences lead me to a very intuitive understanding of identity as performance. Hosting is similarly like being a container or catering to the needs of others."[92] Tsang knows that her "firsthand experiences" of other people's assumptions made about her are not actually about her. Nevertheless, she is ready to host those assumptions, which is to say, she is willing to host other people's "identity issues," which are mediated by assumptions made about her. Full body quotation reflects how Tsang mediates outside of the realm of performance. Her body, racialized and gendered inscrutably, receives and tunes into someone else's frequency, becoming a channel for another, on demand.[93] Tsang's "firsthand experience," then, comes secondhand. In other words, her experience of the self, and her account of the self, are linked to her capacity to be a good host.

Her quotation of another, speaking as another, does not lead to self-estrangement or self-alienation. It lets her encounter herself another way, secondhand, for further learning and study. In playing host, then, Tsang does not merely play someone else. She also enacts what Kandice Chuh describes as the "necessary reflectiveness" constitutive of Asian Americanist critique.[94] Such reflectiveness does not mean Tsang need identify herself as Asian or Asian American. What remains uncommunicable is Tsang's Asianness, and from that incommunicability, Tsang is able to speak as another, as the good host ready to overshare, lending herself to another, but also to receive another's oversharing. As Vivian Huang reminds us, hospitality, as a moral and ethical challenge, incurs its costs for racialized, gendered subjects, particularly for Asian and Asian American women, who are always perceived as serviceable with unconditional limits. Huang does not want to forgo the social possibilities of hospitality, for she proposes "a disidentificatory discourse of hospitality, one that does not vacate or concede the pleasures of giving or saying yes" to what is asked.[95] Hospitality entails taking a risk, of finding out that one might, indeed, have conditional limits, by first saying yes.

In their interview, Tsang tells Lax, "There is a lot of power to hosting and being a host."[96] Hosting is not just about submitting to another's needs. A host can say yes to someone else's request for a need as much as a host can say yes from a position of authority, giving permission for the doors to open at a party or a bar, prompting a DJ's set to begin, or deciding who can skip a line. A host can give and take, and in doing both, the power dynamics keep shifting, between one of power and one of accommodation. A host can take your coat, take your drink ticket, or take your song request (not likely); a host can also give you the space for a party or performance, give you a free drink, give you the microphone for an announcement (also, not likely). Such is the work of being a good host who shows up for their guests.

I want to end by quoting another good host: Nicol, the host of the Platter, introduced in *Wildness*. Cut between footage of her working the door, taking people's cash for the five-dollar entry fee, stamping their hands and wrists, Nicol sits in an armchair for her interview, with legs crossed and hands in her lap. "I can't imagine this place without the Silver Platter," she says in Spanish. "There's a lot of anecdotes that I've had to witness at the door," she explains, "In reality, not everything is family here, not everything is rosy. . . . It's like a game of chess. . . . We are all at play here because we are all a part of it, right, with different jobs, but we all complement the Silver Platter."

As the bar's host, Nicol sees everything at the bar—she sees who comes and goes, how many people show up at which time in the night. She is the keeper of cash but also of anecdotes and gossip, greeting you at the door, and escorting you out, should it be necessary. This is a job, and it is a bar, and therefore it is not all "family" and "rosy." While she had described the Platter as a "living room," everyone is still "at play" with their "different jobs," herself included, as the host tasked with maintaining that sense of play—a good time—while also making sure that everyone knows what role they are there to fill. Although Nicol does not share all that she has seen while working the door of the Platter, her discretion does overshare something else: what is incommunicable about other people's dependence on her and her dependence on them, all of which is required to make a night at the Platter worthwhile for everyone involved. Everyone has their complementary roles, and in order to fit with one another, they have to be willing, in some way, to show up and be used.

3. COLD LEFTOVERS

OUT OF TOUCH WITH ASIATIC FEMININITY'S MATERIAL REMAINS

I begin with what some might not want to touch on again. David Henry Hwang's 1988 play, *M. Butterfly*, opens with the former French diplomat René Gallimard announcing from a prison cell, "I have known, and been loved by . . . the Perfect Woman."[1] Based on Giacomo Puccini's 1904 opera, *Madama Butterfly*, Hwang's play tells the story of Gallimard, who, in Beijing in 1960, has a twenty-year relationship with a Chinese opera singer named Song Liling, "a feminine ideal, beautiful and brave."[2] Gallimard has been imprisoned under the charge of treason, but it seems that this is not what concerns him most, for he himself has been betrayed and is in mourning. He has discovered that Song, his Perfect Woman, is a man and Chinese communist spy, who passed as a woman and gave intelligence to China throughout their relationship. The play is based on a 1986 scandal and legal case in France. A French diplomat named Bernard Boursicot, who was sentenced to six years in jail for espionage, claimed to have never known that his lover, a Chinese opera performer named Shi Pei Pu, was a male spy. Boursicot said that when he had sex with Shi, it was only in the dark, and that because of this he had never seen Shi naked. When asked why he did not find this odd, if not suspicious, he explained, "I thought she was very modest. I thought it was a Chinese custom."[3] The perceived foreignness of Chinese customs and beliefs about a Chinese woman's modesty afforded both Boursicot and Shi a cover story: Asiatic femininity enabled Shi's acts of espionage and masked Boursicot's queer desire and sex under the assertion of his naivete and Shi's deception.

In *M. Butterfly*, Hwang redeploys the Butterfly stereotype to interrogate the durability of Western white fantasies of the Orient played out on the feminized Asiatic body. The play is not actually about Song's womanhood, so much as it is about the "feminine ideal" that Gallimard touches, just barely, and what he chooses (not) to see in the dark. Gallimard's failure to make sense of what lies beyond his fantasy lends a psychic interiority, however pathetic or damning, to his character. In contrast, Song is not afforded the same, representative of a stereotype constituted by surface, not depth. As Rey Chow writes, "The act of stereotyping is always implicated in visuality by virtue of the fact that the other is imagined as and transformed into a (sur)face, a sheer exterior deprived/independent of historical depth."[4] Song's femininity, even when exposed as a spy's cover, obfuscates any glimpse into Song and her desires. We see Gallimard for who he is and who he wants to touch and see, but who is Song? By the play's conclusion, she is still left in the dark.

And yet, there is perception in darkness, there is the possibility of touching and feeling one's way through it. In a momentary loss of vision, one often reflexively reaches out for what might be there, as a stabilizing gesture. While *M. Butterfly*'s use and interrogation of stereotype entails an engagement with visuality, and particularly the flattened "sheer exterior" of a person made into an object marked by difference, I also consider the sensation of touch, which Rizvana Bradley describes as a "singularly violent immediacy."[5] For "touch cuts two ways," Bradley writes, "it might be understood as the gateway to the most intimate experience and exchange of mutuality between subjects, or taken as the fundamental element of the absence of self-ownership."[6] What does Song feel like in the dark? This is something that Gallimard and Boursicot cannot deny knowing, and here, I imagine that what they felt, cut two ways, was coldness. This coldness leads to an embodied way of knowing that clouds vision rather than substitutes for it, messing with the visuality of the stereotype for sensuous, enigmatic materializations of difference and the forms it can take.[7]

In this chapter, filmmaker and scholar Mila Zuo's 2016 short film, *Carnal Orient*, and artist Alison Kuo's work with gelatin across installation, performance, and video deform the Asiatic body by making it go cold at the moment when it is touched and consumed by the voracious appetites and fantasies of others. Deformation does not give way to formlessness. It draws our attention to "the line that we can draw between crude materiality and aesthetic form," Tompkins writes: between what is raw, or untouched, and what is refined and cultivated, touched by the social.[8] I stay with Tompkins's attention to "form as it decays, morphs, and improvises, against and ahead of disciplinary programmatics," and like her, I am inclined toward the instability of "crude matter," as opposed to the pristine, orderly structures that form can construct and impose.[9] If crude matter is "prior to formation," directing us to the "immanent labor of aesthetics" and the "social coherence" of an aesthetic object, an engagement with coldness handles the matter of what is left behind, like Shi and Song in the dark, as remainders of the violence and violation of racial and gender formation.[10] I approach the distinction between matter and form from the other end, not when things are warming up but when things have gone cold, after the line has been drawn between matter and form, in the fallout of forms that cohere in and according to certain social contexts. Whereas crude matter is untouched because it has yet to be processed or refined, cold leftovers are out of touch because they have been used up, if not overused—too obvious and familiar, too rote and depleted.

Cold leftovers are not wholly the provenance of the feminized Asiatic body, nor of Asiatic femininity. Cold leftovers are the materials that have been discarded, shorn, and excreted in order to preserve the fantasy of Orientalized feminine ideals and prevent them from spoiling over time. Cold leftovers can frustrate not only a hungry appetite for racial, gendered fantasies, but also the political desire for relatable, representable forms of Asian American subjecthood. With each iteration of the played-out stereotypes of the pure, self-sacrificing Butterfly or Lotus Blossom, or the corrupt, deceptive Dragon Lady, reemerges the questions: What do we do with Asiatic femininity? How do we want to make it matter, how do we endow it with agency and potentiality, which is to say, how do we approach it as the condition of possibility, self-possession, and identification for a subject, rather than solely the source of a subject's harm and devaluation?

It seems that Asiatic femininity is always in need of rescue and repair. If not, if found in the wrong hands, Asiatic femininity is subject to appropriation and fetishization, subject to another's use. In other words, Asiatic femininity can get spoiled by someone else's fantasy, as someone else's object. Animated by Orientalist fantasies like those of Gallimard and Boursicot, or reduced to the flourish and detail of Orientalism as style, Asiatic femininity can be used to further denigrate Asian women while bolstering liberatory expressions of white gender and sexuality.[11] Asiatic femininity can also face (misogynist) accusations of becoming complicit with the emasculation of Asian men by way of its intimate associations with white heteromasculinity, as the latter's object of desire. Asiatic femininity is approached as already and often mishandled, as that which someone else might take and use for the wrong reasons.

Many feminist Asian Americanist scholars have engaged with social, cultural constructions of Asiatic femininity. They have critiqued its representation as a site of objectification, degradation, and harm, but have also made efforts to reclaim it by way of its hypersexualization, perceived hospitality, and ornamental perihumanity. Celine Parreñas Shimizu argues that Asian American women can enact forms of "productive perversity" that center and prioritize Asian American women's pleasure, power, and desire through, as opposed to against, their hypersexualization.[12] Vivian Huang reads the ways Asian American women artists, in the face of their expected hospitality, can redraw the boundaries of queer and feminist forms of sociality, intimacy, and care.[13] Shimizu and Huang disidentify with the hypersexualized and hospitable Asian woman, attuning to a sense of satisfaction and play that commingles with the pain and constraint of stereotype.

In Anne Anlin Cheng's theory of the "yellow woman," Asiatic femininity constitutes a "highly fabricated figure" as opposed to a subject—a hybrid entity that is "present/absent, organic/synthetic, a figure of civilizational value and a disposable object of decadence."[14] Asiatic femininity becomes exceptional and transformative in relation to the category of "woman of color" but also in relation to constructions of Western modern personhood that are "inextricable from synthetic extensions, art, and commodity."[15] Cheng does not argue for a disidentification with the ornament, or "*ornamental personhood*," and she shifts away from a focus on "real" Asian women in order to consider how the yellow woman haunts and hovers around the desire for a real Asian woman to reveal herself via the ornamental.[16] At the same time, ornamentalism has become a theoretical frame that seductively invites disidentification from Cheng's readers, in part because of the kinds of access to recognizable personhood it promises by way of the "interstitial life" of a racialized, gendered object.[17] Although Cheng impresses ornamentalism's entanglement with the violence of being made into a beautiful object, the theory of the yellow woman has become both a salve and stimulant for feminist Asian Americanist scholars, as well as for Asian American writers and artists who, as Cheng puts it, might feel that Asian American feminist theory is "stuck in the first wave," and suffused with a "critical fatigue."[18] Ornamentalism, which "names an elegant—that is to say, seamless—alchemy between things and persons," has an ameliorative effect because it offers an account of Asiatic femininity that puts it at the center of our understandings of personhood.[19] In other words, a theory of the yellow woman puts Asiatic femininity to good use. Addressing the relationship between the ornamental and Asiatic femininity promises to put theories of Asian American feminism back in time, no longer outside of it. A theory of the yellow woman puts Asiatic femininity in touch, both desirable and within reach. Like hands that palm a packet of butter at a restaurant or bend a new book's spine, the theory of the yellow woman softens the stiff, hard edges of a figure gone cold. Similar to Shimizu and Huang, Cheng holds out the promise of unlocking the political and aesthetic potential of Asiatic femininity, and even though Cheng makes clear that she is not defining the category of Asian woman and that her work is not meant to be prescriptive, her case studies authorize and animate the ornamental artifice of Asiatic femininity, endowing it with a longed-for theoretical heat and rigor.[20]

In the want to make Asiatic femininity a relevant site of theory, I think we might be getting too touchy, too handsy. Put differently, we might be too delicate but also too demanding in our handlings of Asiatic femininity. We want to guard and protect it from objectification, fetishization, and appropriation at the same time that we are eager to seize it, as that which can be imbued with potentiality and freed up for our political, identitarian ends. Zuo and Kuo take a different approach by considering what is out of touch about Asiatic femininity—how it is made to matter as cold leftovers that cannot be salvaged, reheated, and consumed. Instead, it stays cold, ducking our desire and attempts to metabolize it. If disidentification, as José Muñoz quotes Norma Alarcón, is "a nay-saying of the variety of the 'not yet, that's not it,'" alternatively, I think about what comes after such nay-saying: What now? What do we keep?[21] Cold leftovers cannot be retrofitted to an identity or palatable narratives of minoritized subjecthood. So, while I, like Cheng, focus on Asiatic femininity as distinct from Asian woman as a subject position, for me, and for the artists here, the "alchemy between things and persons" is not "seamless"—materials are cast off along the way.

Made to function as a cover—for a spy, for queer desires, or for an object's ornate surface—Asiatic femininity becomes a reminder of the messes made out of the desire for recognition. Asiatic femininity attaches itself to bodies that are historically, materially, psychically, and culturally entangled with fraught processes of Asian racialization. As such, it is not proprietary to any subject or body. For Cheng, this speaks to how Asiatic femininity emerges as a style, "which claims specificity but lends itself to promiscuous transferability."[22] However, this does not mean it can queer or transcend the human or personhood, or abolish gender and sex binaries. I merely mean that such promiscuity continues to make Asiatic femininity politically productive for some and a problem for others. Asiatic femininity has been subject to the work of many people's fantasies. As a diffuse yet recognizable style, everyone touches it and it touches everything. I am interested in what is shed, peeled away, or sloughed off in that touch, not in excess of style and form, but necessary to both because it must fall away, sacrificed and left behind.

Alongside the necessity of spoiling Asiatic femininity as the foundations of Gallimard and other white men's "feminine ideal," I aim to spoil the ways we—as Asian Americanists, feminist scholars, Asian women—idealize Asiatic femininity, as that which can and must be restored and redeemed by and for Asian women, whether through the recognition of subjecthood or disidentification with ornamental personhood. At the same time, I hope it is clear that I am not dismissing the presence, existence, and experience of Asian woman. Rather, I am acknowledging that fantasies of Asiatic femininity and the appetites it provokes are entangled with how Asian women perceive themselves and develop an appetite for their own selves in the process. Shimizu and Zuo write with ambivalence about how their understanding of the self emerges from representations of Asian women made by other people, and how they feel both seen and not, when, for instance, accosted by a stranger on the bus or in the middle of a bad date.[23] In these encounters, the flush of embarrassment or confusion turns cold and what they are left with is loss, whether the loss of a potential lover or the wish for omnipotence and control.

However, as Elizabeth Wilson points out, ambivalence is not prompted by and in response to loss. Ambivalence—which involves love but also hostility and aggression—shapes our relationship to a lost object before we had even lost it.[24] What we lost we also love, not in spite of our hatred but alongside it, mixed with it. Admitting that our ambivalence precedes loss is to recognize our sadistic capacity for destruction, our ability to put our hands on what we have loved, hated, and lost, and in the process, potentially ruined. Here, the loved, hated, and lost object, or ideal, is Asiatic femininity, made to bear Zuo's and Kuo's attacks, as well as mine. In this chapter, Asiatic femininity feels like skin out of touch, sounds like a voice with no origins, and tastes like inedible food. Asiatic femininity materializes as cold leftovers that are not just of white men's own messy making but also ours—specifically Asian women's—in the want to see what can be done with what has gone cold over time. I do not seek to revivify forms of Asiatic femininity, but to see how its materials demand that we encounter the damage we have done to it and the damage we still have yet to do.

Cold Camouflage in *M. Butterfly*

M. Butterfly has become a canonical object for Asian American studies as well as for Asian American theater. Like *Paris Is Burning* in the previous chapter, the play is often encountered in the classroom. Asian Americanist scholars have debated the play's use of the Butterfly that persists from Puccini's opera up until the present through *M. Butterfly*, with David Cronenberg's 1993 film adaptation and a 2017 Broadway revival (as well as the 1989 musical *Miss Saigon*, another adaptation set during the Vietnam War).[25] Karen Shimakawa reads Song's fulfillment of Gallimard's fantasies as a form of critical mimesis.[26] Meanwhile, David Eng points out how the play addresses the material, psychic emasculation of Asian American men and the failures of whiteness to shore up its fantasies of heterosexuality.[27] For Cheng, the play addresses psychic processes of "melancholic racialization," where a minoritized subject's assimilation, enabled by inhabiting a stereotype, does not solely signal powerlessness and internalized self-hatred, but also offers the occasion to "unravel . . . the deeper identificatory operations—and seductions" entangled in the fantasies and desires for minoritized subjects.[28] The play shows how racial and sexual difference are intertwined—how the feminization of Asianness via Orientalist fantasy affects the ways we come to understand Asian Americans in relation to citizenship and the nation, embodied and materialized as the abject, suspicious, foreign, and inscrutable.

M. Butterfly has gone from being widely engaged in Asian Americanist scholarship and discussions of Asian American culture to, in some way, going untouched, as a site of representation and critique that comes from another time. The play debuted in Washington, DC, in 1988 before moving to Broadway, in the midst of multiculturalism's rise as well as the culture wars and canon wars of the late 1980s and 1990s. With its willful perversion of a canonical opera, *M. Butterfly* did not inflame the white conservative Christian right so much as its awards and praise drew critiques from Asian American writers invested in seeking and preserving the ideal of an authentic, more often than not heteromasculinist, Asian American cultural nationalism.[29] *M. Butterfly* bears remnants of a not-so-distant past, mired in moralizing calls for respectability that have never quite left our present.[30]

What happens when we return to *M. Butterfly*? Not with the purpose of adapting it to the contemporary moment, but as that which over the years has gone cold? To say this is not an aesthetic judgment of the play so much as a means of addressing the shift in contemporary cultural and political investments in Asian American representation, and how *M. Butterfly* becomes evidence of another time, when a surge of visibility necessitated new modes of critique. The feelings of difficulty and fatigue that attach themselves to canonical objects like *M. Butterfly* mean they have not outlived us, even if we feel they have outlived their use. They might, however, feel or seem somewhat untouchable. It is this sense of the untouchable that I hold on to for the ways it undercuts that touchiness and "handsyness" that I have described, and which, to an extent, irritates me. This also gives me a way of entering back into the play with an attention not on visual representation but on sensation, and specifically the sensation of coldness.

When discussing *M. Butterfly*, critics and scholars turn toward the visual reveal of Song's nude body at the end of the play. This moment is understood to disrupt the ruse of the Butterfly, jolting the audience, removing them from fantasy and placing them within the real. I move away from this moment that reduces the play's epiphanies to the visuality of the racialized, feminized body, and specifically a fixation on Song's genitalia. Taking into account Boursicot's claims to not seeing and only feeling Shi in the dark, I read Asiatic femininity in the play within the realm of sensation, felt and experienced as the affect and temperature of coldness under cover, in the dark, mediating between the insularity of the subject via bodily autonomy and the exteriority of the body via its objectification that invites another's touch.

Coldness is a sensation of temperature and a metaphor for emotion. As Amber Musser writes, coldness, as a sensation, engenders embodied forms of difference in and of the body but also external to it, as "both individual and impersonal."[31] Attempts to narrate what it feels like—how it is experienced and perceived from within and without—are irreducible to identitarian categories. Instead, coldness becomes a source of nonidentitarian forms of knowledge. At the same time, sensation and the forms of knowledge it makes possible are inextricable from the workings of power. They can yoke differentially marked bodies to racialized, gendered, sexed notions of capacity, debility, plasticity, animacy, the visceral, and "impressibility."[32] Sensation is not pure potentiality that can transcend biopolitical governance and the production and management of difference. Sensation is the site where the matter and meaning of differentially marked bodies are constituted and contested, shaped by broader structures of power as well as the more quotidian and atmospheric, like an upset stomach or chilly weather. Coldness is the slow, drawn-out reshaping of the body's composition. Coldness causes the body to prickle with goosebumps, to go numb and stiff. When we are cold, our joints creak, our breath becomes short and shallow, and our teeth chatter. When we are cold, our body defensively turns in on itself to conserve heat. Coldness also constricts—shrinking and taking up less space, causing the body to pull away and withdraw from its unfriendly, hostile environment.[33]

Affectively, coldness shapes a bitchy disposition. Cold bitchiness is the feminized, alienating assertion of difference and distance from another. For Simone de Beauvoir, coldness is a symptom of objectification by way of masochism, and "a true masochism is to be observed in certain women."[34] As Beauvoir saw it, masochism in women is not wholly pathological because it is somewhat expected, given women's limited choices within and against the constraints of patriarchy. Frigidity in women sets in over time, from when they are young to when they grow up. As young girls, women start to submit themselves to others, "to be made purely a thing under the conscious will of others, to see [themselves] as a thing, to play at being a thing," and because of this, they grow up to become narcissists, desirous of their own objectification as a beautiful thing praised and affirmed by others.[35] As women age, they feel ashamed and humiliated, and blame themselves for becoming an object for another. Musser writes that what Beauvoir describes as frigidity is women's feeling of complicity with patriarchy and their own powerlessness. Complicity, rife with bitterness and resentment, results in what Beauvoir calls an "insulting coldness," whereby women punish themselves with their own objectification while also punishing their lover or partner.[36] Frigidity is a form of "vengeance" wrought on themselves and others that alienates women from their pleasure, further hindering their freedom and the possibility of developing (heterosexual) relationships built on mutuality.[37]

Beauvoir writes in response to studies from the early twentieth century by sexologist Havelock Ellis and psychoanalyst Wilhelm Stekel, who described frigidity as a sexual perversion in women.[38] In her reading of Ellis, Xine Yao describes frigid women as those with a "queer unwomanliness," who "lack . . . appropriate affective and somatic responsiveness to the imperatives of heterosexual desire and reproduction."[39] As such, frigidity becomes "a technology of disaffection" used by women in the nineteenth century to manage a perceived objectivity, particularly in professional contexts.[40] Similarly, Mila Zuo turns to modes of "likable deflection" and "frigid ornamentation" tasted and felt as the "salty-cool" of the "Chinese femme" in film, who must confront the projection of Western fantasies, like those of Gallimard's, and the heat of the US multicultural melting pot.[41] Like Song in *M. Butterfly*, the Chinese femme, as Zuo argues, makes use of the ways she is rendered an "object-surface."[42] Coldness and coolness render women's affectability inaccessible and opaque.

If, for Beauvoir, frigidity in women obstructs liberatory, ethical, reciprocal heterosexual relationships, for Yao and Zuo, coldness grounds productive modes of queer and feminist critique unbeholden to the promises that heterosexism makes. While my interest in Asiatic femininity is in the hostility of frigidity, coldness, and coolness, like Musser, I hesitate to reclaim frigidity and coldness as empowering strategies of refusal and resistance. For her, coldness is the embodied manifestation of women's ambivalence in the face of their submission. It is a symptom of women's complicity with their own disempowerment by way of objectification, at the same time that it also promises to empower and protect them with the unbothered, hardened appearance of detachment. Coldness, "as a property of being in one's body while simultaneously being alienated from it," moves between agency and subjectlessness, as a mode of self-making and unmaking that reveals a sensuous trace of one's interior life reaching out to be felt by another, for another's pleasure.[43]

In Gilles Deleuze's essay on Leopold von Sacher-Masoch's *Venus in Furs*, the character of the Ideal Mistress—the dominant to the male masochist—is always cold, always sneezing, and prefers to cover her "marble body" in furs.[44] Such furs, along with the Ideal Mistress's high heels, become what Musser describes as "the aesthetic dimension [that] camouflages [her] inner vulnerability."[45] As armor and adornment, indulging in the hostility in and of alterity, I think of coldness as camouflage, lending visuality to sensation and texture to surface. Camouflage conveys dimension and depth while confusing perception in ways not uncommon from the immersive, all-encompassing feeling of complicity. Taking into account how camouflage can be a "militaristic texture," Christina León writes that camouflage, as an "ambivalent hermeneutic," is a "militancy that takes so-called natural background as its cover."[46] In the case of coldness, the background is body, and camouflage is not an encasement of feeling, protected and sealed within the body, as Deleuze might suggest, so much as it affords a different mode of reveal.[47] To me, camouflage is more sheer than opaque—a surface that suggests, more so than obstructs. In his study on the "sexual impulses" of women, Ellis described frigidity as "sexual anesthesia" and "erotic blindness."[48] Such blindness can be a different attunement to one's senses, as opposed to a lack of vision. As camouflage, coldness alters vision through its conflation with touch and its ability to render indistinguishable knowing from feeling, texture from pattern, depth from surface, sheerness from opacity.

A women's desire to become an object to be looked at and handled by another is bound to the aesthetic and the cosmetic, to what a woman puts on to become the object of another's desire. Coldness is not about the exposure of bare surface, but about the careful cultivation of that surface's coverings.

As Musser writes, "Learning to submit, it seems, begins with learning what to wear."[49] Yet, when we look to Song in the play, learning to submit becomes indistinguishable from teaching another how to see and feel a particular way—of training and guiding another's gaze so that they may not see what one prefers to keep hidden. Who, then, can be said to experience an "erotic blindness"? The frigid woman or the other who encounters her? Throughout the play, Song's femininity is constituted not by furs—not by and as the "gleaming things" of the ornamental—but by sheer, suggestive fabrics that are not to be touched or removed, as the trappings of "modest Chinese customs."[50] The stage directions in *M. Butterfly* include costume descriptions that repeatedly draw attention to the partial reveal of Song's body, covered in "a sheer dressing gown," "a sheer robe," "simple baggy clothes," or an "elegant black gown": a stitching together of fabrics in formless shapes described and located within the private spaces of a dressing room or Song's flat.[51] Song's garments lure hungry eyes, at the same time that, like camouflage, they blur the shape of a figure and its surface, whether naked and bare or ornamental and decorated.[52]

Gleaned from these stage directions are the materials needed to adorn Asiatic femininity as deceptive cover, but also the ephemeral acts of simultaneous covering and uncovering when wearing these sheer garments. There are small yet significant gestures of adjustment: pulling down a sleeve over the wrist, tugging the shoulder of a draped robe, clutching a loose neckline close over the chest, smoothing out a dress's hem over a bare calf and ankle. This play upon surface flirts with the boundaries between the invisible and visible, between garments and the body they are tasked with concealing yet risk laying bare. Fabric on skin intimates the possibility of reveal at the same time that Song's gestures of adjustment prevent such reveals from happening. Song must artfully touch her garments—she must know how to handle herself—so that Gallimard cannot. She calls attention to what he cannot touch through the posturing of skin cold to the touch.

Early in the play, Gallimard comes to Song's flat to profess his feelings for her. His declaration also becomes her own admission that she is his Butterfly, couched within a sensorial discourse of skin and the temperature and temporalities of touch:

> GALLIMARD: Are you my Butterfly?
> *Silence; he crosses the room and begins to touch her hair.*
> I want from you honesty. There should be nothing false between us. No false pride.
> *Pause.*

SONG: Yes, I am. I am your Butterfly.
He starts to kiss her roughly. She resists slightly.

SONG: No . . . no . . . gently . . . please, I've never . . .

GALLIMARD: No?

SONG: I've tried to appear experienced, but . . . the truth is . . . no.

GALLIMARD: Are you cold?

SONG: Yes. Cold.

GALLIMARD: Then we will go very, very slowly.
He starts to caress her; her gown begins to open.

SONG: No . . . let me keep my clothes . . .

GALLIMARD: But . . .

SONG: Please . . . it all frightens me. I'm a modest Chinese girl.

GALLIMARD: My poor little treasure.

SONG: I am your treasure.[53]

This scene can read as Song's capitulation to Gallimard's desires. She becomes his object, possessed and hoarded. And yet, the sensation of coldness comes between them, warding off Gallimard's physical advances at the same time that it caters to them with perceived modesty. Whatever acts of affirmation she is expected to provide—like the heat of a passionate embrace—are not given. Nevertheless, Gallimard feels assured of her submission. Song does not say that she is cold. Gallimard misreads Song's hesitation as feeling cold, as if there could be no other reason she would not desire his advances. To speak for her, to animate her via his own words, becomes her alibi. By claiming what is projected on to her, Song takes up what Uri McMillan describes as performances of objecthood.[54] Her loss of words undermines Gallimard's power over and in the encounter. Underneath the skin-crawling discomfort of Gallimard's coaxing and Song's hesitations, coldness encroaches on the silent omission that could otherwise enable a coercive encounter, stalling without outright refusal. Song's coldness as a spy's calculating cover renders Asiatic femininity not just through and as the iterability of performance, but also as racialized matter left untouched and enfolded within the sheer seduction of fabrics. Asiatic femininity remains under cover, as an answer to a question—"Are you cold?"—which Song does not need to answer or protest.

M. Butterfly is about Asiatic femininity, insofar as it is about a fantasy cold to the touch that can only be reanimated by Gallimard, for himself and by himself. In the final scene of the play, Gallimard makes himself up into the Butterfly for which he still longs. Gallimard tells the audience that in order to find another ending to his story, one where he can return to his Butterfly, he finds his way back through the scenes and music of Puccini's *Madama Butterfly* and its "vision of the Orient."[55] While the score from the final scene of *Madama Butterfly* plays, Gallimard wistfully tells of a land filled with resilient, self-sacrificing women. As he speaks, he begins to put on one of Song's kimonos and a wig of black hair. In Michael Cronenberg's film adaptation, Gallimard (played by Jeremy Irons) dresses himself and ceremoniously spreads thick swaths of white makeup, eye shadow, and lipstick on his face. When his face is covered, Gallimard declares, "My name is René Gallimard—also known as Madame Butterfly."[56] In the play's stage directions, Gallimard takes a knife and stabs himself, performing seppuku, an honorable suicide in the face of a dishonorable life, mirroring Puccini's opera. Except this time, the Butterfly does not die—only the person who could not live without the fantasy of her does. The Butterfly, and the Orientalized feminine ideal she represents, remains on stage and in the film, as her dressings she left behind, which, this time, can be touched, and even tried on. However, without the cover of darkness, we might not want to anymore.

The Inedible Dishes and Cold Voice of *Carnal Orient*

Watching Gallimard apply different pots of makeup to his face at the end of Cronenberg's *M. Butterfly* feels like watching him make himself into a frosted cake for his own fatal consumption. The white men in Zuo's *Carnal Orient* do the same, in a way, and to a different effect. In Zuo's film, Asiatic femininity materializes in a moment of what Tompkins calls "racial indigestion," when the white body, with its appetite to eat and dominate difference, comes up against the racialized body that gets "sticky" and "chokes."[57] Here, cold leftovers cannot be relied on to mediate cross-cultural encounters, where diverse tastes bring people together at a lively, warm multicultural communal dinner table, nor can they fit within narratives about smelly non-American lunches at school (a well-worn metaphor that has also gone cold). If anything, this is because cold leftovers are often times eaten alone. For me, at least, they are primarily eaten cold, as a meal of defeat, consumed without the wherewithal to cook because I am too tired or lazy.

Eating cold leftovers alone could fairly be described as abject, and leftovers, especially those sitting in one's refrigerator for too long, could be called abject materials. For Julia Kristeva, the abject is located in and of the body, necessary to its ability to live, yet expelled from it, like "corpses" and "dung."[58] The abject confronts us with the limits of the body's borders. Karen Shimakawa argues that Asian Americanness emerges in US culture via processes of national abjection, whereby Asian Americans are expelled or "jettisoned" from the national imaginary at the same time that they are ambivalently and conditionally included within it.[59] In Shimakawa's reading of Kristeva, the corpse encapsulates the abject because "our bodies are continuously approaching that state, and waste marks the presence of mortality and decay *within us*."[60] It is the "paradoxical recognition of the abhorrent as already internalized," Shimakawa writes.[61] It is that which we do not want any part of but cannot part from. Here, the abject names a feeling and material we would prefer to leave alone for the sake of shoring up a representational subject, as the site of processes of "paradoxical recognition," mixed with desire, need, and disgust.

Such feelings were certainly entangled with the conception of *Carnal Orient*, directed by Zuo, and cowritten by Zuo and her collaborator Angela Seo, known for playing in the indie band Xiu Xiu. They made *Carnal Orient* after a music video for a song titled "Asian Girlz," by a band named Day Above Ground, had gone viral online in 2013.[62] While the song never became popular, it became a source of controversy for its tacky lyrics about Asian girls with their "creamy yellow thighs" and "slanty eyes." The video was taken off media platforms, however it still exists on the internet as a bootleg copy in degraded form. It seems fitting that the video lives on as the audiovisual remains of a bad, corny, racist, sexist joke, in worse quality than it had been before. Zuo and Seo wanted to make a film in response to the music video, but they did not want to merely correct its bad representation. Alternatively, they wanted to follow the song to its (il)logical conclusion, when a fantasy cannot possibly last, or stay fresh, and instead bares its own rottenness. Zuo explains that she is interested in the "investment in the notion of the bad object to labor and feel on behalf of the representational subject."[63] She neither disavows the bad object nor disidentifies with it. She touches it and keeps it too close for comfort in order to wear it out, rendering it into a proxy, eroded and deformed. Like Song, who lets Gallimard speak on her behalf, Zuo lets the bad object "labor" and "feel" on her behalf. The subject—the Asian woman—is left alone, relieved from showing up. She gets to stay left in the dark, untouched, too. And yet, in *Carnal Orient*, she becomes the cold matter of indigestion, but also the chilling, sadistic presence of a cold voice that asserts itself from beyond the film's frame.

Carnal Orient opens on an industrial kitchen, with stainless steel surfaces awash in neon green and pink lights, which flicker and buzz amid the sound of pots and pans that angrily simmer and boil on a stovetop. A young Asian man holding a defeathered, raw, pink chicken enters the kitchen. He wears white plastic gloves, a white tank top revealing tattoos creeping up and down his arms, and a white apron. The film cuts to a close-up of a few dirty small serving dishes on a cooking board, strewn around a small red Buddha figurine that sits on a ledge above them. The Oriental kitsch oddity as the out-of-place racialized object placed in proximity to the unclean serving ware lets us know what kind of food this kitchen prepares. The figurine racializes the smears and dregs of condiments—threatening to touch them, or animate them, as Mel Chen might say, with the toxicity of difference.[64] In turn, the condiments' remnants associate the figurine with the unhygienic: with unattended dirty dishes and dried-up bits of food left out for too long. Between the moment when a consumable dish goes cold and becomes inedible, but not yet disposed, difference threatens to emerge.

The film cuts to a wider shot of the kitchen, where the man hunches over with a lit cigarette dangling from his mouth. With gloved hands, he grasps the chicken, slowly and disinterestedly pulling and tearing skin from flesh, flesh from bone, contorting its limbs to get a better angle as slippery skin resists his grip. The sound of a gong reverberates, overlaying the gurgle of hot liquids and the ripping of skin, as the cook picks up a butcher knife and begins cutting the chicken. As vibrations of metal, the gong clangs and the knife chops along its hard edge, causing us to flinch at the blows of knife and gong, sparking a metallic taste on the edge of our teeth. The gong is not visible, and yet we need not wonder why it is heard or where it is. The Orientalist imagery has necessitated the sound as common sense to the scene.

The sheen of the cook's sweaty skin draws unseemly, unsanitary comparisons with the skin of the chicken he holds. While the Buddha figurine, dirty dishes, and hardened condiments stir up dis-ease in their difference, here, the cook and the chicken invoke similar feelings by way of their unsettling sameness. What separates cook from chicken? Visually, very little. The ripple and pull of the cook's muscles as he exerts force on the chicken, and the squish and stretch of the butchered chicken's skin, sonically produce a comparable effect. We wonder what kind of violence is enacted here and to whom, or what? That we might not be able to distinguish one from the other speaks to the contamination of racial difference—how it can seep into the scene, creating unlikely associations and proximities where figures and objects eat and tear into one another.

With another ring of the gong, the film cuts to a restaurant space, adorned with paper lanterns, panel screens, and a red mask looking maliciously down on the scene. White men sit waiting for their meals, each at their own individual tables. This is not a scene of communal eating, even though they are all there for a piece of the same thing. The food that the cook sets down before each customer, with the slide and slam of dishes on table, jiggles and shudders, repulsing with its movements that suggest liveliness, or not quite deathliness. The food is shown in low red light, like darkrooms protecting film from light, or bar bathrooms that hide the filth and grime they accumulate on a weekend night. The dishes served are not meant to look familiar or appealing to a Western viewer, nor are they meant to entice an adventurous, fearless foodie. The men, however, look down at their places with menacing, greedy grins, or at the very least, with wide-eyed curiosity.

What these men hold in their chopsticks or in between fingers trembles with fear, or pleasure. So, too, do these men's dry, thin lips as they place the food in their mouth to bite, suck, and chew. Close-ups of the men's faces and their mouths bring attention to the act of eating, and more specifically to the mess these men make. While the first chapter looked to the mouth as a site of autoerotic pleasure, here men's mouths become a site of hostility directed outward toward others. As Tompkins writes of orality, their mouths become a "stage" and "a public space whereupon the racialized erotics of the modern encounter are played out."[65] Within this encounter, one notices the crumbs and bits of food left on these men's lips, in the corners of their mouths, or stuck in their teeth. What drops or slips out between chopsticks, fingers, teeth, and mouths becomes the visceral points of the scene tugging under the visual field. These material remains are evidence of the encounter's racialized erotics, as the waste these men's appetites produce and leave behind on the plate and table.

As they eat, one man pauses, wrinkles his nose, and turns his head to look elsewhere. He is drawn to the scent of something appetizing, and at the same time, it might also be something Zuo describes as pungent, which, like "spice and its irritating qualities," or someone's "piquant body odor," aggressively impinges on the self, drawing the line between what is tolerable or intolerable about something or someone different from and foreign to one's self.[66] Zuo writes that pungency can be atmospheric, yet it is embodied, and given its manifestation as smell, it demands our time: when confronted with it, one has no choice but to wait for it to fade away, on its own schedule. Who demands these men's time and stomachs in the restaurant appears to be an Asian woman at the head of the room. I will refer to her as the performer, since she does not represent a real Asian woman, but her animated figure.[67] Initially, the film only shows her figure from behind, as a silhouette that languidly moves toward the stage. While she walks, out of focus in the background, the men never let her leave their sight, as they eat their meals in focus in the foreground. Overheard are the cries, coos, and growls of predatory animals taunting their prey, as well as the buzzing of insects swarming around a decaying corpse. In the noise, we can also hear crunches and cracks, like the breaking of bones, as if with each step, the performer becomes more mangled and out of sorts, limbs popping out of sockets, in pain and disarray.

When the performer reaches the stage, a man grabs her hand, pulling her toward him as he stands to whisper something in her ear that we cannot hear. This man sneers with curled lips, taunting her with what we can only imagine is a threat, or else a seduction, out of spite. His aggression is not masked with muteness, so much as it manifests *as* muteness, as an expression of what Barbara Johnson calls the "muteness envy" of men.[68] For Johnson, men desire muteness—and particularly women's muteness—as an aesthetic ideal. Such muteness, attributed to Greek mythological figures like the nymph Daphne, who escaped the god Apollo's unwanted advances, or to feminized objects, like John Keats's Grecian urn, renders women's rape or ecstasy—their "pleasure" and their "violation"—indistinguishable from one another.[69] The silent unknowability of what women feel becomes men's loss and source of suffering (not women's), and as such, it affords men a moment of aesthetic possibility: a way of turning their perceived helplessness at the hands of women into art, or perhaps a grossly decadent meal. In *Carnal Orient*, this man whispering into the performer's ear, pulling on her hand, is akin to Keats addressing his Grecian urn, who awaits and has yet to be captured or in rapture.

While Johnson speaks of muteness, her turn to Daphne, who transforms into a laurel tree to protect herself from being raped by Apollo, necessitates a consideration of touch as a site of pleasure and violence. This moment of transformation under duress is famously depicted in Gian Lorenzo Bernini's baroque marble sculpture *Apollo and Daphne* (1622–25). Daphne's mouth opens in terror, her hands are raised into leafy branches (one of which Apollo subsequently plucks—a souvenir of a failed rape turned into "a sign of artist achievement").[70] Apollo's left arm reaches around Daphne's nude torso, and his left hand grabs her hip from behind, making an indentation in her flesh.[71]

In *Carnal Orient*, there is only a brief shot of this man grabbing the performer. In the scene that follows, we cannot see how they touch—how he holds her down by the hand or the wrist. Instead, we sense the touch of muteness, of the air dampened by this man's stale breath, couched in the cramped, claustrophobic space of the close-up that contains the man's face and the performer's ear and cheek. The performer is subject to a violence—an embrace, an utterance—that remains inaudible.

While the man's mouth moves, his muteness conveys stillness, or the "still" of the "still unravish'd bride," which implies, as Johnson writes, that such ravishment is inevitable, on the verge of taking place once the scene changes and the narrative progresses.[72] Such inevitably leaks through the film, as shots of the man's mouth speaking are interlaced with shots of the other men's mouths chewing their food. At the site of the mouth, speaking is conflated with eating. The violence of verbal assault, as words aggressively thrown at another, converge with the violence of consumption, as attempts to take another in. Here, the moment of feminized muteness and aesthetic possibility, much like Keats's ode and Apollo's pursuit, is "a freeze frame just prior to ravishment."[73] Johnson is writing in visual terms, yet I infuse her wording with the sensation of coldness, and the frigidity that arrests the frame into a mute, immobilizing display of these men's relation to the performer, who, in the context of the film, remains food "still unravish'd," or still uneaten. The men's muteness expresses the want to claim and destroy the performer, and while we might be tempted to read the performer's muteness as radical refusal, we must keep in mind that such muteness also signals the omission of pain and pleasure, or the bleeding of one into the other.

After this man has had his say, he sits back down. The performer turns to her audience and the camera, as music begins to play. She wears a dress made of vibrantly colored paper fans and yellowface prosthetics caked onto her cheeks that protrude and pull unevenly as she begins to sing with a smile. Her makeup is not dissimilar from the makeup Gallimard applied, which fails to pass as skin, but perhaps something that tastes sweeter. The clumpy, tacky textures of the performer's makeup simultaneously repel and attract our touch and taste. The performer's pained yet sinister smile and her glitchy movements press up against the stiff constraints of her makeup and dress. Everything is effortful, there is no grace given. Then, her muteness is broken. The only voice we hear in the film is the performer's, as she begins to sing.

Zuo lends her voice to the song, written by Seo. As we watch, we do not know this. Her voice becomes what Michel Chion calls an "acousmatic" one: a voice that cannot be placed or traced back to an originary source.[74] As Mladen Dolar writes, the acousmatic voice is "a voice in search of an origin, in search of a body, but even when it finds its body, it turns out that this doesn't quite work, the voice doesn't quite stick to the body, it is an excrescence which doesn't match the body."[75] In his study of the voice as partial object, Dolar turns away from the singing voice because it reduces the voice to a fetish object, as the site of aesthetic pleasure and appreciation that promises to transcend the structure of language with deeper meaning and truer feeling.[76] Zuo's voice risks the possibility of (racial) fetishization, and yet, I hear her voice, and experience it, as the "excrescence" of the performer's body she ventriloquizes, and which labors on her behalf.

Zuo's voice ludically animates the performer on screen. We could read the performer as the cold object of masochism, representative of Asiatic femininity's pain and submission. But when I listen to Zuo's voice, I hear something else going on. As the acousmatic, Zuo's voice becomes a sadistic presence that asserts its omniscience and omnipotence, which we, the men, and the performer, must learn to stomach. If we do not know where her voice comes from—from the position of above or below, inside or outside—we cannot say her voice flips or subverts the meaning of the lyrics or the film's scenes of objectification and consumption, thereby endowing the performer with subjectivity. Saketopoulou writes that exigent sadism, as an ethical kind of sadism, is "independent of positionality (whether one is the top or the bottom)."[77] I hear Zuo out as the exigent sadist, whose voice, camouflaged and covered by the performer's body, coldly resonates through us. "Exigent sadism," Saketopoulou explains, "is not an imposition on the other but an offering, and it may or [may] not be accepted."[78] Zuo's voice is her offering to us, which breaks up our "ossified relationship" to racist representations of Asiatic femininity and the pain they might cause.[79] In the process, Zuo does not promise to deliver the "good outcome" of a healing narrative of reclamation.[80] In lieu of this, she relinquishes control over how we interpret her voice as it misfires from a wounded figure she does not claim as her own.

The performer sings,

In my place
made up and pure
I can grow
I'm seed
You're dirt
I don't feel
until you have me hurt.

Through lyric and voice, distinctions between damaged object and injured subject are contaminated, bleeding into each other like wounds touching. To be pure, the performer must be "made up," constructed and sullied by the "dirt" of others. These others include the men in the restaurant, Zuo, and us. We inflict harm—we touch the psychic, historical wounds the film presents to us on a platter, in the form of an enticing, edible body. For Dolar,

> the voice as the bearer of a deeper sense, of some profound message, is a structural illusion, the core of a fantasy that the singing voice might cure the wound inflicted by culture, restore the loss that we suffered by the assumption of the symbolic order. This deceptive promise disavows the fact that the voice owes its fascination to this wound, and that its allegedly miraculous force stems from its being situated in this gap.[81]

It would seem that the structure of language (i.e., "culture") has created a wound, which cuts us off from some "deeper sense" or "profound message" of the self that the voice is tasked with healing. Yet as Dolar points out, the wound lends the voice its fantastical qualities. It is where the voice, as a site of wonder, festers and resides.

Zuo's singing voice in *Carnal Orient* flirts with fantasy, as does the performer's body on stage, but Zuo knows that her voice is not a healing source for Asiatic femininity, for those who claim it or identify it as perhaps the source of that "deeper sense" of self. Therefore, the lyrics "I don't feel / until you have me hurt" can be a masochistic bid for recognition, and alternatively, they can also be the sadistic assertion of the acousmatic voice, as an overwhelming proximity that oversteps its bounds. Zuo's voice, which is everywhere and nowhere, does not transcend so much as protrude from and into the gut of the misfitting body, with and as its "excrescence." It is a voice that spoils, whether from top or bottom, from within and without the film's frame. It gives way to the voice as "the remainder that doesn't make sense, a leftover, a cast-off," Dolar writes, and then asks, "shall we say an excrement of the signifier?"[82] I take such corporeal, visceral language of excrescence and excrement literally—a site of wounding, of food waste—and say yes.

As Zuo sings, the film cuts to shots of the men hovering over the performer, obscuring her body as they feed on her flesh. Synchronized with the song's rhythm, punctuated by the jolt of the song's synthesizers, the film shifts between images of the performer, close-ups of the raw chicken and other foods, and the carnage that blurs into her performance. During the montage, it becomes harder for us to separate what comes before and after the figure's performance, between who and what is ingesting or being ingested—between figure and food, Asian woman and white men. The montage speeds up, visually propelling the film, like bile moving food back up the alimentary tract in nausea and discontent. When the song has finished, the film offers a wider shot of the men, who back away with shock and disgust to reveal something not so exotic or delicious at all. For once the men have dispersed, we see the remains of what they had been eating this whole time: just another average, bland, white man. Like Gallimard's Butterfly, these men's meals have turned into themselves. The stabbed gut becomes a churning, heaving one repelled by the realization of cannibalism, of eating sameness, not difference. They are stuck with their mess, now consumed and roiling in the darkness of the gut.

We might consider what instinctively happens next, once the film is over: the body might gag, spit, or vomit. In *M. Butterfly*, while Gallimard transforms himself using Song's leftovers, he tells his audience that throughout the trial, he never confessed to knowing Song was a man. He states, "This brings me headlines, and is a source of great embarrassment to my French colleagues, who can now be sent into a coughing fit by the mere mention of Chinese food."[83] This coughing fit is brought on by the conflation of Chinese bodies with Chinese food that takes place in the throat. Tompkins might describe this moment as one of "racial indigestion," where the racialized, gendered subject as (in)edible object asserts the self by way of a "queer alimentarity."[84]

Dolar also reminds us that coughing is a vocal expression—"a break in speech, a disruption of the ascent toward meaning, an intrusion of physiology into structure."[85] Coughing might hinder social interactions, and yet it might also initiate them. For instance, as Dolar describes, someone might cough to announce one's presence or to draw someone's attention in order to speak. Whether as a bodily response or vocal expression, coughing is not external to the structures of the body, speech, and language, but internal to them and their function. It is uncomfortable and antagonizing, in both social and physical contexts, while at the same time it is ameliorative in both, insofar as coughing can be a way of easing into a social interaction, but also a way of expelling something bad or unpleasant from one's body, like phlegm, or the cold leftovers of Chinese food. Perhaps watching *Carnal Orient* also provokes a coughing fit. Not out of fear or intolerance of spice and flavor (and the racial differences they so often stand in for), but as an expression of a destructive capacity within one's body that acts on itself and outward toward others, wracking the body and causing its borders to collapse, as its own kind of sadistic attack inside and out.

The Cold Comforts of Giving Up (Your Flavor and Form)

> The ambiguity of the phrase "giving up" in English is instructive: to give is always to give something up; something or someone is sacrificed. And sacrifice, whatever else it is, is a sadistic pleasure. To put it another way, perhaps we should not underestimate the pleasures of giving up, however forbidden or shameful they may seem to be.—Adam Phillips, *On Giving Up* (2024)

Here, Song's garments reappear in a different context. I revisit them as a palate cleanser, of sorts, and as impersonal materials that allow us to encounter what Eve Kosofsky Sedgwick calls "the middle ranges of agency."[86] In her essay "Making Things, Practicing Emptiness," Sedgwick writes of the textile artmaking practice she took up around the time of her second diagnosis with cancer.[87] Drawing from Tibetan Buddhism and Melanie Klein, Sedgwick's work with textiles become a means of handling notions of emptiness and nonbeing, contingent on one's relinquishment of the fantasy of omnipotence.[88] Sedgwick has always loved working with textiles, stating, "The feel of any kind of fiber between my thumb and fingers . . . just is the rub of reality, for me."[89] However, somewhere between the initial misdiagnosis of her physical pain and its subsequent correct diagnosis, her relation to textile artmaking changed:

> I think I was finally giving up the pretext of self-ornamentation, to which my love of textiles had always clung before. For instance, I had all these gorgeous silk clothes I'd bought or made but never ever wore. . . . Apparently the notion of a visual or tactile beauty that might be impersonal, dislinked from the need to present a first-person self to the world, came as news to me—late, late news. But exciting! My fingers were very hungry to be handling a reality, a beauty, that wasn't myself, wasn't any self, and didn't want to be.[90]

With this new realization, she writes, "I just found myself cutting up fabrics, especially old kimonos, which I've always been fond of, to make into other fabrics."[91] Once Sedgwick gives up this pretext that the purpose of clothes like "old kimonos" is to adorn the self, her love for these clothes clings differently, no longer building up the self but unraveling it, reweaving it, and unraveling it again. I have always been drawn to the way Sedgwick describes the destructive act of cutting up old kimonos that leads to the creation of something new. I have also always been hung up on the kimonos themselves, as objects Sedgwick is fond of, and which, out of her fondness for them, she destroys. Sedgwick describes a hunger felt in her fingers, not her mouth, as if her body, in experiencing pain and uncertainty, redistributes its senses. She is not detached from her body, only from a sense of beauty tethered to a "first-person self." She attempts to touch something other than herself. She describes the brief sensation of an impersonal touch: a touch between hungry fingers and cut-up fabric that is not about her.

Sedgwick has written elsewhere of her affinity with Buddhism, which, I think, no one knows how to talk about quite yet, specifically in relation to the question of Orientalism.[92] I do not point this out to excuse or admonish Sedgwick's attachment to Buddhism or her kimonos, nor to say that we need to expose this and get to the bottom of what this all means. I mention this in order to address the awkwardness of ambivalence—the same kind of ambivalence that informs Sedgwick's handling of her kimonos. If we follow Sedgwick's Kleinian thinking, we know that her love for her kimonos is already mixed with hate, with the inevitability that what is loved will bear, and must survive, her destructive acts, like cutting and pulling fabric and thread. Sedgwick's aesthetic practice rests on a hostility toward the kimonos as beautiful objects, but moreover, the idealized, autonomous, able-bodied self they are expected to adorn.

The association Sedgwick makes between her kimonos and ornamentation can be thought of alongside Cheng's theorizations of ornamentalism, and particularly how Asiatic femininity, as a style, often appears where Asian women do not. It is not difficult to see how this could apply to Sedgwick's essay—how the spectral figure of the yellow woman haunts its margins, gets interwoven and tangled up within her textiles. Instead of trying to free up the yellow woman to then, somehow, free actual Asian women in turn, I let her stay where she is, just out of view, in the dark. Like Sedgwick, we "give up," except we do not give up "the pretext of self-ornamentation," but the expectation of a recovered subjectivity, of furnishing and constructing "a first-person self to the world." Sedgwick gives up her kimonos, destroying them and their function as garments, but she also gives herself up to them, feeling out the "second-by-second negotiations with the material properties of what I'm working on."[93] "What will it let me do?" Sedgwick asks, "What does it want to do?"[94] For Sedgwick, in accordance with Klein, giving up is the relinquishment of the fantasy of omnipotence, and the realization that one is vulnerable to others, as well as to pain, illness, and death. To give up in this way can be hard, yet as Sedgwick writes, it can also be "exciting" and, moreover, something like a relief.

Adam Phillips diverges from Sedgwick's engagement with Klein, although, similar to the letting go of a "first-person self," he views giving up as a form of self-sacrifice, where the self is made to encounter its own "dependence" and "the sign of an ultimate and defining realism, of what we call 'knowing our limitations.'"[95] I do not think this means such limitations are immovable and etched in stone, never to be breached. To know our limitations is not to steel ourselves from harm. To know our limitations is to acknowledge that we are vulnerable and susceptible to harm in the first place—that in our dependence, we are subject to another's destructive capacities as much as others are open to ours. Giving up idealized notions of autonomy and independency can afford something like a cold comfort. To call something a cold comfort usually, in fact, offers very little comfort. A cold comfort is a concession, consolation, crumbs. In "knowing our limitations," we know that there is a limit to what level of comfort is possible; it is to recognize comfort, however minimal, within constraint. We see the structure we are in, the power dynamics at play, who is giving to whom and who is taking what.

Zuo gives up her voice and Sedgwick gives up her kimonos, and both, in different ways, and with different stakes, give up a particular orientation to the self and its representation via Asiatic femininity. Kuo gives up her body as the site of the self by giving it to gelatin in performance, video, and art installation. What she gives up is her flavor and form. For her, this "gift-giving" is a sacrifice bound up with "sensuality" and "aspiration," all of which are notions entangled with the Butterfly who, in her willingness to sacrifice herself, becomes alluring as an honorable, feminine ideal.[96]

Kuo's sacrifice, however, is not a totalizing act of self-annihilation like Gallimard's or the Butterfly's. For her, the racialized, feminized act of giving in is not akin to powerlessness, but, as I see it, more aligned with the pleasurable forms of receptivity that self-identified femme lesbian Amber Hollibaugh describes as a way of demanding to a partner: "'Love me enough to let me go where I need to go and take me there.... Give me a way to be so in my body that I don't have to think; that you can fantasize for the both of us.'"[97] To say "Let me go" is to permit one's self to remain open in giving up power and the fantasy of control. At the same time, "Let me go" gives permission to another to take that power for the sake of enacting and taking part in a shared fantasy. To "let me" is to also "let you," and the other way around, too. In her work with gelatin, Kuo gives up and lets go for her own cold comfort—it is impersonal in its letting, at the limits of the self's fantasies of omnipotence. Phillips writes, "It is as though at certain moments in our lives we are given the order 'Give up!' or 'Give it up!' and so begins an obscure kind of wishing and hoping and bargaining."[98] In Kuo's work, gelatin, like Sedgwick's textiles, orders her to "Give up!" and "Give it up!" not with defeat and resignation, but with a renewed devotion to figuring out what one makes a sacrifice for: what one wishes and hopes for within an exchange between fingers and fabric, body and gelatin.

Kuo's work with gelatin does not explicitly focus on the fantasies of representations of Asiatic femininity like *M. Butterfly* and *Carnal Orient*. To riff on Chuh's critiques of "aboutness," if Kuo's work with gelatin is "about anything," it is not exactly "about" Asiatic femininity.[99] Yet, alongside an annoyance felt around such expectations of aboutness, I am compelled by how Asiatic femininity is implicated and suggested, or rather touched upon, through Kuo's use of gelatin, as matter that needs and aspires to Kuo's flavor and form. In *M. Butterfly* and *Carnal Orient*, spoiled white men feast on the fantasy of Asiatic femininity, consuming themselves in the process. In Kuo's work with gelatin, she spoils herself, which is to say that she gives up and finds cold comfort at the limits of the self, at its seeping edges.

In her 2017 performance, *Bone Bath*, Kuo lets gelatin consume her over time by taking a bath in it. In the marble white bathroom of a luxury apartment overlooking New York City's High Line, Kuo, in nude-colored underwear and blue toenail polish, cast herself in a bathtub filled with undyed, unflavored Knox-brand gelatin for three hours. The performance was a part of "Timeshare," a site-specific exhibition that took place in four new luxury apartments, which were the last project the architect Zaha Hadid had worked on before she passed away in 2016. The exhibition put the apartments on display for visitors, tourists, and prospective homeowners, adding to real estate value with the trace the artworks, performances, and films left behind.

Onlookers shuffled in and out of the bathroom as Kuo laid on her back in the tub, while Williamson Brasfield played an original live score from the shower—a place where sound always sounds smoother, softened by its reverberation. In an interview, Kuo says, "What I didn't expect, lying there in a weird collagen golem that I spent days preparing, is that it would be so supremely comfortable."[100] It must have been apparent, for Kuo remembers one woman who, during the performance, approached her to tell her "I like your comfort."[101] Given her comfort, her performance differs from other kinds of durational performance that bring the body to the limits of debility and capacity. Kuo's body is held and suspended, not strained, and she lies in repose. She draws comfort from bathing, and yet, it is a comfort that comes with sacrifice. Her stillness draws attention to the touch of gelatin, as a substance that needs her to give up her flavor and form because it needs both to support and compose itself. Kuo's body is not visibly or physically worn down, yet something of her body is offered up and given the longer she lies there. Looking at Kuo, we wonder what Kuo might taste like, as if she were, in fact, a body and an object made edible in her contact with gelatin, ready to be set in a gelatin mold, presented at a dining table.

Beginning in 2017, Kuo became preoccupied with the history, material properties, and sensations of gelatin. As Tompkins writes, "Gelatin . . . has a complex history tied both to waste management and to the management of the poor."[102] Developed in the early nineteenth century in the United States, gelatin is an animal byproduct made from meat, bone collagen, and connective tissue. Initial experiments with gelatin were for the purposes of discerning whether it could be used as a "cheap meat alternative" to feed the poor, until it was ultimately found, after more research and study, that "gelatin could not sustain life."[103] Nevertheless, gelatin became a common ingredient in the United States during the mid-twentieth century, as a part of postwar rationing, leading to the publication of various cookbooks promoting its versatility. In a time of scarcity, recovery, and war overseas, gelatin promised domestic ease as well as abundance. One need only picture the decadence of colorful gelatin dishes with other food like slices of hardboiled eggs or pineapple suspended in its innards. If gelatin could not provide ample nutrition to live, it could hold other food within it, displayed like edible trinkets.

Images of these dishes abound in midcentury cookbooks, which Kuo collected as a part of her research and fascination with all things gelatinous. While reading through these old cookbooks, Kuo found that to use gelatin at that time was, she writes, "a duty of citizenship: to maintain the bodies of young Americans; to *stretch* food; to avoid waste and the appearance of having less than is needed to live well."[104] Gelatin made devalued, disposable, unsavory parts of animals' bodies edible, but also morally right, as a sign of modesty and efficiency, rather than deprivation and impoverishment. If gelatin could not sustain life, then it could be made valuable as the economical, as a sign of frugal resourcefulness in service to a nation in need of healing. Gelatin did not have clear nutritional value, yet it did nourish a nation's image of itself and the bodies within its borders.

Gelatin is a demanding, desiring substance. It is formed by the surroundings it absorbs, envelopes, and molds itself around. It needs you to give up something to it; *it lets*. It needs and aspires to the flavor and form of something else in order to have a definable taste and settle into a particular shape. It is created in heat, then cooled. Coldness is required for it to set and retain the form it has been given and also takes. Kuo's body in the gelatin enacts what Adrian Piper would call "catalysis": the process of increasing the rate and outcome of a chemical reaction caused in a substance by a catalytic agent that is itself not changed or affected.[105] Like Piper's series of performances *Catalysis* (1970–73), Kuo makes herself the art object as catalytic agent, which provokes a reaction in the gelatin.

The violence of gelatin's material properties accompanies the history of the High Line, an elevated linear park created on what had originally been a part of the New York Central Railroad. Built in 1846, the railroad was used for freight trains that transported meat, produce, and dairy, serving the meatpacking plants around Tenth Avenue. These trains, traveling along street-level tracks, caused so many deaths (more than 540 by 1910) that Tenth Avenue earned the nickname "Death Avenue."[106] In 1929, due to the ongoing deaths and public outcry, the railroad was elevated thirty feet above the street, reopened in 1933, and renamed the West Side Elevated Line.[107] The traffic on the line began to decline during the 1970s, and by the early 1980s, the line stopped running and had become abandoned, left to fall into disrepair. In 1999, under the threat of demolition, the elevated rail line was made into a public park owned by the city and maintained by a nonprofit organization, Friends of the High Line. Since then, it has remained a popular tourist attraction.

While Kuo's performance for "Timeshare" was meant to increase the value of luxury apartments along the newly revitalized High Line, Kuo insists on the material remains of the surrounding area's history: the cargo of meat that the freight trains carried, cutting into cross streets and other traffic, the detritus of the meatpacking plants along Tenth Avenue, and the victims of the train's fatal accidents. For Kuo, the area, and particularly the rail line's history of commerce, is tied to meat and its history as Death Avenue, as well as to the structure of the High Line and its conservation of urban wildlife that could only grow in the wake of the railroad's neglect. The High Line's ruin became something of value to a city always in need of more green spaces; it promised a different kind of vitality for the city, particularly for those who could afford to live in Chelsea, and for tourists who came to visit. In her accompanying statement for the performance, Kuo states, "Cattle to the meat packer, oranges to the market, milk, vegetables. Nourishment for an alive city with a visceral dash of collateral damage was the norm."[108] In *Bone Bath*, Kuo lays her body down in gelatin, as if she were there waiting for an oncoming train. Kuo puts herself on the line, along Tenth Avenue, where nourishment and damage, life and death came hand in hand.

Kuo's performance is one of stillness, yet there is gelatin's movement to consider. It ripples, shakes, and quivers. It reacts and responds as affectable yet resilient materials. While gelatin is constituted by the dead and disposable, and made in attempts to sustain the lives of populations also deemed disposable, what interrupts the presumed unliveliness of such disposability is gelatin's movements and sounds. As Tompkins writes, "the aesthetic power of gelatinousness is the potential that these materials hold for forms of movement and shifts in sensory organization that undo the animacy hierarchies that traditional prioritize agentic, individualized, human selfhood and rather imagine relational forms of inhuman and human collectivity."[109] The gelatinous does not behave like it should, which is to say, like food that is neither alive nor lively. Sometimes, given its "uncanny responsiveness to its sensory surroundings," it acts all too human.[110] It does not act like itself. This speaks to its ability to withstand and give in to the "stress of deformation" and "the deformative pressures of the everyday."[111] The gelatinous, Tompkins writes, "is in fact quite exquisitely relational in its materiality: gelatinous materials manifest and materialize forms of touch that are otherwise not visible to the eye, and they manifest the nature of that contact in and as movement."[112] Touch can be seen, and sometimes it can be uncomfortable because gelatin's movements and sounds suggest, at one moment, a trembling body, and at the next, its innards. The cold comfort of Kuo's performance becomes the site of exquisite relationality: the site of letting go and giving up, of touching what might need something from you, making you aware of your bodily and psychic limitations.

When Kuo first touched the gelatin in *Bone Bath*, she realized there were so many other ways to handle it, play with it, and draw out its desire and violence. This led to Kuo's 2019 one-off performance and a video, both titled *The New Joys of Gellies*. In the performance, gelatin molds on trays and a large plastic storage bin full of gelatin are placed on a steel table, which Kuo stands over. A microphone hovers over the gelatin to amplify the sounds it makes as Kuo jiggles it with her hands, cuts it with utensils, digs her fingers into it and squeezes its bits into in her fists, letting it ooze out between her fingers. She breaks up the large molds into smaller pieces, which she gathers in her arms, bringing all of it closer to her chest while bracing against the gelatin's weight and leaning into the table for support. The gelatin spills over the table's edge onto the floor, and Kuo loses her footing as her feet slide on its slime. Where there was once the stillness of soaking and being soaked in a bath, now there is exertion and strain. Giving up becomes a struggle. Cold comfort takes effort and can make you work up a sweat.

The ten-minute video for *The New Joys of Gellies* is akin to videos circulating in online video sharing and social media platforms like YouTube that are made to trigger an autonomous sensory meridian response (ASMR). The idea for the video first occurred to Kuo after joining a Facebook group called "Show Me Your Aspics," made up of members who share materials like vintage photographs of gelatin dishes in cookbooks and ASMR videos. The term *ASMR* first appeared in online discussion boards in 2010, and is often described as a calming, pleasurable, "tingling sensation" that runs up down the head and the spine.[113] One might say it produces a feeling of supreme comfort. As Rob Gallagher writes, "ASMR is often associated with scenes of intimacy and concentrated attention: it might be brought on by watching someone performing a meticulous task, by the cadence of a voice, by whispering and soft sounds or by expressions of care, interest and affirmation."[114] The internet and social media platforms have countless videos made to activate one's ASMR. These videos can center around the auditory, but also the visual, with videos of hands that carefully and slowly crinkle a paper bag, fold a piece of paper, or gently tap a hard surface with the soft bed of fingers tips and nails.

The New Joys of Gellies is divided into three chapters. The first chapter is a close-up of the surface of gelatin, textured with air bubbles. Kuo's hand enters the frame to press down on the surface, first gently, then with more force. She shakes it, rubs it, and digs into it with her fingers. Her touch is tender before it turns aggressive, with strokes and slaps. In the video's second chapter, a wider shot shows a plastic tub of gelatin sitting on top of a white marble countertop surface. Kuo's arms and hands enter the frame to slowly push and pull the gelatin out of the tub, which slides out with resistance, almost resentfully. Kuo bends the gelatin until it breaks into blocks that she stacks one on top of the other, letting them slide, rip, and fall. The third chapter reveals a close-up of the gelatin in its heated liquid form as a whisk spins it into a smoky, frothy, white texture. Gelatin aspires to another's flavor and form, and in the context of an ASMR video, we might aspire to its qualities, too. We might wish we were also good at being under pressure. Phillips tells us that we give something up when we desire change and feel that we are in need of something new. Watching gelatin move in *The New Joy of Gellies* might soothe us with the promise of its bounce, with the way it rebounds under duress and withstands Kuo's attacks.

I first encountered Kuo's 2020 installation, *I Remember You*, from my phone's screen, while sitting at a dining table I had borrowed from my parents after a last-minute move back home to LA in the summer of 2020. I sat at that table alone every day, eating and working, sometimes working without eating, but rarely eating without working. The fantasy of a work-life balance had faded. This seemed like the right context for encountering Kuo's installation, especially given the theme of the group exhibition for which it was commissioned. On view at the Hessel Museum at Bard College, "Somatic's Grocery," curated by Brooke Nicholas, interrogated how "the body's capacity to store and process emotion is similar to the experience of cooking, eating, and digesting food."[115] What was I processing, psychically and physically, as I sat working and eating at that dining table at all hours? Nicholas thought about what the body can take, where art became food, and how to work was to eat. Because of COVID-19, I was not able to travel from Los Angeles to upstate New York to see the show in person. While Kuo had to remain in Brooklyn, where she lives, Nicholas had to receive instructions from the artists in the exhibition to manage and oversee all of the works' installation. Upon the show's opening, Nicholas offered to give me a tour of the exhibition on FaceTime. I sat at the dining table as she walked me through the space.

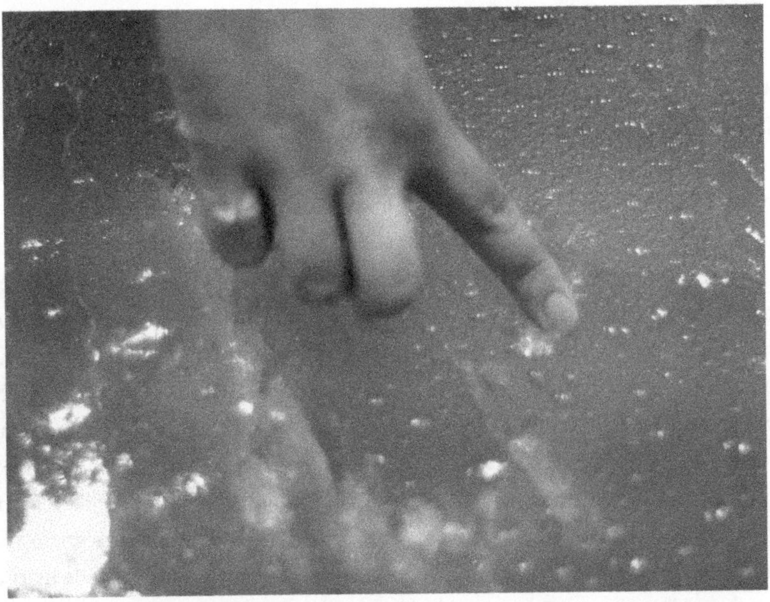

FIGURE 3.1. Still from *The New Joys of Gellies*, Alison Kuo, 2017. Director of photography: Williamson Brasfield. Courtesy of the artist.

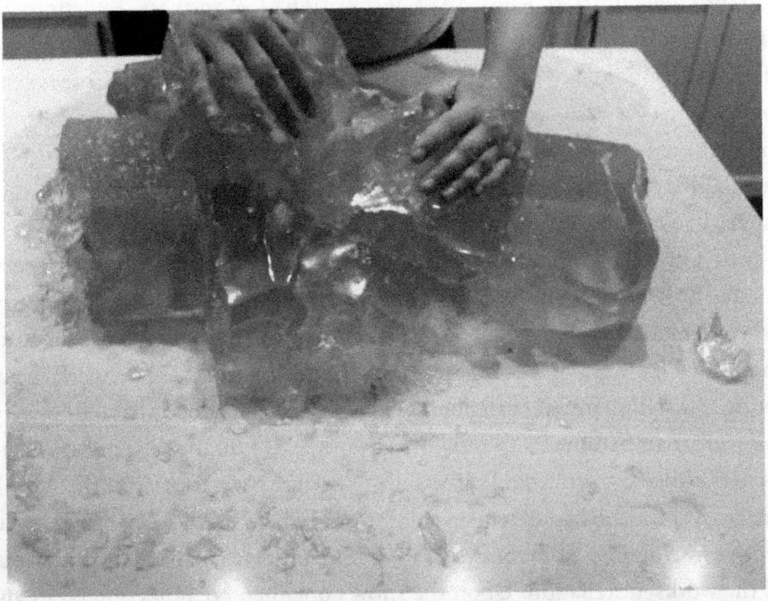

FIGURE 3.2. Still from *The New Joys of Gellies*, Alison Kuo, 2017. Director of photography: Williamson Brasfield. Courtesy of the artist.

In *I Remember You*, Kuo's body is not involved, only invoked. Gelatin stands in for her body, and her body stands in for her grandmother, who had passed away in 2017 in Hong Kong. Kuo made the installation as a recollection and restaging of her grandmother's funeral in Hong Kong, which she attended. For the funeral, her grandmother had been laid out and preserved in an air-conditioned glass chamber for viewers to say their farewells and pay their respects. In our correspondence, Kuo wrote, "her body was the vessel for her life and spending time with her body was an important cultural tradition to say goodbye."[116] "I was thinking about how bodies are made of proteins," she continued, "just as proteins from cattle bodies become gelatin powder and then get reconstituted to some kind of fleshy form."[117] Kuo prepares gelatin like a body prepared for the duration in and of loved ones' mourning. In the same way that gelatin can stretch the matter and use of food waste, Kuo's use of gelatin in *I Remember You* stretches the matter of time and how mourning moves through it. Kuo filled a large chest freezer—"coffin-like," she describes it—with an amount of unflavored Knox-brand gelatin equal to her weight.[118] For the run of the exhibition throughout that summer, the gelatin sat rotting, congealing, splitting, and cracking.

I Remember You presents the ritual of mourning as the process of decay. The work is reminiscent of Felix Gonzalez-Torres's *Untitled (Portrait of Ross in L.A.)* (1991), in which a pile of colorful wrapped candies sits on the floor, weighing a total of 175 pounds, equivalent to the weight of Ross Laycock, Gonzalez-Torres's lover, who died due to complications from AIDS that same year. Those encountering the work are invited to take a candy to keep as a souvenir or to unwrap and eat, letting it dissolve into their mouth, into their body. Gonzalez-Torres's mourning and remembrance of Laycock is made into a public, collective ritual. At the end of each day, more candy is added to the pile so that it returns to its original weight, reminding us of Laycock's absent presence anew. Whether consisting of piles of candy or frozen gelatin, the absence of a loved one is heavy. There is a weight to loss, akin to the weight of the body left behind as a vessel reconstituted into a different kind of "fleshy form." In Gonzalez-Torres's work, the memory of a lover tastes sweet before melting away. There is no process of decay, but there is the consumption and dissolve of form. Kuo's work stays untouchable, without sweetness, sealed into a cold coffin partially to protect the space and people in its proximity, and yet, as the growth of bacteria is inevitable, it is vulnerable to contamination. Purity is impossible, and so is preservation. This in itself is a cold comfort—no matter how many candies are taken and eaten, no matter how rotten the gelatin gets, the loss they materialize is not forgotten, and always within reach, in touch.

In art school, Kuo liked working with food. However, her professors often told her that the goal was to make an object that has a gallery life, which is another way of saying it should have lasting value. An art object is not for letting go, or rather, not unless we want to, and usually for a certain price. As Kuo puts it, her professors asked, "How do you translate [your art] into something that will be easy to show and sustain you financially?"[119] Art is expected to appreciate in value; a buyer or collector, most of the time, understands art to be an investment. Kuo was faced with the question of how to preserve the life of something perishable to make it more financially sustainable—to stretch its own value as gelatin does with animal byproduct. She could put her work in the refrigerator, but it would still go bad, becoming an inconvenience at best and a health risk at worst. It might become cold leftovers, rather than an art object. *I Remember You* addressed Kuo's frustrations with this advice she had been given. Letting this advice marinate over time, she wanted to play with the finite life of perishable goods. Kuo knew what happened with gelatin over time. Even when refrigerated, it melts down into slime. It molds and begins to smell.

In preparation for the work, Kuo met with an art conservator, usually tasked with the restoration of valuable artworks, to ask how they might conserve gelatin "without it turning into a petri dish in the gallery."[120] Gallery spaces had health restrictions that prohibited the handling of food, a challenge that frequently presented itself in some of Kuo's other work. The conservator had come up with the idea of spraying an ethanol solution on the gelatin, as well as including desiccant beads that absorbed moisture to keep its surrounds as dry as possible. The conservator also decided that the gelatin had to be chilled at all times on the freezer's lowest setting, and therefore could not be in open air. As a solution, Kuo kept the freezer lid open, but had plexiglass fitted over the top so that viewers could see how the gelatin spoiled over time, which it did. Coldness could offer protection, but only to a certain degree.

When I asked Kuo for images of *I Remember You*, she also shared footage of the work's deinstallation. Unlike its installation, she was tasked with taking it down, which, given its material, necessitated the work's destruction, rather than its storage and transportation. Kuo sent two videos showing her hands, in blue latex surgical gloves, clasping a large sledgehammer, which she used to slam a crowbar and chisel into the frozen mass of protein flakes, breaking up its surface. These videos seemed like sequels, of a sort, to *The New Joys of Gellies*. With the deinstallation, Kuo's attacks on gelatin escalated, from the strokes and pokes of bare skin on jiggling gelatin to hacking and hammering frigid gelatin with gloved hands. In these videos, the gelatin is harder and more stubborn, but ultimately it shatters, it gives up. Kuo's treatment of the gelatin is similar to

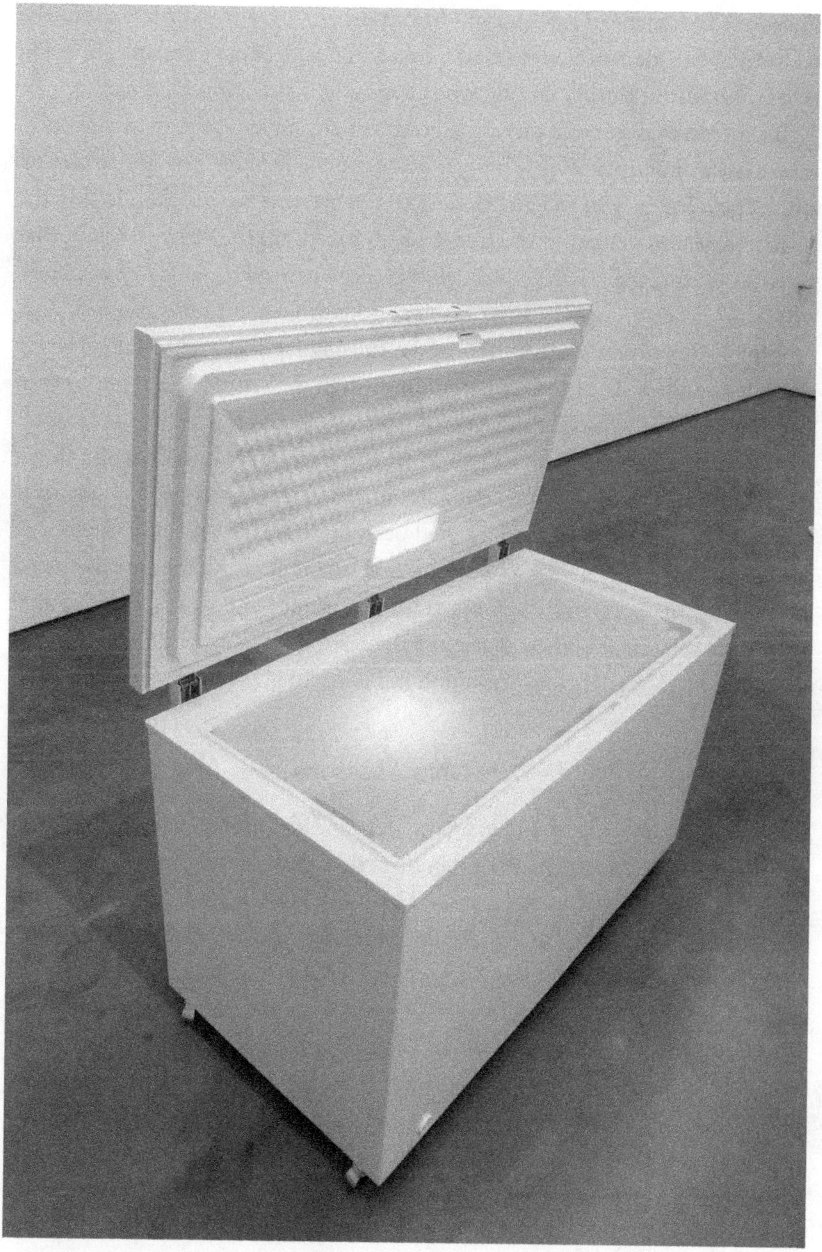

FIGURE 3.3. Alison Kuo, *I Remember You*, 2020. Courtesy of the artist.

the cook's treatment of raw chicken in *Carnal Orient*, which brings about the realization that destruction does not only come at the end, after an exhibition is over, but also at the beginning, when a meal or installation is prepared.

If the freezer is a coffin and if the gelatin stands in for more than one body, we are left wondering: Whose body is being touched? Who is having to give up and let go? The gelatin to Kuo, or Kuo to the gelatin? Rather than letting the gelatin thaw and defrost in the freezer, Kuo speeds up the process. In another video Kuo sent, she cradles the smaller pieces of frozen gelatin in her hands, which she holds up to the camera. She digs her fingers into the gelatin before rubbing its icy pieces against each other, causing ice shavings to fall, creating the soft sound of brushing and friction, bringing to mind the sounds of an ASMR video. But what qualities do we aspire to here? Once all of the freezer's remains were removed, Kuo put all of it in large garbage bags that she threw away. The work's gallery life ended, along with whatever value it might have held and accrued. After the gelatin had been disposed of, Kuo gave the freezer to an artist she knew who was working with roadkill. Thus, the freezer would continue to preserve and carry the trace of violence and death, from animal byproduct to animal bodies. It remained a resting place, which one might say is another kind of cold comfort, found in the act of giving up and letting go.

Cold Object Lessons

This chapter came out of a talk I gave as a candidate for tenure-track jobs in Asian American studies. At the time, I worried about my legibility within the field. I came to Asian American studies late, and I felt behind. I tried to anticipate the expectations of search committees and departments, and what they might think constitutes Asian Americanist scholarship. Like everyone on the academic job market, I was anxious about making the right kinds of impactful yet palatable interventions in the field. This came down to my case studies: How do I showcase my knowledge of Asian American studies through my selection of and engagement with certain cultural objects? Curation might be akin to practices of care, but to select objects for the genre of the job talk felt more cold, extractive, and calculating. Given this, how could I warm up to my objects? In grasping for an object worthy of Asian American studies—something from the canon—I thought of Hwang's *M. Butterfly*, which I had first read as an undergraduate student. I found my old copy of the play, with all my younger self's annotations indelibly made in pen, much to my embarrassment, and I began to read it again.

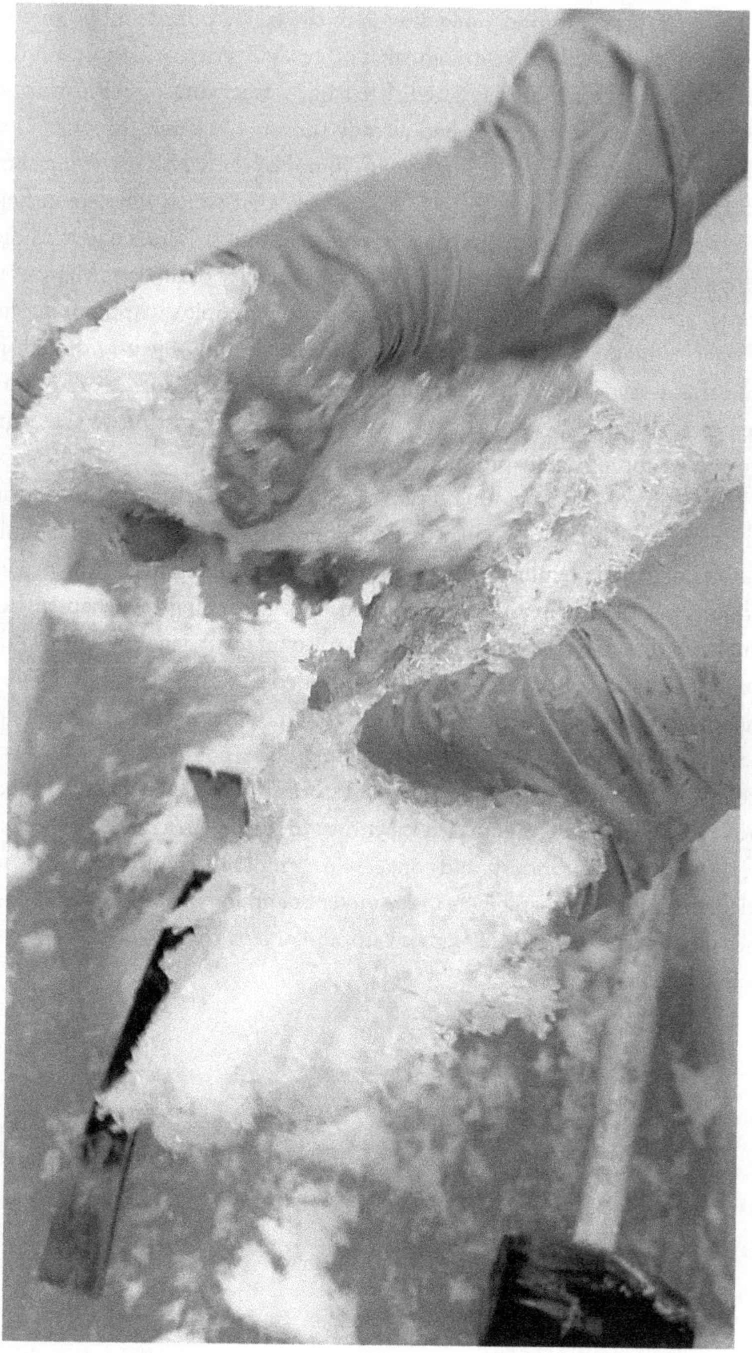

FIGURE 3.4. Still from a video of the deinstallation of Alison Kuo, *I Remember You*. Courtesy of the artist.

As I read, I tried to find a new way in to the play. I poked and prodded to see what might give. I read through what others had written about it. Reading made me feel irksome and agitated. I felt like I was working with what felt picked over, with what others had already thoroughly sifted through. These feelings were not the fault of the play itself, nor of the scholars writing about it. Rather, I attribute these feelings to the ways that we, as scholars in fields like Asian American studies, critical race and ethnic studies, gender studies, and queer studies, are often confronted with a scarcity of objects. Many of us, I think, are hesitant to touch the remains of other people's work, not because we want to be the only ones who write about a certain object (although for some, that is the case), but because if more than one of us does, a canon starts to emerge, and along with it, the traps and affordances of institutional recognition and its appropriately productive "object lessons."[121]

I offer this context as another means of addressing the fraught stakes of material remains—of a canonized play that continues to stick around, or of fatiguing fantasies of Asiatic femininity that fail to become thriving sites of theory and critique, and for that reason, stick around, too. In writing this chapter, I did not search for a new discovery to claim as my own for Asian American studies and its discussions of Asiatic femininity. I wanted to stay with what remains in place, what has remained spoiled, in the dark, almost like a secret. As Zuo notes, a secret secretes. It is "not only a container but also a contagion which . . . is an attempt to spread, touch, infect, and transform."[122] A secret spoils. It blocks one's view of what lies underneath sheer robes, it jiggles on a plate, gets stuck in the throat, rots in the mouth, and congeals in comfort and mourning. These material remains are inseparable from the violence and loss that has spoiled them. They offer the cold comforts of giving up, and of letting, still.

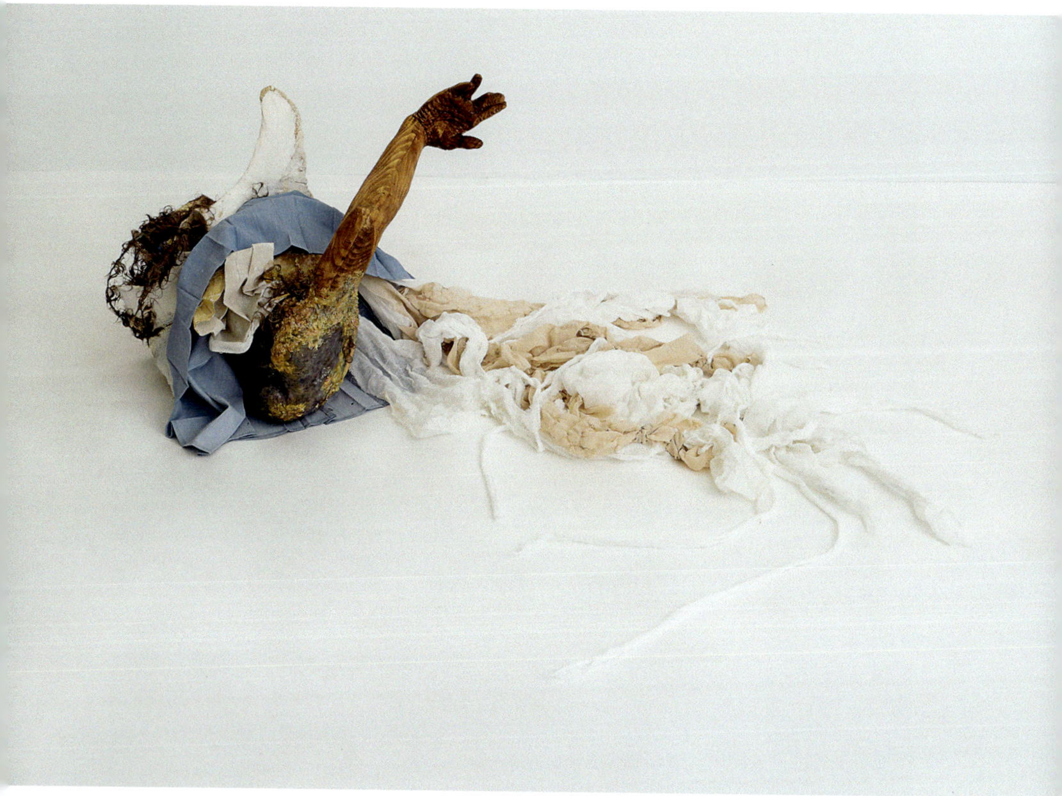

PLATE 1. Cato Ouyang, *Kicked Madonna (Crystal)*, 2022. Wood, mustang pelvis, epoxy clay, hydrocal, gypsum, papier-mâché, beeswax, oyster shells, horsehair, polyester, cotton gauze, 50 × 36 × 21 in. No Place Gallery, Columbus. Photo: Jacob Collier. Courtesy of the artist.

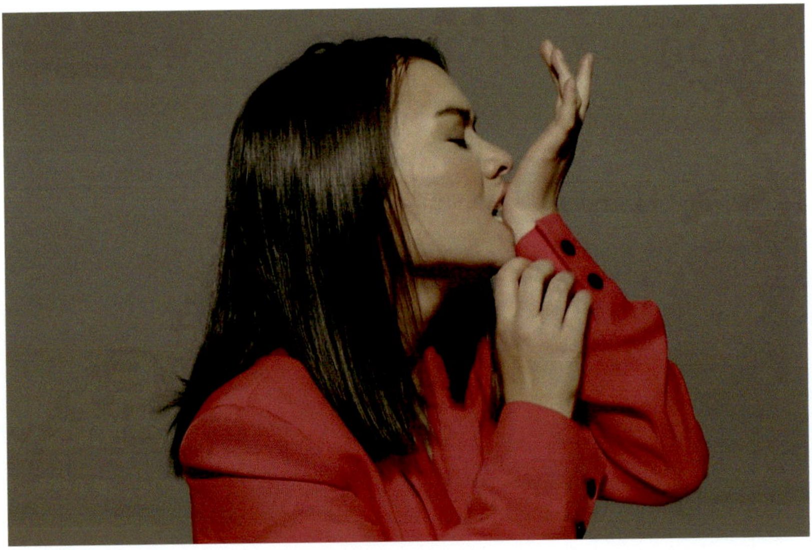

PLATE 2. Still from Mitski, "All-American Girl," 2016.

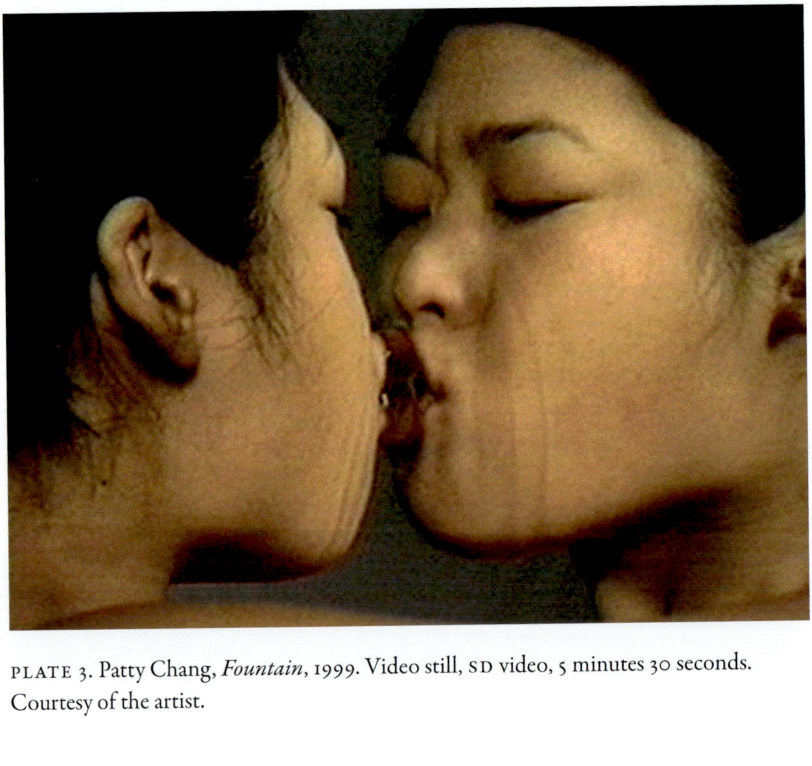

PLATE 3. Patty Chang, *Fountain*, 1999. Video still, SD video, 5 minutes 30 seconds. Courtesy of the artist.

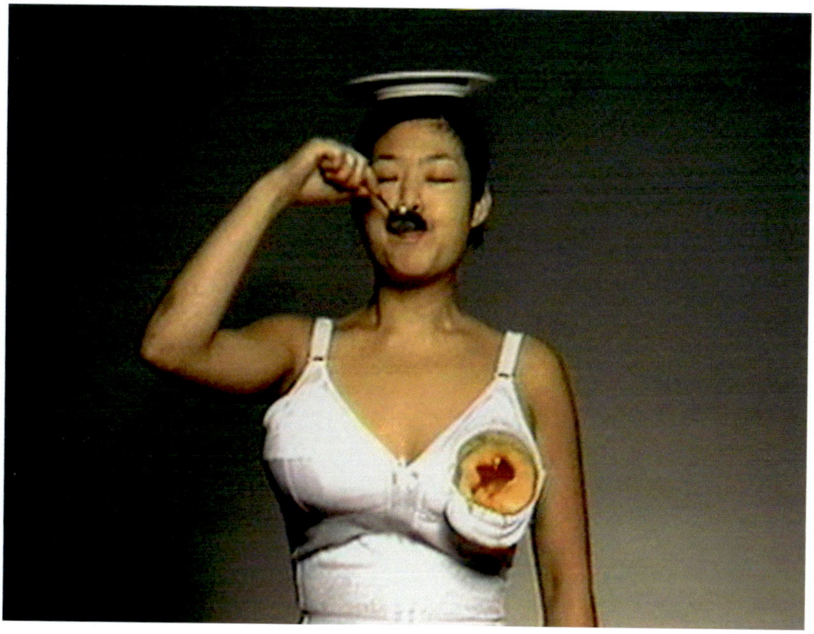

PLATE 4. Patty Chang, *Melons (At a Loss)*, 1998. Video still, SD video, 3 minutes, 47 seconds. Courtesy of the artist.

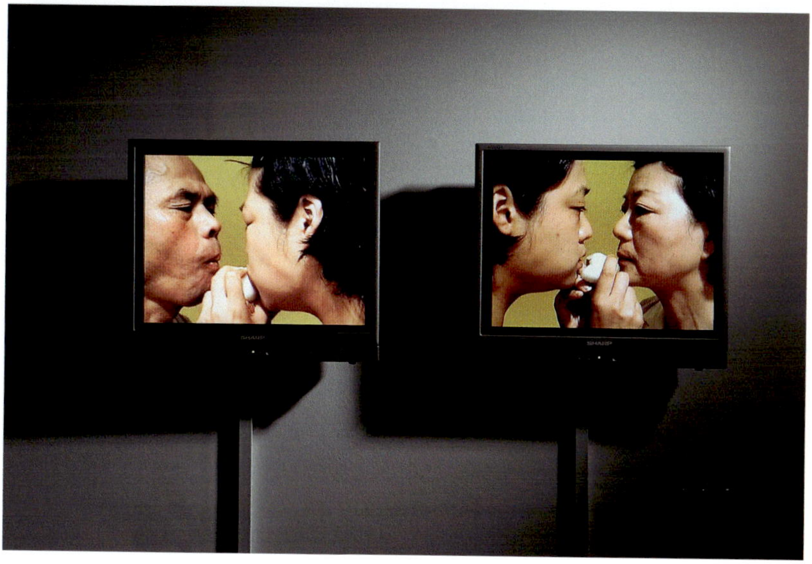

PLATE 5. Patty Chang, *In Love*, 2001. Two-channel video installation, TRT, 3 minutes, 28 seconds. Courtesy of the artist.

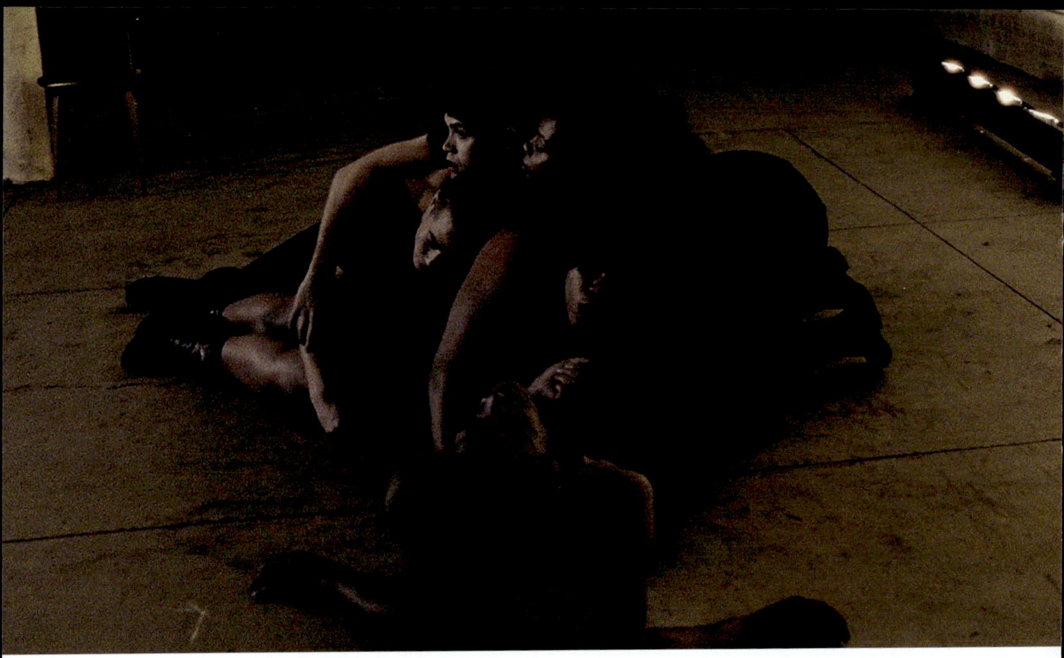

PLATE 6. Wu Tsang, *For how we perceived a life (Take 3)*, 2008. Courtesy of Electronic Arts Intermix (EAI), New York.

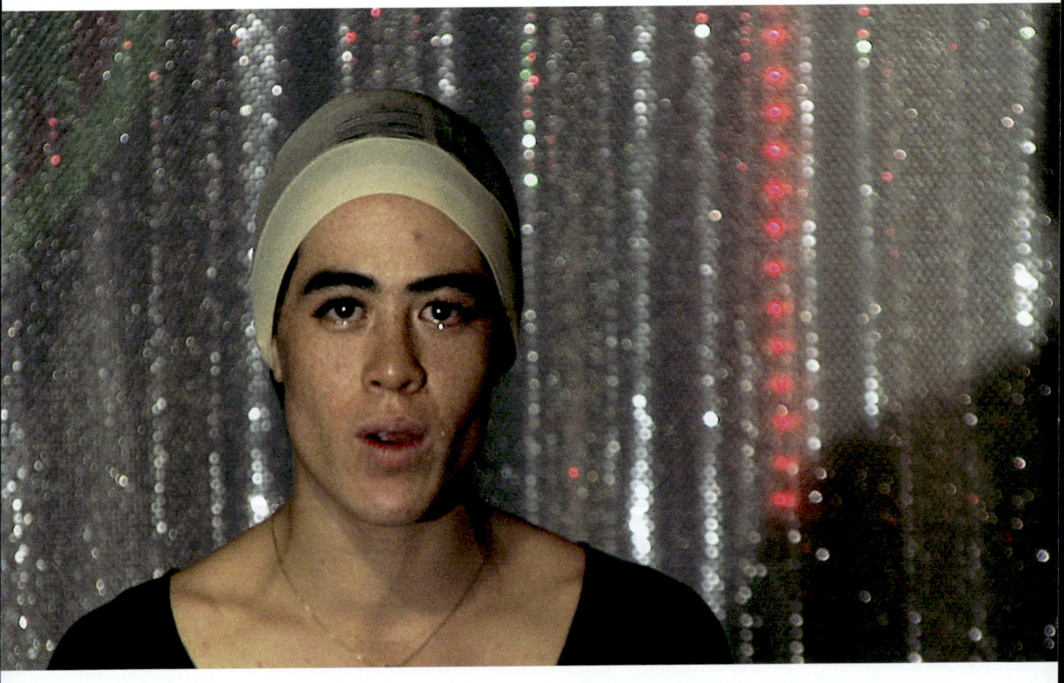

PLATE 7. Wu Tsang, *Shape of the Right Statement*, 2008. Courtesy of Electronic Arts Intermix (EAI), New York.

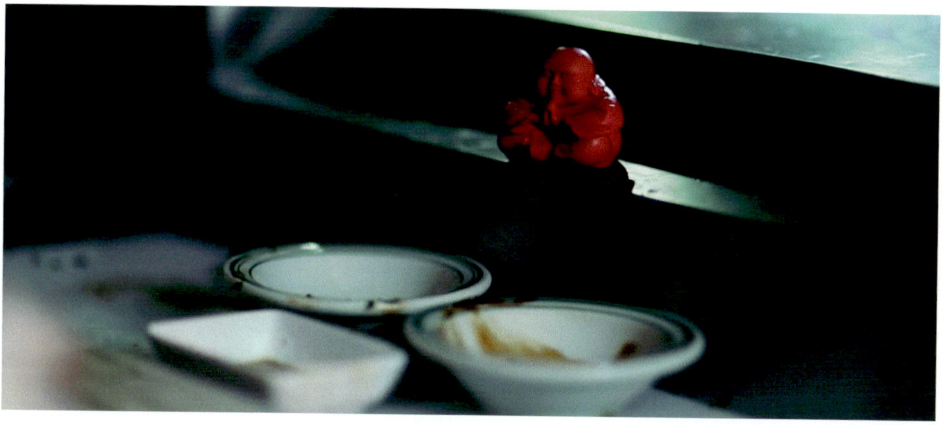

PLATE 8. Still from *Carnal Orient*, dir. Mila Zuo, 2016. Courtesy of the artist.

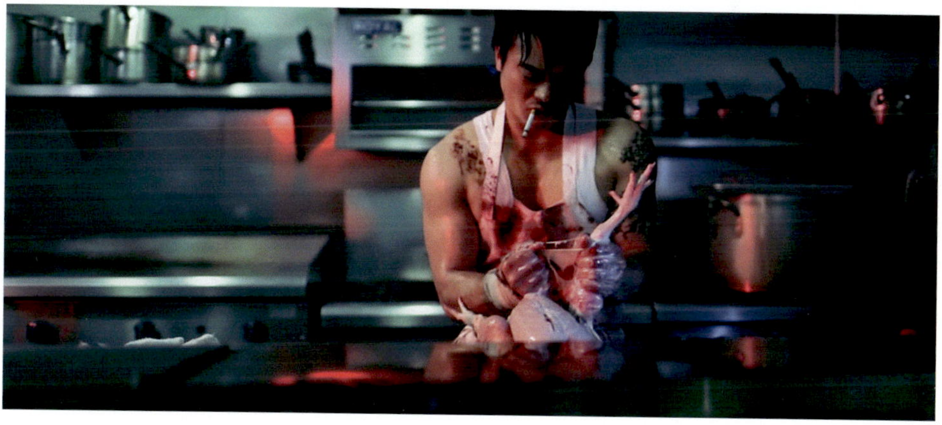

PLATE 9. Still from *Carnal Orient*, dir. Mila Zuo, 2016. Courtesy of the artist.

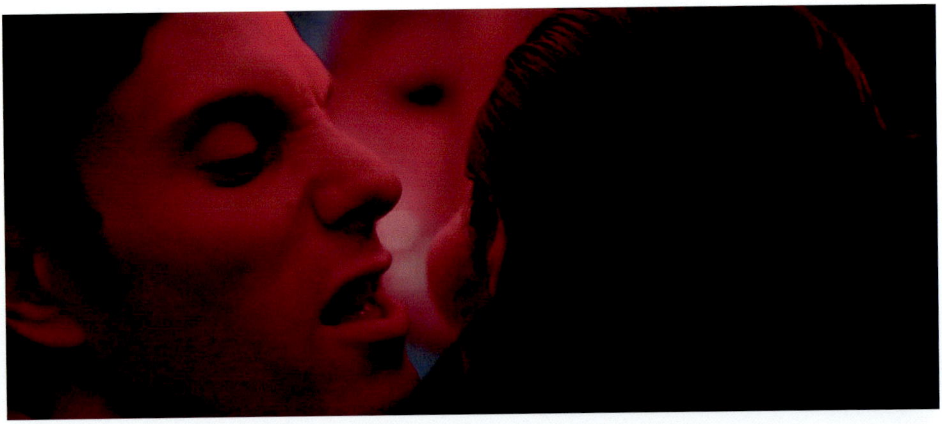

PLATE 10. Still from *Carnal Orient*, dir. Mila Zuo, 2016. Courtesy of the artist.

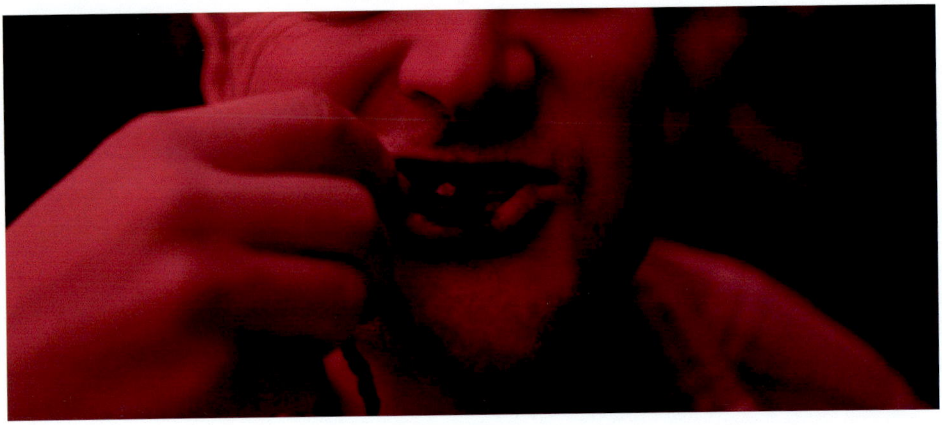

PLATE 11. Still from *Carnal Orient*, dir. Mila Zuo, 2016. Courtesy of the artist.

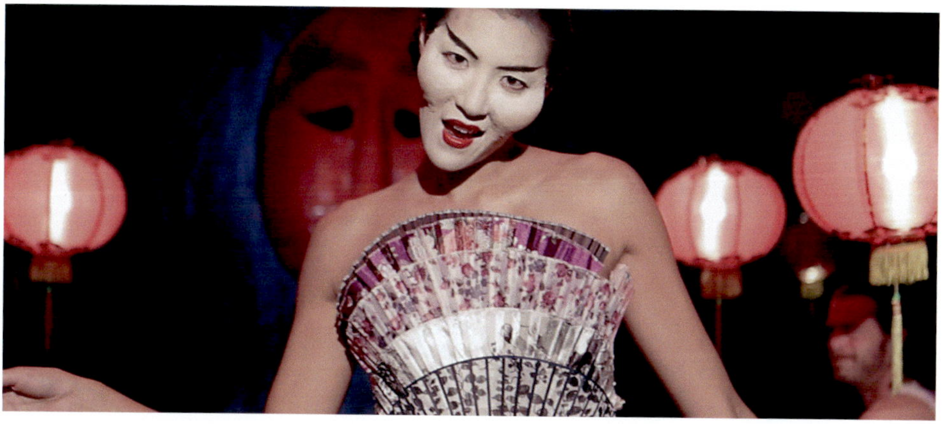

PLATE 12. Still from *Carnal Orient*, dir. Mila Zuo, 2016. Courtesy of the artist.

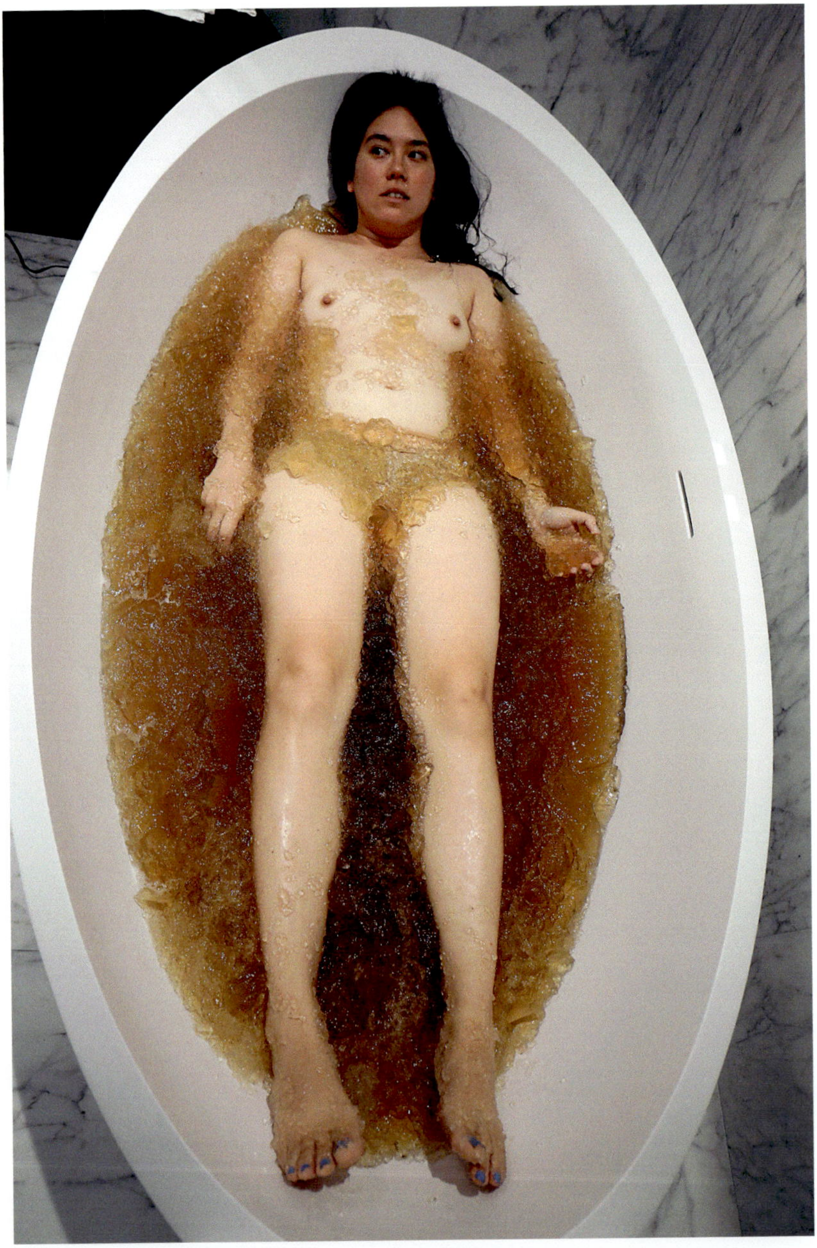

PLATE 13. Alison Kuo, *Bone Bath*, 2017. Photo: Williamson Brasfield. Courtesy of the artist.

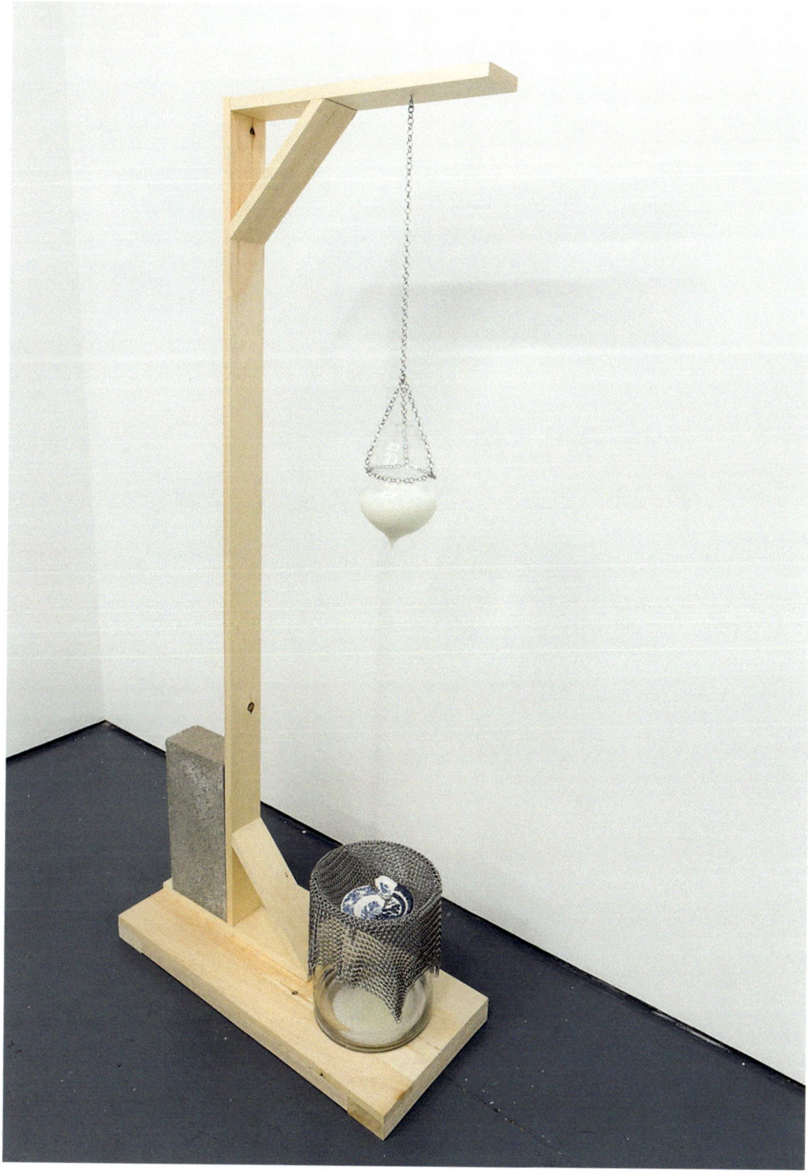

PLATE 14. TJ Shin, *Untitled (torture)*, 2019. Milk, porcelain, handblown glass, wood, metal, cement. Courtesy of the artist.

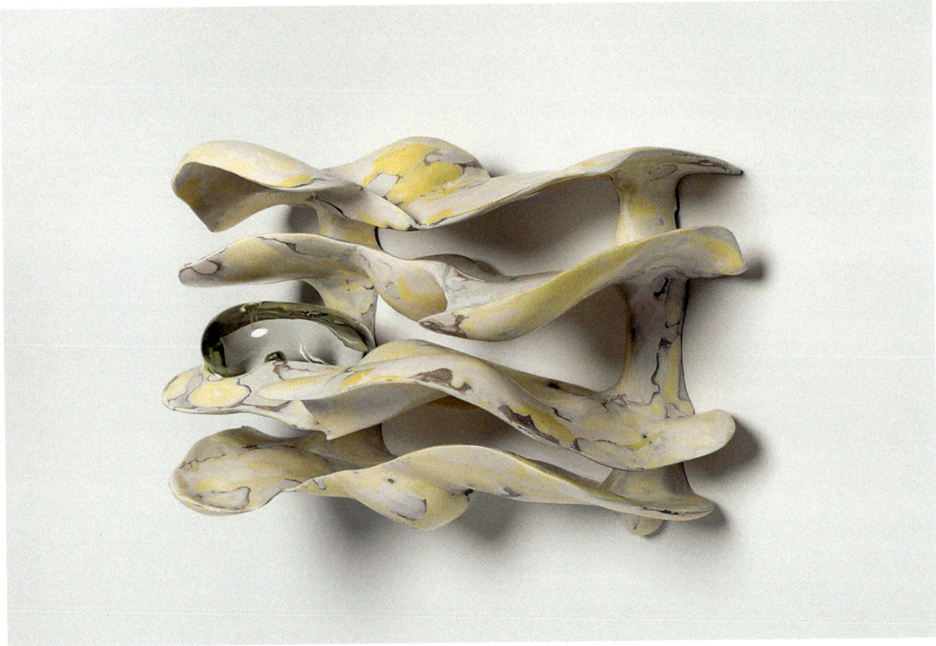

PLATE 15. Jes Fan, *Diagram XI*, 2020. Resin, selenium glass, pigment, 30.5 × 50.8 × 48.3 cm. Courtesy of the artist.

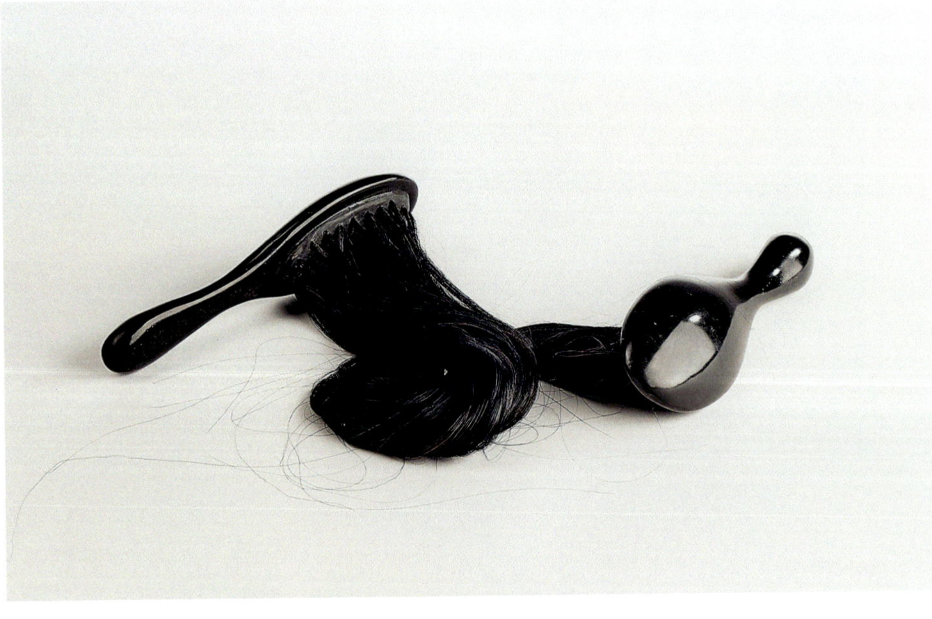

PLATE 16. Jes Fan, *Stranded Between One Act and Another*, 2016. Hair and resin, 15 × 7 × 4 in. Courtesy of the artist.

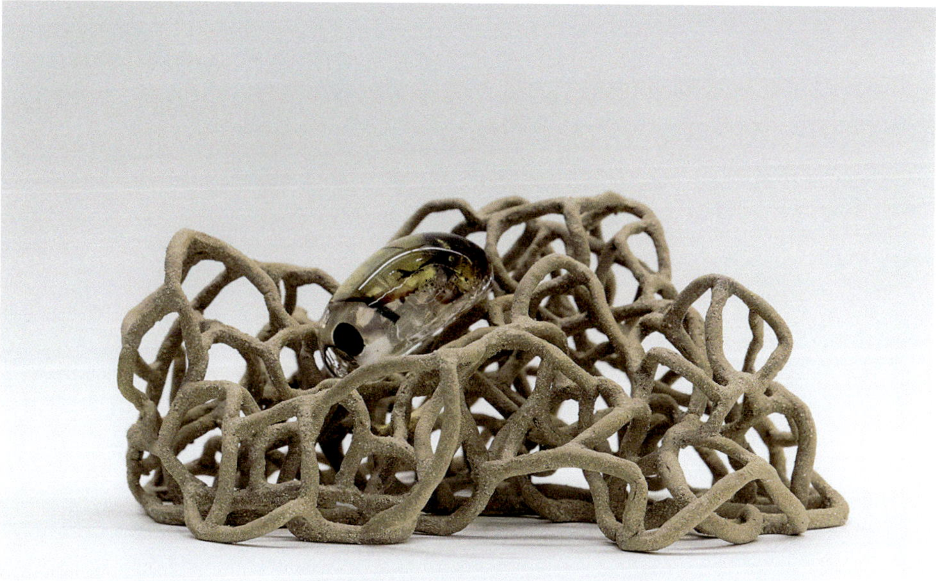

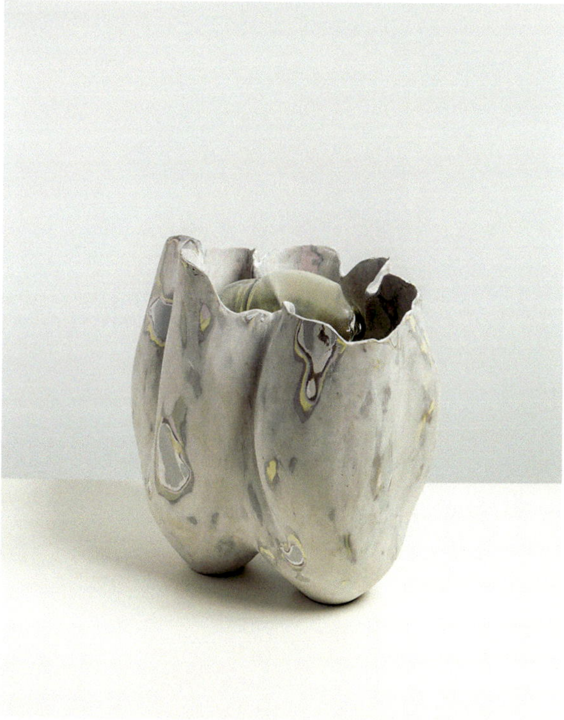

PLATE 17. Jes Fan, *I think about Lam Qua everyday III*, 2019. Ceramic, glass, melanin, silicone, 30.5 × 28.2 × 13.8 cm. Courtesy of the artist.

PLATE 18. Jes Fan, *Left and right knee, grafted*, 2023. Aqua-Resin, glass, pigment, 12 × 9 × 12 in. Courtesy of the artist.

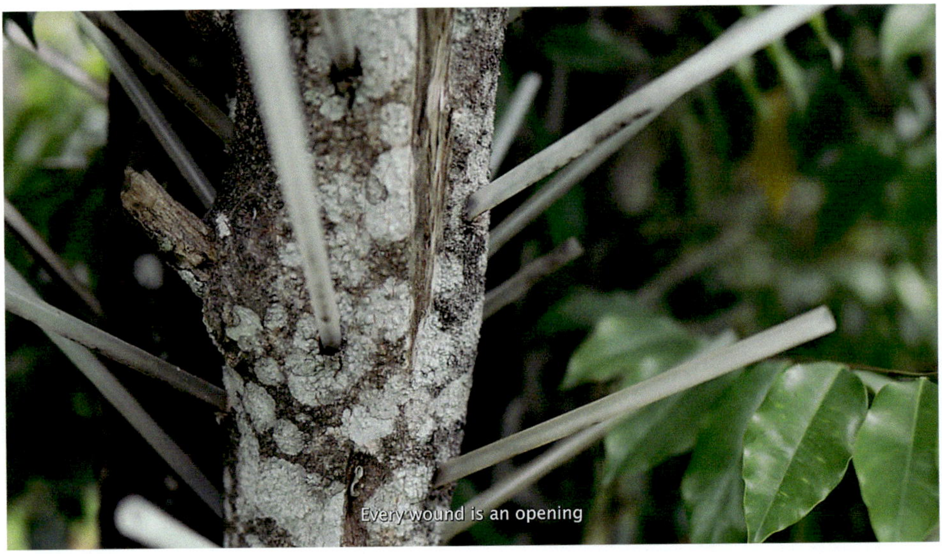

PLATE 19. Still from Jes Fan, *Viscera*, 2023. 4K Color, with sound, 6 minutes. Courtesy of the artist.

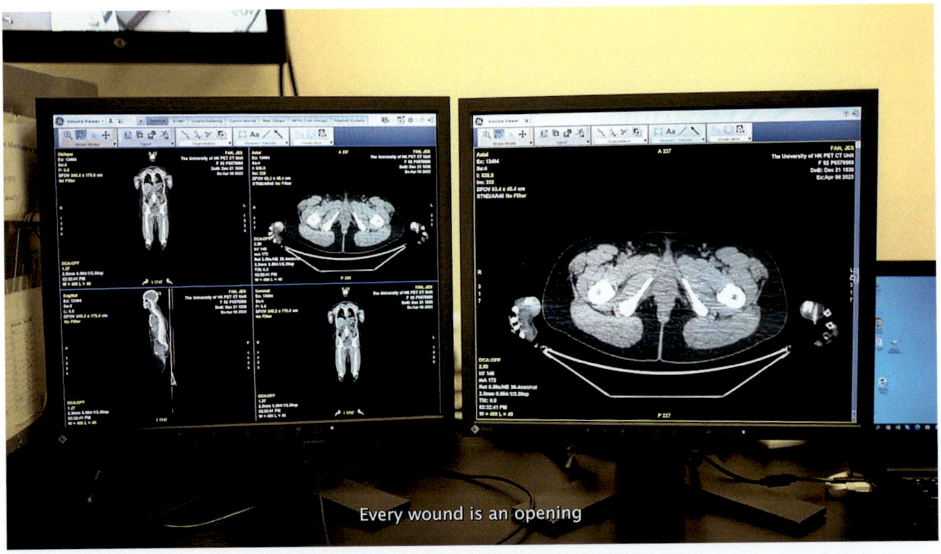

PLATE 20. Still from Jes Fan, *Viscera*, 2023. 4K Color, with sound, 6 minutes. Courtesy of the artist.

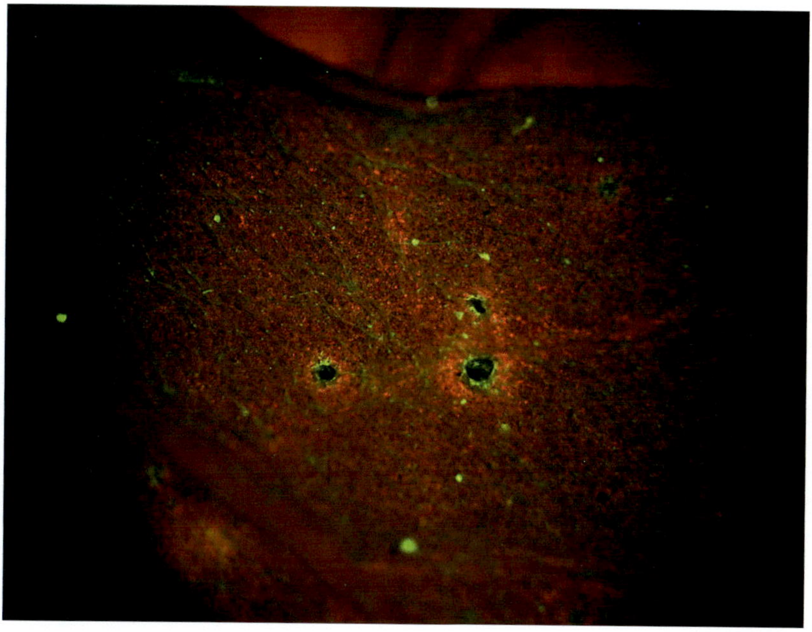

PLATE 21. TJ Shin, *Untitled (Self-Portrait 1)*, 2022. Digital print from microscope scans. Courtesy of the artist.

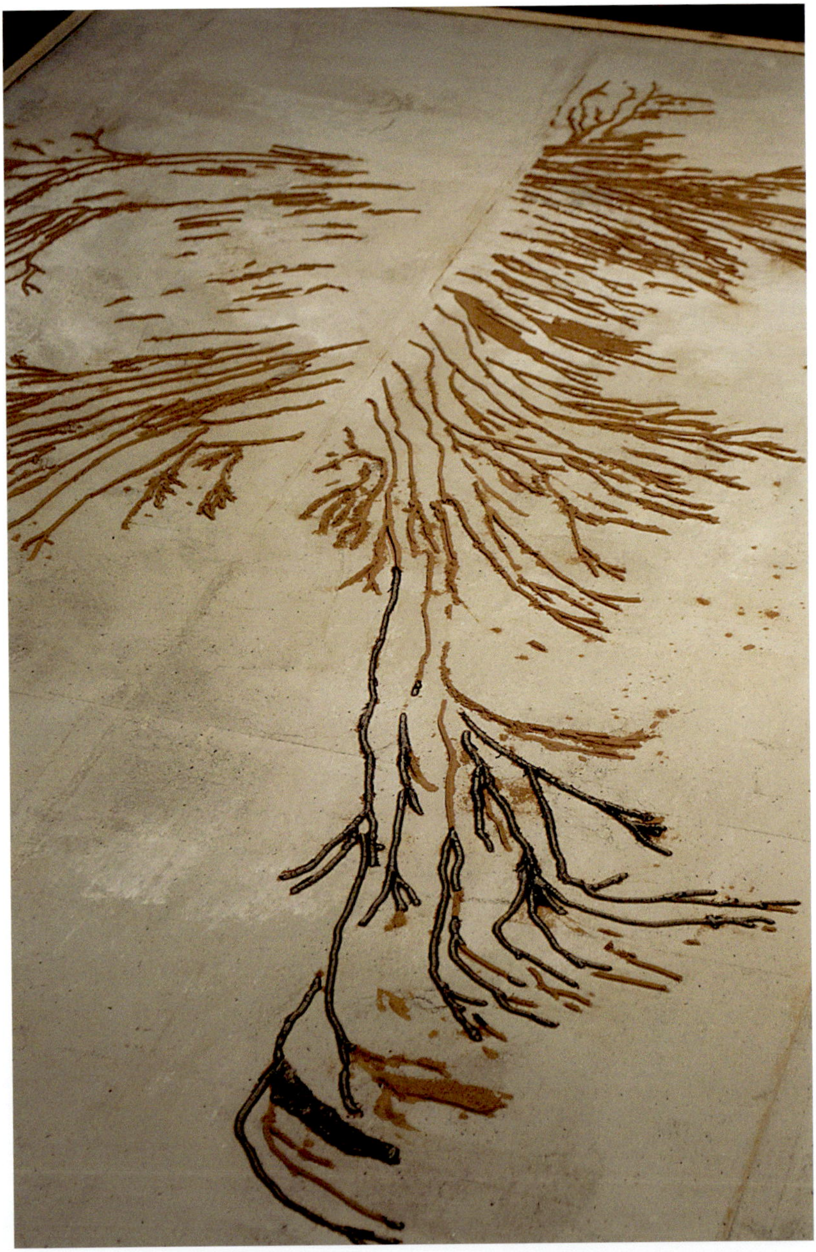

PLATE 22. TJ Shin, *Untitled (100 days of solemnity)*, 2022. Transfected mugwort, cinchona, makko, oak, wild cherry, sandalwood, ash, diatomaceous earth, wood. Courtesy of the artist.

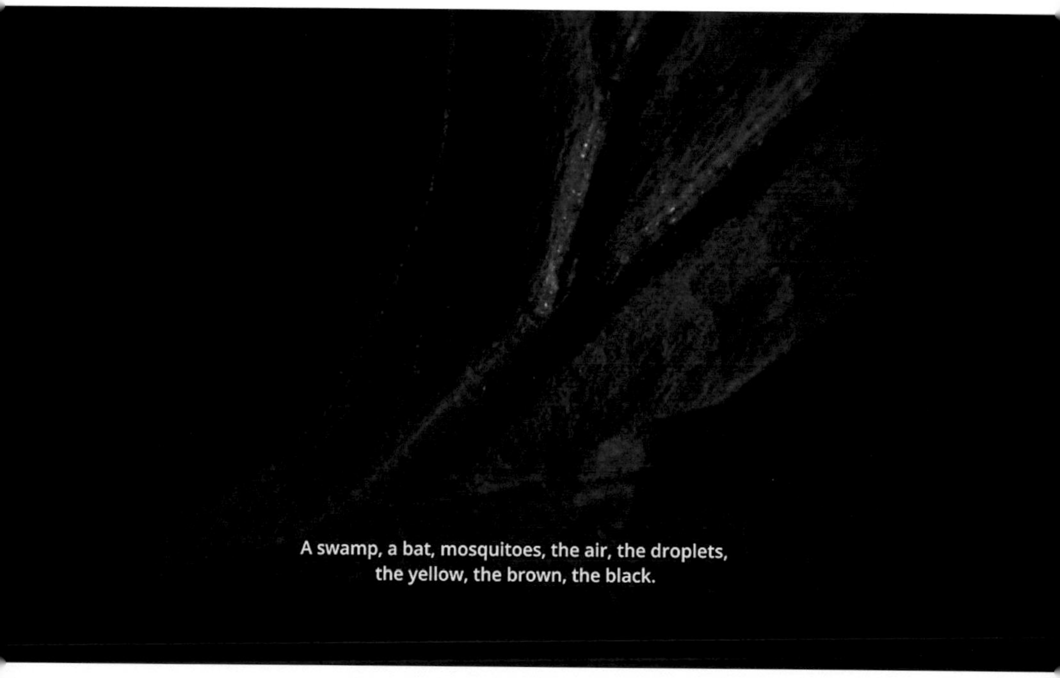

PLATE 23. Still from TJ Shin, *Anthropology of a Phytomorphist*, 2021–2022. Video, 14 minutes. Courtesy of the artist.

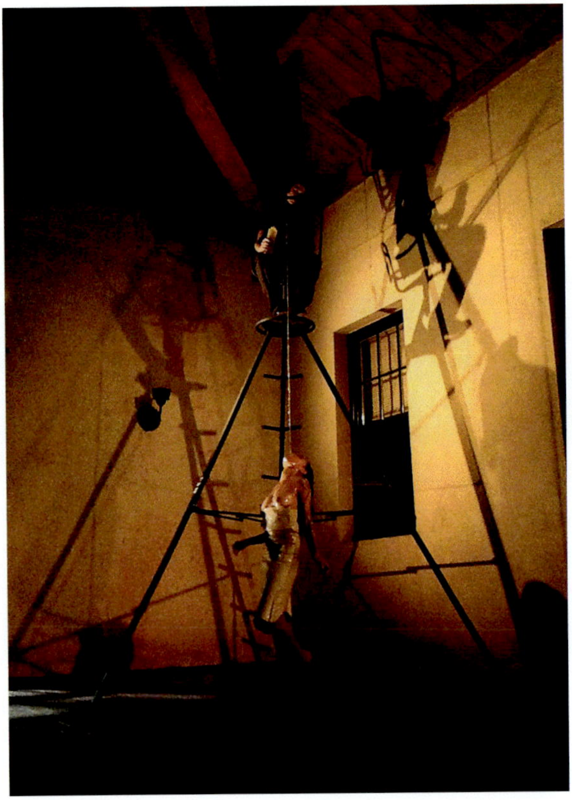

PLATE 24. Julie Tolentino, *HONEY*, June 28, 2013. Part of the Performance Studies International Conference at Stanford University. Performers: J Tolentino and Stosh Fila. Photograph taken by author.

4. INJURED ENOUGH

DEPENDING ON THE WOUNDS OF ANALOGY

> The space occupied by analogies is really a space of radiation. Man is surrounded by it on every side; but, inversely, he transmits these resemblances back into the world from which he receives them. He is the great fulcrum of proportions—the centre upon which relations are concentrated and from which they are once again reflected.—Michel Foucault, *The Order of Things* (1966)

Artist TJ Shin's installation *Untitled (torture)* (2019) features a rounded glass vessel filled with milk, like a swollen breast. It is wrapped and suspended by a silver metal chain attached to a wood structure reminiscent of gallows. The wood is unvarnished, weighed down by a cement block resting on its base. From the bottom tip of the vessel, milk drips. The breast lactates, or, given how the chain wraps around the vessel, digging into its sides, perhaps its milk is squeezed out by force. The milk falls onto four broken pieces of porcelain plates, laid out on a sheet of chainmail draped over a glass vat that catches what sifts through porcelain and chain. There is no identifiable body here, yet the work's parenthetical "(*torture*)" and its milk urges us to look for its substitute, to endow the suggestive shape of the glass vessel with meaning and weight. We string together a series of associations drawn from the installation's materials and objects: gallows with body, body with vessel, vessel with breast, breast with milk. What is being tortured? Or, rather, who?

In 2020, artist Jes Fan began making his series of *Diagram* sculptures. He asked his friends, lovers, ex-lovers, and collaborators if he could create molds of their anatomical features, like their pectorals, biceps, nape, or clavicle. He cast these molds in aqua resin, which he proceeded to duplicate, cut, and stack, flipping them on their side or turning them over, sanding them down by hand. Fan placed glass works shaped into organic, bulbous forms on top of these manipulated, deformed casts. He did not secure the glass with adhesive, and instead relied on the contours of the casts to hold the glass in place, without slipping or breaking. Knowing where to place the glass required feeling out what his loved ones could carry and support, once a piece of them had been removed from their context and made into abstract parts. *Diagram XI* (2020) consists of two casts of his ex-lover's breasts, which he sliced in half, creating four pieces stacked on top of one another, like shelves. On the second lowest shelf, a glass work shaped like a kidney sits to the left, interrupting the undulating parallel lines of lacerated breast. The *Diagram* series relies on the care and discernment needed to place a fragile object, to make a mold of someone's body part for one's own ends. At the same time, the excision of an anatomical feature, alienated from the body from which it originates, entails the body's destruction and defamiliarization, as a violence borne of love.

Shin alludes to the torture of a body that never appears. Fan molds, casts, and manipulates his loved ones' body parts with brutal affection. In their work, the racialized, gendered body, produced by way of injury, becomes perceptible through abstract objects as opposed to recognizable, discrete figures. Their work is *of* the body—making use of its matter and form—but it is also *like* the body, made analogous to it. This likeness is my focus here. Through Shin's and Fan's work, I look to the hostile forms of relation and recognition that the Asiatic body creates in the injurious process of being made comparable to objects, as well as to the bodies of others different from itself. Shin and Fan do not physically harm their own bodies or the bodies of other people. However, they do damage to the Asiatic body as well as to the things they conceive of and construct as analogous to it. They attend to analogy, as an artistic and political practice Asian Americans have come to lean on, particularly in a moment when Asian Americans'—and especially East Asian Americans'—legibility as a minoritized group seem less clear and defined, and more like an open question. That is, following a question posed by Kandice Chuh—"Asians are the new . . . what?"—we should take seriously how an attempt to answer, to figure out what newer version of something else Asians are, requires the use of analogy, and that this is something not to deny and disavow but to approach as integral to the production of Asian as a racial category in the United States.[1]

This book has been interested in the ways that artists have overstepped the bounds and limits of the self and other, whether by staying in, speaking as another, or going cold. This final chapter continues in this vein, with a consideration of how Asian American uses of analogy do the same, by spoiling the categorical integrity we attribute to and hope for Asianness, and also the categorical integrity of whatever else comes into contact with it. In this chapter, analogy spoils and is spoiled in its need and reliance on another. Shin and Fan experiment with the semblance and suggestion of the Asiatic body as that which depends on the wounds of analogy: on the wounds inflicted in the act of being made comparable to something else that has (already) been destroyed. Analogy, and the forms it produces by way of comparison, makes the wounds of racial injury legible and thus worthy of sympathy and repair, at the same time that it inflicts wounds through extraction, appropriation, contamination, and generalization.

Shin and Fan make forms that bear the spoiled trace of a smudge, drip, cut, puncture, or stain made analogous to the wounds of racial injury. Both artists touch on processes of objectification that have shaped perceptions of the Asiatic body and histories of Asian racialization. However, they do not aim to recuperate the Asian American subject as a healed whole, in the regard of another. Through analogy, and the damage it makes in moving through and across forms of difference made comparable to each other, Shin and Fan show that to be held in the regard of another, to be recognized by another, can be a source of wounding, both for one's self and for another.

In the contemporary moment, what injury looks like for Asian Americans as a marginalized, minority group presents a problem. There is anxiety, frustration, and anger around the fact that Asian American experiences of discrimination, inequality, and violence are not taken seriously, or rather, they are not taken as seriously as the experiences of other marginalized, minority groups. Forms of anti-Asian racism must be compared to other forms of racism—a point to which I will return. Asian American injury, then, and the recognition and legitimacy of it, is mediated by analogy, which positions Asian Americans as either those forgotten within the Black-white binarism of US racial logics, or uniquely suited to intervene and move beyond the rigidity of such logics. The uses of analogy have been critiqued and approached with suspicion for the ways analogy can assume and privilege a relation of similarity between groups of people that runs the risk of flattening myriad forms of difference.

Given these critiques, in Asian Americanist scholarship, there can be a hesitation, if not defensive unwillingness, to claim the role analogy plays in making Asian Americans recognizable as a marginalized, minority group. There tends to be a preference for language that emphasizes kinship, affinity, and solidarity over that of analogy, as if analogy should be contained and cordoned off from the rest. Shin and Fan offer a way to think about Asian Americans' need for analogy and what kinds of destruction and contamination can occur as a part of analogy's logic. Rather than assuaging or disproving the suspicions surrounding analogy and its centrality to understandings of Asian racialization, Shin and Fan mine these suspicions by making use of the hostilities it is charged with inciting. They tap into the impulse to make objects analogous to the Asiatic body with work that straddles the particular and general, the concrete and abstract, by way of the cut, alteration, disfigurement, and defamiliarization—through the wounds that analogy represents, but also inflicts.

Shin and Fan take up an abstractionist aesthetics, which, as Phillip Brian Harper writes, works against a realist aesthetics that represents the harms inflicted on racialized subjects in the real world in positive, affirmative terms via "figural verisimilitude" and the moral claims it enables.[2] An abstractionist aesthetics, in contrast, breaks from the real afforded by the figural. It obstructs moral claims that inspire the "inertial passivity" of empathy by defamiliarizing the figure of the body and its materials, alienating them from their context and assumed form.[3] Shin's and Fan's modes of abstraction enact the violence of negating and undoing "figural verisimilitude," by severing the part from the whole, the body from its figure. For them, representing racial injury provides the opportunity to spoil the notion that repair and restoration should be the ideal outcome and objective of recognition for minoritized subjects. If recognition is contingent on injuries made legible through analogy, Shin and Fan stick with the damage of analogy as opposed to fixing it, approaching such damage not as that which asserts the necessity of sympathy and healing to arrive at autonomous political subjecthood, but as that which asserts the necessity of our dependence on others, in analogous relation to them.

Analogy's Risk

What does racial injury look, feel, and sound like for the Asian American subject? For Frank Chin and Jeffery Paul Chan, it feels like "racist love," "the cloying overwhelming love of a protective, coddling mother" that renders the Asian American (and specifically for them, the Chinese American) "womanly, effeminate,"[4] "an emotionally stunted, dependent child."[5] The infantile, feminine, and queer become evidence of racial injury, sabotaging the possibility of an oppositional (heteromasculinist) Asian American cultural nationalism.[6] Anne Anlin Cheng writes that racial injury is beautiful and aesthetically pleasing when it manifests as the racialized femininity that the figure of the "yellow woman" evokes. This yellow woman is "simultaneously consecrated and desecrated as an inherently aesthetic object."[7] Given this, she asks, "Is the yellow woman injured—or is she injured enough?"[8] If such injury is encountered through the aesthetics of the ornamental, the answer might be no: this kind of injury will never be "enough" because we are not able to recognize the devastation of such injury. We are, instead, too distracted by its beauty, with "the collusion between abstraction and racial embodiment."[9]

The injurious processes of Asian racialization become enlivened through things, ranging from everyday household items to art. While racial injury, for Cheng, is beautiful, for Leslie Bow, it is cute. Attraction is the form anti-Asian racism takes, manifest in the powerlessness of anthropomorphized animals and objects like toys, dolls, or cartoon animals that call out to be held, cared for, and dominated by another.[10] Racialized objects of affection undergird contemporary understandings of Asiatic difference, acting as analogs for Asian American subjects that show "the simultaneous saturation and displacement of racial meaning, its ability to be abstracted from human embodiment."[11] Expanding on Chin and Chan's articulations of "racist love," Bow argues that the presumably positive feelings surrounding Asian Americans perpetuate anti-Asian racism, and that these feelings are projected not onto Asians and Asian Americans, but onto their "nonhuman proxies."[12] Processes of Asian racialization produce fantasies that animate objects by way of their abstraction, enacted through "metonymic signs, the part for the whole."[13] Cheng and Bow see aesthetically pleasing objects, and our positive or ambivalent affective response to them, as the evidence and effect of anti-Asian racism and violence.

A study of the violence of Asian racialization as the reduction of persons to objects is indebted to scholars working on the history and afterlives of slavery, as well as Black aesthetics and performance. For Zakiyyah Iman

Jackson, "thingification," alongside "bestialization," is "the process of imagining black people as an empty vessel, a nonbeing, a nothing, an ontological zero, coupled with the violent impositions of colonial myths and racial hierarchy."[14] Black people, the black(ened), are not excluded from the category of the human subject, but violently appropriated by it. Uri McMillan takes into account the history of the objectification of blackness as the "primal site of injury" to consider the ways that Black feminist artists have performed objecthood as an aesthetic strategy, thereby making use of racialization's wounds.[15] As Fred Moten writes, "the history of blackness is testament to the fact that objects can and do resist."[16] In line with these scholars, Asian Americanists have critiqued the beautiful and the cute as aesthetic categories simultaneously constituting and obstructing racial injury, but they have also wondered if the possibility of resistance lies therein.

Not wholly unlike Chin and Chan, who strove for an Asian American cultural nationalism inspired by Black cultural nationalism, Cheng's work on ornamental Asiatic femininity and Bow's articulations of the feel-good objectification of "racist love" are placed in analogous relation to the terror, pain, and violence of the objectification of Black women and their bodies, reduced to flesh. In the opening of *Ornamentalism*, Cheng positions her theory of the "yellow woman" as an alternative to theories of Black women's flesh by Hortense Spillers and of epidermalization by Frantz Fanon.[17] For Cheng, both have "hardened" over time and crowded out another conceptualization of racial embodiment and modern personhood made graspable through the injuries of the "yellow woman."[18] "*Like* the proverbial Ming vase, [the yellow woman] is at once ethereal and base, an object of value and a hackneyed trope," Cheng writes, and "*like* the black woman, she has suffered a long history of painful denigration" (emphasis added).[19] Note here how the likeness of the yellow woman shuttles between the vase and the Black woman, emerging as a figure within and through them. In a similar turn, Bow compares segregation-era racist kitsch embodying Black people with anthropomorphic, cute Asianized objects bought and sold in the United States at the turn of the twenty-first century. She points out that while a mammy cookie jar instigates negative feelings, a citrus squeezer made to look like a smiling "Mandarin," or a Pixar animation of a talking car made to look like a geisha, elude the same kinds of legibility as racist kitsch because they provoke fuzzier, warm feelings.[20] The former is met with disgust; the latter is met with affection.

Within the conceptual frameworks of *Ornamentalism* and *Racist Love*, blackness and the violence of its objectification, enfleshment, and epidermalization are more legible and recognizable as such, compared to the "racist love" of the deceptively affirming, beautiful ornamentality of Asianness. These comparisons, particularly in the context of Asian American studies, speak to the primacy of analogy in discerning Asian Americanness and the racial injuries it bears. As Colleen Lye writes, "The Asian American, which is surely the premier example of a racial concept of the Asian, has always been a comparative identity" set up to intervene or "move beyond race as a matter of black and white."[21] The most prominent example of this can be found in Claire Jean Kim's 1999 essay, "The Racial Triangulation of Asian Americans," which argues that Asian Americans are in a triangulated relationship to white and Black people within a "field of racial positions."[22] Kim provided Asian Americanists a framework for mapping Asian American racialization via "civic ostracism" in relation to and distinction from Black racialization via "relative devalorization," both of which uphold the dominance and privilege of whiteness.

However, as Lye writes, through this comparative framework, "the Asian American is more easily evoked as a third term to trouble binary habits of racial classification and analysis than to illustrate the genuine multiplicity of racial logics and racisms."[23] Asian Americans are not white and not Black, but some other third category within preexisting racial logics organized around white supremacist ideology and antiblackness. For Lye, this approach essentializes anti-Black racism, so that in the need to have Asian American experiences of discrimination, inequality, and violence taken seriously, it is either implicitly or explicitly understood that such experiences must be taken as seriously as the experiences of, specifically, Black people. Asian Americans have to contend with "the frustrations of the analogical status of Asiatic racial form" or what Lye also refers to as an "Asian American analogical dependency," made evident in the comparisons drawn between Asian and Black subjects (made into objects), as well as between anti-Asian and anti-Black racism and violence, spanning from the earlier work of Chin, Chan, and Kim, to more recent work by Cheng and Bow.[24]

Within the school of thought named Afropessimism, Frank B. Wilderson argues that this dependency speaks to "the ruse of analogy," wherein blackness is violently brought into an anti-Black world founded on blackness's ontological impossibility.[25] Analogy leads to the "mystification" and "erasure" of "Blackness's grammar of suffering."[26] While Lye takes issue with Asian American analogical dependency because of how, on the level of the historical, it enforces "the foundational status of antiblackness in conceptualizations of racism,"[27] Wilderson, at the level of the ontological, critiques this dependency because of how blackness, in analogous relation to, for instance, Asian Americans (or "Whites and colored immigrants, respectively"),[28] is made to carry symbolic value and meaning, not only for Black people but also for non-Black people.

For Wilderson, antiblackness is precisely the foundational violence that Lye wants to put into question, yet despite their differences, both view analogy as a problem. What I offer here is not an Afropessimist critique nor an engagement with the ontological. However, I keep in mind these critiques of analogy, as that which risks abstracting the suffering and injury of some by making it comparable to the different kinds of suffering and injury of others. Given the analogical dependency of Asian Americanness, these critiques affect how we give accounts of Asian racialization, which, as Lye writes, remains "the unfinished business of the twentieth century."[29]

This unfinished business shows itself in Cheng's *Ornamentalism*, which is bookended with theorizations of the injuries of the yellow ornament in analogous relation to the injuries of Black flesh. In the book's introduction, there is a passage that, as Cheng describes it, "echo[es] and depart[s]"[30] from the well-known opening of Hortense Spillers's 1987 essay, "Mama's Baby, Papa's Maybe: An American Grammar Book," before making comparisons between "two iconic nineteenth-century images" of Sarah "Saartjie" Baartman, called the Hottentot Venus, and Afong Moy, known as the Chinese Lady.[31] Cheng then ends the book with a coda that returns to this comparison of the yellow ornament with Black women's flesh through a reading of the "horrifying scars and wounds [that] abound" in Toni Morrison's *Beloved*.[32] This comparison emerges at the site of the chokecherry tree on Sethe's back, as the literal and allegorical reminder of the violence and brutality Sethe experienced as an enslaved woman. Cheng argues that through Sethe's claiming of the chokecherry-as-ornament, she arrives at her own personhood. "It is precisely when flesh has been defiled and radically severed from its own sense of humanity that the path back requires mediation," Cheng writes, "the flesh that passes through objecthood needs 'ornament' as a way back to itself."[33]

Cheng initially states that ornamentalism, as the theory of the yellow woman, is not meant to preserve the figure of a real Asian woman. However, it seems that by the book's end, this theory does have a restorative function insofar as the ornamental, as the means of mediation, promises a way back to the realness of such a figure. Ornamental personhood is a hybrid of the organic and synthetic, but as Cheng's argument unfolds, the ornament becomes less hybrid and more analogical, sliding between being and being *like* other things, all of which become comparable to one another in the process: the yellow woman is like a vase, a body, a doll, a dress. In its analogical capacity, the ornament repairs the cut between flesh and humanity, mending the tear between object and body, thereby leading a person back to herself, to her agency and subjecthood. The Asian woman appears through the yellow woman and her analogs, all of which carry and make legible the extent of her injuries. Through the ornament, the Asian woman might become injured enough after all.

The ornament promises to repair Asian women and Black women too, turning both, as objects of violence, into healed subjects. By extending her readings to include Morrison's novel, Cheng aims to elevate the status of the ornament from analogy to theory. This is what we want out of analogy most of the time: we bring two different objects together in hopes of producing a theory of and as some other intervening, third thing. Considering arguments made about Asian Americanness that position it as that which can "move beyond race as a matter of black and white," Asiatic racial form becomes that other third thing.[34] This does not make Asiatic racial form exceptional, transcending the Black-white racial binarism; this makes it dependent, implicated, and involved. If Asian Americanness needs analogy, it is because through analogy, Asian Americanness can become that recognizable third mediating thing, like the ornament that enables the path back to personhood. Even the comparisons Cheng makes between Asian women and Black women produce the yellow ornament—or the yellow woman—as a figure distinct from both subject positions, and yet, as she argues, the yellow woman, as analogical object, is integral to Asian and Black women's formation and repair in the wake of racial violence.

Rather than try to make Asiatic racial form the grounds of an independent theory—a third thing that can stand on its own, beyond Black and white, beyond analogy—I stay with Asiatic racial form's analogical status constituted by dependency, as well as by the frustration and anxiety such dependency entails. In this respect, I am in keeping with Yogita Goyal's work on the logic of analogy. For her, modern slave narratives are analogs which, in moving across time and space, reinvent form and create the possibility of an "ethical globalism," by making human rights abuses in the global present recognizable via the afterlives of slavery.[35] What interests me here are the ways that analogy might afford sites of ethical relation by way of the recognition of injury, which in turn can also necessitate the reinvention of form. "To make analogy work, we need a clear sense of both correspondence and difference," Goyal writes.[36] To my mind, this correspondence and difference lies in analogy's hope for equivalence that always fails. Therefore, while I do lay out the discomforts, awkwardness, and encroachments of Asian American analogical dependency, I am not saying analogy's uses and logics are only a "ruse." At the same time, analogy cannot only be thought of as that which creates healing, inoffensive, affirming forms of relation and solidarity. Put differently, if and when analogy does make forms of relation possible, it might not always feel good or welcome. I take seriously how analogy is used as a bid for recognition. The use of analogy makes legible one's own injury, and invites the possibility that in making that bid, in desiring to be recognized by another by becoming comparable to another in the want to forge a connection, one risks doing some damage to one's self and others.

Shin and Fan do not make work that intends to refine and smooth out the tense, fraught analogous relations made between body and person, object and subject, part and whole. They call attention to such troublesome relations by way of the other third thing. They bring to the fore how discussions of anti-Asian racism and violence—and what it looks, feels, and sounds like—presents a problem for modes of aesthetic interpretation and judgment, but also for how we give an account of shifting processes of Asian racialization in the United States. I do not overlook how relating through shared experiences of marginalization and common, overlapping struggles were and still are instrumental to a decolonial politics rooted in Afro-Asian solidarities, and what had been envisioned as Third World studies.[37] However, as Gary Okihiro reminds us, Third World studies, and its grounding in anticolonialism and anticapitalism, had been passed over in the late 1960s for the liberalism of ethnic studies and its focus on the United States.[38] Given this liberal turn that has come to shape the present, we cannot operate under the assumption that analogy works only in service to these kinds of solidarities, even if we hold out for the hope that they have yet to be realized.

We should remain critical of analogies made for the sake of lending legibility to Asian racial injury that presume such moves are always frictionless when in service to the right politics, for the right reasons. Yet, as I have been saying, this does not mean analogy is something to avoid. It means we should acknowledge that analogy, and its attempts to forge relations through and in the differences between objects, people, and ideas, can be destructive. In the analogous relationship between objects and Asiatic bodies, Shin and Fan show us what that destruction makes possible. Following Shin's and Fan's lead, I depend on analogy in my readings, seeking out the hostile assertions that come up in relying on comparisons for my own argument, too.

Do Not Trust the Figure

In Shin's *Untitled (torture)*, instead of body parts, there are pieces of broken porcelain plates. These pieces of plates play on associations made by artists and scholars, including Candice Lin and Anne Cheng, between porcelain's durable yet porous surfaces and racialized skin.[39] Shin's use of broken porcelain plates locate the matter of Asiatic feminized skin in the context of the history of the porcelain trade between Europe and Asia from the fourteenth century to the eighteenth century.[40] Once called "white gold," porcelain recalls a refined Victorian sensibility informed by Western imperial relations with Asia, bringing attention to how such sensibilities are contingent on the enfleshment of racialized, Orientalist commodities in place of the bodies they suggest.[41] In *Untitled (torture)*, the pieces of plate are analogous to a body broken. After all, as Anna Storti notes, porcelain is a mixture of the "flesh" of petunse and the "bones" of kaolin clay.[42] Thus, the broken plate pieces are endowed with a "corporeal life" of flesh and bone.[43]

The work brings together the history of the porcelain trade with the history of the stigmatization and pathologization of the Asiatic body, and specifically, the Chinese body. This body is unsanitary and unhealthy as a carrier of disease, but it also has what Eric Hayot describes as a "biologically impossible body" indifferent to pain.[44] In eighteenth-century Europe, the circulation of images of smallpox in China furthered the belief that the disease originated in China,[45] and in the nineteenth century, Chinatowns in the United States were seen as sites of contagion, blamed for the source of smallpox, syphilis, and the bubonic plague, leading to the implementation of public health policies and staunch sanitary regulations.[46] In the twenty-first century, with the COVID-19 pandemic, anti-Chinese sentiment grew as conspiracy theories spread that the disease originated from China, either as the result of a lab leak or from the wet market.[47] These perceptions have implicated not just those who are Chinese, but also those who are assumed to be, which is also to say, those who look like they might be. This is not a stretch, given how often non-Asian people think all Asian people look alike. (I can confirm this, particularly in a time when wearing face masks in the United States has become more common: when I wear a mask, I become unrecognizable to people I know or recognizable to people I do not.) Shin, who is Korean Canadian, and Fan, who is Chinese Canadian, play on the contaminated, infectious associations afforded in looking alike, looking akin, and looking like kin, between Chinese and Asian, subject and object, people and things, tortured body and broken plate. For Shin, as well as for Fan, to be akin and a kin to so many other subjects and objects makes the Asiatic body a site from which to consider how susceptibility to contamination and infection, as a vector and carrier of disease, shifts what is at stake in recognizing racial injury as the grounds of recognizing another.

In *Untitled (torture)*, the broken pieces of plate on top of the chainmail are mismatched. The detail in their designs do not align; they cannot be put back together to make one plate because they never made a whole plate in the first place. But the milk that drips tries to make it so. Casein proteins, commonly found in mammalian milk, are created when enough lactic acid bacteria is produced from the fermentation of lactose caused by bacteria. Lactic acid bacteria is a probiotic microorganism, which, when consumed in fermented foods, can fortify one's gastric lining. It is also an antioxidant and chemical exfoliant with healing properties, so that when applied appropriately to the skin, it can increase cell turnover, eliminate the accumulation of dead skin cells, smooth the skin's surface, and even out the skin's hyperpigmentation.[48] The milk that drips over time might hope to mend the flesh and bone of broken porcelain plates to create a smooth surface, free of blemishes, scars, or cracks. Eking from a glass breast, the milk promises to nurse these broken pieces back to wholeness. However, the pieces of plate remain, and in the failure to repair, the milk might congeal, turn sour, and curdle, while the vat underneath becomes a vestibule for other kinds of bacteria to grow. The hard chain presses up against soft liquids, delicate ceramic, and fragile glass. At the same time, the metal's indestructibility, as material used for constraint and protection, is undermined by the milk that is able to seep through it. The milk, while expected to bond the separate pieces of plate together, also exposes the chainmail's porousness as a weakness. The suggestion of the body—a tortured figure—leaks into the installation by way of milk, slipping past what would otherwise attempt to capture it, falling through the cracks of the porcelain's flesh and bone.

The suspicions and fears surrounding the leaky Asiatic body and what it is perceived to carry and transmit can be analogous to the same suspicions and fears that surround the boundaries of the category "Asian American" and its dependence on others. In Asian Americanist critique and Asian American cultural production, Rachel Lee notices a preoccupation with the "cutting, tearing, disassembling of the human body" into its parts.[49] While Asian Americanist critique in the late twentieth century set out to "expose an injustice or breach of ethics, thereby seeming to correct the injurious act" of racial violence, in the twenty-first century, "it relishes the affects circulating—the ballistic force—from these tactile cuts, tears from context, and plastic transformations."[50] This is not for the purposes of utter annihilation, but to make, Lee writes, "*ethical, political, and moral claims vis-à-vis these body parts . . . that putatively returns the extracted body part to the violated racialized whole—a move that naturalizes a prior state of organic intactness and individuality to that racialized body.*"[51] The hostile, destructive acts that shape an aesthetic and critical reading practice end up constructing—via narratives of loss and restoration—a body as coherent as the category of "Asian American" to which it might be assigned and which a subject might claim. The relishing of the fragment of the Asiatic body, as Lee sees it, collides with fraught perceptions of the fragmentation of Asian Americanness as a site of incongruity and possibility.

For Lee, this necessitates and enables a consideration of the biological body "in informational, molecular, and posthuman terms."[52] Shin and Fan experiment within these terms, disassembling the body without making such ethical, political, and moral claims on the parts they excise and create. Their work breaks apart distinctions between part and whole that might fit too neatly into narratives of healing and wholeness. Whereas a body part is understood to belong to the body as a whole, the analogical object depends on its relation to other people, bodies, and things, or otherwise it is incomplete, unfinished. Shin and Fan take up the body via its biological parts and matter as a means of "relishing the fragment."[53] I understand such destructive relishing within a psychoanalytic framework as what Juliana Chang calls "traumatic enjoyment": "a violent yet blissful shattering of the self," akin to jouissance.[54] Traumatic enjoyment names the ways we take pleasure in the inhuman, which for Chang means the nonhuman as well as the sadistic and cruel—what causes suffering and is morally wrong or reprehensible. We might enjoy the inhuman (examples Chang gives are the figures of "the villain, the outlaw") because we are masochists seeking out punishment, and we might also identify with the inhuman, which is traumatizing in itself because it causes us to "call into question our own status as ethical and rational beings, as human."[55] Rather than reject the dehumanization of the racialized subject as the inhumane, and rather than disavow our traumatic enjoyment, Chang argues that we inhabit the conditions of both. Shin and Fan take part in this traumatic enjoyment that spoils the self.

In an interview, Fan states, "I don't trust the figure."[56] This distrust fuels Fan's practice of working with glass, silicon, plastic, resin, and wax, alongside depo-testosterone, progesterone, estradiol, estrogen, melanin, urine, and semen to make abstract sculptures and installations.[57] He removes biological materials from their assumed contexts, taking form apart from function. In his practice, biological matter is made hostile toward normative categorizations of race, sex, and gender that attach themselves to the biological body in order to maintain their efficacy and meaning. Such matter, as the site of a category's spoilage as opposed to its coherence, is used to contaminate and confuse the formal integrity of what Fan creates. As seen in his *Diagram* series, his sculptures and installations frequently carry glass works in bloated, distended shapes, which he injects with biological substances, and which sag and droop as if in gluttony or defeat. He builds lattice-like structures resembling dizzying organizational systems, networks, scaffolding, and shelves made of wood or pipes and covered in resin.

In addition to castings of aqua resin that suggest the body, he fabricates an array of recognizable, everyday objects made strange. *Disposed to Add* (2019) includes barbells of soft, limp silicon in different skin tones of beige, tan, and brown, which can be laid out or hung on a wall in various positions given their flexibility. *Testo Candle* (2016) displays a candle made of beeswax and depo-testosterone, and *Testo-soap* (2017) features a bar of soap made from lye and depo-testosterone. Both the candle and soap are placed on fleshy pink silicone bases next to empty glass medical bottles used to store and preserve the hormones which, in these works, have found a new form, other than a human body, to seep into. Fan's work draws unlikely comparisons between objects and materials that might seem antagonistic to one another, like oil and water, like metal and silicone, like wax, lye, and hormones. Things and materials are not mixed correctly, connections are asserted between a barbell that is like a body's limb, or hormones that are applied to the body like a bar of soap.

With a sense of play, Fan cultivates what he describes as both the "banal" and "absurd."[58] He finds all the ways to use biological matter that are decidedly not right, which is also to say, not in service to maintaining and defining categories of racial, gender, and sex difference. He knows that the substances he uses are politically contested, fraught with irresolvable meanings and ends that are obscured by the notion that such substances belong to some bodies and not others. Fan asks what happens to biological matter, bodies, and categories of difference when their associations with one another start to spoil, converge, and collide. For Fan, it is not that these materials and categories lose their meaning once removed from their more familiar normative contexts. Fan relies on the fact that what he works with will still carry the residue of their meanings—their difference—like the stubborn blemish or splotch of blood and melanin shifting shadily in glass. Despite the damage he exacts and what he infects, Fan knows the mark of difference remains. He does not claim to radically abolish race or gender. His work hinges on the realization that to some extent, and with much ambivalence, we rely on the materials he uses to be recognizable to others in the ways we want to be recognized, indeed in the most "banal" and "absurd" yet vital ways.

Briefly, I return to a figure, or two of them drawn and repelled by the other, as each other's analogous objects. In introducing her concept of traumatic enjoyment, Chang describes the "sadistic satisfaction" she felt when reading a well-known scene from Maxine Hong Kingston's *The Woman Warrior*.[59] The narrator, as a young girl, explains how she and other Chinese American girls in her school "invented an American-feminine speaking personality" in order to better assimilate—that is, except for one "quiet girl."[60] One day after school, the quiet girl follows the narrator into the school bathroom, where the narrator starts to bully her. The narrator yells at the quiet girl to speak;

she pinches the quiet girl's cheeks so hard that she starts to cry. Then, the narrator pulls and yanks the quiet girl's "China doll hair cut," which she so hates.[61] Chang addresses how scholars' analyses of this moment argue that "the narrator's torture of the girl conforms to the logic of self-punishment and self-discipline," and extends this reading by confronting the enjoyment drawn from the scene.[62] While Chang lays out the ways the reader's identification shifts from the narrator to her victim, I wonder if we might hold in tension this move from one to the other, from two figures made to be each other's uncanny, shameful double, as a kind of taut, suspended identification with another, between another, as alike and analogous.

I see this scene in *The Woman Warrior* restaged in one of Fan's earlier works, *Stranded Between One Act and Another* (2016). Two hairbrushes made of polished black resin are attached to one another by a swath of long, black, straight hair grafted on to the heads of each brush. Since the hair is attached to both brush's heads, it is impossible to know where the strands of hair grow and where they become split, dead ends. Like two young girls who see themselves in the other, one of whom pinches the other's flesh and pulls at her hair in not knowing where her self begins and ends, so, too, do these hairbrushes find themselves tied to each other, pulled at each other's roots, caught in "sadistic satisfaction." The head of a hairbrush becomes a head of hair, and when looking at it, one cannot help but think of the overly familiar image of the Asian head of hair that frequently dons the covers of books written by Asian authors, as a particular genre of book cover, which writer Tony Tulathimutte designates "Hair Without a Face."[63] On these book covers, black hair is slick and shiny like oil or water, or blurred like the stroke of a calligraphy brush.[64] The seam of a hairline runs down the length of a scalp. Hair might hang in a braid, cascade down the side of a blank space where a face should be, or it might blow in some meaningful yet nonspecified direction surrounded by mysterious, alluring debris like leaves or the demure petals of a cherry blossom. The Asian head draws a reader to the book, who mines the Asian head for what it knows. The Asian head becomes an abstract racial form and feature, in place of a racial figure.

Another way of looking at *Stranded* is to realize that the hair, no longer attached to a body, has become its detritus. It is not the beautiful wisps of hair that appear on a book cover, but more like the clumps of hair left accumulating on top of the drain after taking a shower. It is dead matter that disgusts, a reminder of what the body sheds. *Stranded* plucks strands of hair from a stranded body to which it once belonged, and for which it now perhaps longs. The work stays tangled in abstraction's rupture of meaning and interpretation, dredging up comparisons between an artwork, a hairbrush, hair, a head, a book's cover, and a book's content. That space of severance and separation between form and figure is unbreachable, gesturing toward that other third thing analogy is expected to produce, which cannot be disentangled from its comparable objects.

"WHO HURT YOU?"

At the time I am writing this, there is a billboard in Hollywood at the intersection of Santa Monica Boulevard and Highland Avenue that asks, "WHO HURT YOU?" The billboard directs me, and anyone else looking, to a website for accident attorneys ready to seek damages on your behalf. When I see the billboard, I am amused by its dramatic all-capital-letter shouting address that masquerades, not without humor, as an expression of care. To be asked, "WHO HURT YOU?" whether by accident attorneys or by anyone else, is a confrontational, funny, aggressive form of recognition. The question hails someone via their injury, making the injury and the suffering it caused worthy of someone else's time (for these accident attorneys, financially so). While surely the billboard was made in the hopes of going viral on the internet, it also, in the end, hails those who recognize themselves in the question, and therefore in their injury, however much it might cost.

The privileging of injury as the grounds of recognition necessitates distinguishing the kind of woundedness Shin and Fan inflict in and on their work from the woundedness of ressentiment, or what Wendy Brown calls the "wounded attachments" of contemporary identity politics.[65] Wounded attachments confine minoritized subjects, and the identities they mobilize and claim, to a desire for recognition yoked to historical and ongoing pain. This iteration of identity politics, Brown states, "can hold out no future—for itself and others—that triumphs over this pain."[66] For Brown, the minoritized subject is stuck in the impasse of their own unending, ever-repeating suffering. Wounded attachments are symptoms of the liberal individual subject that obstruct shared action toward a transformative, democratic politics and more just future. A minoritized subject with wounded attachments, then, is spoiled, stuck gazing at their own navel, never looking up to become a part of a collective, common whole.

But an attachment to woundedness does not always foreclose relation and the social. José Esteban Muñoz argues that Brown's theory of wounded attachments assumes the closed-off "stalled singularity" of a subject incapable of affecting and being affected by a broader social world.[67] He takes issue with how Brown views the minoritized subject's relation to their own woundedness as pathological in its repetition, rather than a critical practice—a repetition with a difference—that reaches past the present and outward from the self. Woundedness is not solely wielded for the consolidation and repair of an identity built on the recognition of a suffering subject's moral superiority. For "recognition, across antagonisms within the social such as sex, race, and still other modalities of difference, is often more than simply a tacit admission of vulnerability. . . . Indeed, it is often a moment of being wounded."[68] The recognition of suffering and of woundedness for the minoritized subject is not always healing. It can be damaging, but in a way that lets the subject know they are among others, from within a social world, not removed from it. Muñoz is primarily thinking about how feelings produced by and circulating around the particularity of woundedness for the minoritized subject can "resonate" beyond the individual to shape a public.[69] We can also think about the vulnerability of a "resonant specificity" as a corporeal site of contagion, infection, and contamination—affected by more than any "stalled singularity" could hope to ward off.[70]

In Fan's series of three sculptures, *I think about Lam Qua everyday I–III* (2019), what resonates from and as the specificity of a body marked by difference are tumors, or rather, glass forms made analogous to them. The sculptures are built of a bundle of nerves, which can also be a way of describing someone as anxious and sensitive. Fan's glass forms sit on small tangled masses of ceramic. Some of the glass forms are speckled with dark spots of melanin, which Fan grew from genetically modified *E. coli* bacteria and fungi, then injected into the glass and mixed with silicone. The forms protrude politely, yet even so, the glass forms look like unwelcome, foreign disruptions—like tumors pressing down on the nerves tasked with carrying them, causing pain and discomfort. In *I think about Lam Qua everyday III*, glass forms glare with a spot of melanin that looks like the pupil of an eye. These forms are a coolly sterile vessel for the biological matter contained inside, at the same time that its organic shape implies the warmth and movement of a body as well as Fan's own touch. There is a fragility to the work. Do we approach it as such because we fear its infectious materials might harm us, or because we are afraid we might harm the work ourselves? Who needs protection, the person viewing the work, or the work itself?

As the series' titles suggest, Fan made these works with the nineteenth-century Chinese painter Lam Qua (Guan Qiaochang) on his mind. Between 1836 and 1852, in Canton (Guangzhou), Lam Qua was commissioned by Peter Parker, a US surgeon, ophthalmologist, and Protestant medical missionary, to paint Western-style portraits of Parker's Chinese patients who had large tumors. Parker came to China in the midst of the Opium Wars, when China's borders were opening to foreign travel, trade, and Christian missionaries. Parker founded a hospital in Canton, where he and his colleagues treated patients for various injuries, illnesses, and diseases. When he died, Parker left behind his medical case studies, letters, sermons, and journals, and while there is no record of given testimonies by his patients, there are at least 115 oil portraits of approximately 80 of them, all painted by Lam Qua.[71] Lam Qua's portraits depart from typical nineteenth-century medical illustrations that feature the entirety of an anonymized nude body, labeled, measured, and reduced to parts, with the face cropped out. Most of Lam Qua's portraits, alternatively, include patients' faces, either directly meeting the viewer's gaze, or turned away and shielded from view by a patient's hand held up in protest or modesty, or both.[72] Lam Qua did not expose a patient's nude figure. He painted them fully dressed, in different poses and accompanying landscapes as if to complement the tumor, displayed like a "patient's prop," or an ornament, peeking through the folds of a garment.[73]

Lam Qua's portraits were shown to Western donors and displayed in Parker's hospital.[74] They served Parker's belief that Western medicine could heal the Chinese body and soul. As Ari Heinrich points out, Lam Qua's use of Western techniques and styles in his portraits produce and represent the pathology and the character of the Chinese, in need of Western medical treatment as a form of Christian compassion.[75] Parker believed that one such characteristic was an "absence of nerves," or an insensitivity to pain.[76] Given this, one might see how the paintings draw attention to what lies on the exteriority of the body, at the same time that they deflect attention away from their subjects' interiority. A visual dissonance occurs between tumors that appear painful, or at the very least burdensome, and the patients' facial expressions that seem calm or serene, showing no evidence of experiencing pain or discomfort.

Fan's glass forms analogous to tumors do not attempt to resolve and smooth out this dissonance. Akin to the anatomical features of his friends and lovers in the *Diagram* series, Fan made tumors without the figure of the racialized body to which they would be attached. Through his glass forms comparable to tumors, Fan does not try to humanize the subjects of Lam Qua's portraits, as a reparative gesture to rescue figures from their own objectification and stigmatization. Alternatively, Fan draws attention to the dissonance between tumor and facial expression as a site of wounding. It is there, at the cut, and on the side of the tumor rather than the body, that Fan's glass works emerge as abstract, inhuman objects. Recall that for Harper, an abstractionist aesthetics enables a break from the realness of figural verisimilitude and the moral superiority claimed on its behalf, and that for Chang, the inhuman is not just the nonhuman. The inhuman is also the cruel and destructive, going against what is considered humane. Fan's glass forms insist on their own inhumane presence, on the severance suffered, as hostile, needy objects poised to spoil the idealization of the Asiatic subject in need of compassion and repair. If the tumor abstracted the pathological Chinese body in need of a cure, Fan's glass tumors continue to risk that process of abstraction, pushing the woundedness of recognition past the limits of the figure, the human, and the humane.

"There's something about Chineseness here," Fan muses, when talking about the tumors Lam Qua painted and his own analogical objects.[77] "What are the technologies that [are] involved in creating this idea of the Other?"[78] If there is something Chinese about these tumors, it is by association, but what makes that association possible? Is it their attachment or their excision? Parker made similar associations, for he believed that his approach to surgery offered a "radical cure" for tumors, as well as for the character of the Chinese.[79] With Lam Qua's paintings, Heinrich writes, "we get a special glimpse into an ironic reconceptualization of Chinese identity for this period: surgery as a means of becoming whole."[80] One must remove an unwelcome presence in and on the body in order to preserve it. Fan reconstructs and preserves these tumors by making objects that are analogous to them. To make them analogous, he injects them and warps them with heat and volatile materials. Analogy inflicts injury; in its wounding, analogy risks undoing whatever and whoever it tries to compare. In attending to the tumor—what is to be removed with Western medicine yet memorialized with Lam Qua's paintings—Fan's glass works are reminders of how that which is perceived as an incurable (racialized) characteristic, emerges through wounding, which is to say, through analogy. By holding on to the tumor's analogous objects, Fan handles what the figure of the Asiatic body is expected to leave behind in order to become whole.

"Every Wound Is an Opening"

Fan continued thinking about what injury creates in *Sites of Wounding*, an ongoing project conceived in multiple chapters. Fan researched and experimented with species native to Hong Kong that are known to produce "precious materials" by way of "processes of contamination, penetration, and incorporation."[81] Fan takes up such processes, considering how his artistic practice might become acts of wounding. Fan draws comparisons between native species and postcolonial subjectivity in Hong Kong, as a former colony of the British Empire from 1841; during the First Opium War, from 1839 to 1842; to 1997, when it became a special administrative region of China as it still is today. Given its history as a city-state, where one cannot technically be a citizen, and where one faces surveillance, censorship, and violence from the Hong Kong government and police in cooperation with the Chinese government, a sense of belonging or groundedness can feel incomplete, without closure, like an open wound. Through this project, Fan asks how certain species' ability to create something "precious" out of injury might tell us something about the ability of the postcolonial subject to make something out of their injury, too. For Fan, as for the species he works with, sites of wounding become traumatized terrains or landscapes. Fan's engagement with the traumatic is what Saketopoulou calls "traumatophilic."[82] Unlike "traumatophobia," which presumes the necessity of getting over trauma and healing from the wounds it inflicts, "traumatophilia" lingers in the wound, in "the touching of wounds" as openings for the sensuous and erotic within "trauma's afterlife."[83]

The first chapter of *Sites of Wounding*, presented at Empty Gallery's Hong Kong location, shows Fan's work with the *Pinctada fucata* oyster, also called the Akoya oyster, a mollusk species used for freshwater pearl farming in Hong Kong. For almost three years, beginning in 2020, Fan collaborated with scientist Wa-Tat Yan at the University of Hong Kong, who has been trying to revive the pearl farming industry in Hong Kong. Yan's research shows that the earliest mention of pearl fishing in Hong Kong appeared during the Southern Han Dynasty (AD 917–971).[84] While the Chinese were the first to develop techniques of pearl cultivation using freshwater oysters in the eleventh to thirteenth centuries, the modern pearl-cultivation industry began in Japan in the early twentieth century. Following World War II, the Hong Kong government worked with Japanese companies to experiment with pearl cultivation in the 1950s, but ultimately, due to overfishing and a competitive global market, Hong Kong's last pearl farm closed in 1981.

The exhibition at Empty Gallery includes a video, *Palimpsest* (2023), which documents how pearls are made and farmed, narrated with silent, lyrical captions displayed over images of an oyster's fleshy, iridescent innards, oysters shucked or tangled in a net, as well as images of Hong Kong's cityscape and harbor, shown mediated and at a remove, whether as a reflection on the surface of water, in a mirror of a shopping mall's ceiling, or through a dirty, smudged window. The video's captions explain that pearls are created as a result of an oyster's defense mechanism in response to a foreign object or irritant entering its body. To neutralize the foreign object, the oyster secretes nacre, which allows it to absorb the object into its own body. An outside object that spoils the oyster's bodily integrity becomes a part of it and an object of beauty; hostile matter makes for a precious pearl. Fan embedded the Chinese characters for "The Pearl of the Orient" into the pearls he made, taking up a "perverse calligraphy, a kind of traumatic writing," where the meaning of a place is irrevocably engraved with the violence that produced it as such.[85]

Yan speaks of the revitalization of pearl farming in Hong Kong as a means of offering fisherman a source of income.[86] Additionally, given Hong Kong's colonial moniker—"The Pearl of the Orient"—the desire to cultivate pearls in Hong Kong is also the desire to reclaim the pearl's historical significance to the region, preserving its connection to Hong Kong and conserving the life of the oysters themselves. The pearl of the oyster is the pearl of the Orient, and what lends them their association with each other is their historical and material injury. What Fan does to these oysters, as the perverse and traumatic, works against the ways that conservation and preservation can idealize the pursuit of the proper, right use of nature in the case of the former, and its purity and protection with regard to the latter. Fan does not hope to recover a precolonial Hong Kong past, but to linger in past wounds in the present. He does not intend to heal what has been inflicted on a place or in an oyster. He pokes and strokes the wounds he inflicts. Indeed, in *Palimpsest* we see his fingers swirl around the insides of an oyster, playing with the pearls that emerge from its fleshy folds. The layers and traces of text that make a palimpsest are rematerialized, made analogous to the layers and traces of nacre covering foreign objects in an oyster.

The rest of Fan's exhibition includes a series of abstract sculptures made from casts of his knees, chest, or torso, which, like his *Diagram* series, are covered in aqua resin, and have been reconfigured and defamiliarized through their duplication, flipping, or layering. These sculptures hold Fan's glass works, which, here, are akin to pearls, not tumors. The sculpture *Left and right knee, grafted* (2023), comes closest to representing the form of the oyster and pearl that he handles in *Palimpsest*, except as the title of the work clarifies, what is mistaken for the ridges of an oyster's shell is the arch of Fan's knees, grafted one onto the other, as the product of another kind of surgical cut, of shape and surface. Otherwise, the oysters and pearls are not displayed in the exhibition, only their trace. *C is for you* (2023) is composed of a metal shelving unit that contains individual oyster shells embalmed between two plates and fired in a kiln. What is preserved is destroyed, and what is left behind are ashes and charred marks where shells had once been. "The Pearl of the Orient," and its inscription in and as pearl matter, are destroyed by the project's end.

The Cantonese name for Hong Kong translates to "Fragrant Harbor." The name derives from Hong Kong's harbors, which, as early as the Sung Dynasty (AD 619–970), exported a dark, fragrant, resinous wood harvested from the heartwood of *Aquilaria sinensis*, or the agarwood tree, and used to make incense. Fan's second chapter of *Sites of Wounding* turns to agarwood harvesting. Agarwood trees were first brought to China from Southeast Asia in the third century, and by the twelfth century, they had become an expensive, luxurious import, equal in value to silver in southern China and Southeast Asia.[87] Although the tree is an endangered species due to the destruction of its habitat and overharvesting, it can still be found in Hong Kong and other parts of southern China. This chapter of the project, shown at the M+ Museum in Hong Kong, included a short video, *Viscera* (2023). Akin to *Palimpsest*, *Viscera* silently narrates with captions the process of harvesting agarwood. Agarwood's valuable, fragrant resin is the product of a microbial fungal infection in sick or injured agarwood trees. When an agarwood tree is wounded and becomes infected with fungus, it secretes aromatic resins as an immune response—a "stress-induced aroma"—in the heartwood called aloes, also referred to as "tears."[88] The resins coagulate around the wound, accumulating in their secretion to resemble scar tissue. To harvest agarwood, farmers injure the trees just enough to provoke their immune response. They do so by tapping holes throughout the tree's trunk and inserting tubes to pump the tree's arteries with a solution made of a mix of sugar, fungus, and water. Then, the heartwood is removed and its aromatic oils are extracted in a lab.

Viscera tells of the process of agarwood harvesting, with close-ups that pan the details of an agarwood tree's trunk adorned with the textures and colors of its bark, as well as long shots of the tree's green leaves and the wounds the tree bears, which the captions describe as "A tear / A gash / A laceration / A cut / A slit / An amputation." With each type of wound, the video cuts to images of an agarwood tree's chopped-off branches, as well as the drilled holes, burns, and slices in its bark, at times splintering or going deeper into the trunk's core, to its heart. These intrusive markings interrupt the serene surfaces of the tree trunk, and at the same time, they suggest an openness to what wounding makes possible. Throughout the video, attention is given to the opening of the wound as well as the processes of contamination and penetration it endures.

Parallels are drawn between the surface of the agarwood tree and the insides of Fan's body, made visible with a computerized tomography (CT) scan, which uses a combination of X-ray and computer technology to penetrate the body and produce three-dimensional images of its insides. The landscapes of a forest populated with agarwood trees are compared to the interior landscape of Fan's body and its parts, including his stomach, vertebrae, and leg muscles. In the exhibition, sculptures covered in brown, tan, and beige resin—like tree bark—are cast from the interior parts of Fan's body mapped and exposed with a CT scan, laying bare the shape of what lies underneath the surface of skin. These parts' materialization as abstract three-dimensional forms are the result of the opening of the body, shown in the video as the blurred, nondescript image of fleshly orifices and folds, and the tunnel of a CT scanner, as another orifice that Fan passes through, so that the electromagnetic radiation of the X-ray can penetrate his body. Both the agarwood tree and Fan have been disassembled and turned inside out. They are made akin to one another through their openings and whatever enters in.

"Every wound is an opening to ingest the injury," the video's captions read. An image of the trunk of an agarwood tree accompanies the text. The trunk is covered in tubes jutting out from its body, before the video shifts to footage of what, presumably, are the shiny pink insides of Fan's body. The video's transition from the tree's exterior to Fan's interior draws a sliding association between body and tree, torso and trunk, heartwood and gut, where one is related to the other by what they take in, whether poison or X-rays. Through the sequence of images, we are brought to the space of analogy, which, as Michel Foucault reminds us, is one of radiation, with the capacity to penetrate and pass through a body and its cells, compromising its integrity. If the wound is an opening that ingests, the wound is a mouth that consumes itself. As that which ingests and consumes, the wound has an appetite for itself, spoiling itself with a desire for recognition that resonates, or accretes and leaks, like the nacre of an oyster or the resin of the agarwood tree. The final captions of the video offer a refrain, and then a variation: "Every wound is an opening to transform / to scar / to regenerate / to congeal / to change / to go inward / to morph / to name." In the video, two computer screens show Fan's CT scans. On the left screen, the figure of Fan's body is laid out—displayed from the front, back, and side—and on the right screen, the moving image captures an abstract rounded form, reminiscent of Fan's glass works, which, like these scans, skew the relation between figure and part. The video continues to shuttle back and forth between Fan and agarwood trees, between images of his skeleton and muscle, to an agarwood tree's trunk, no longer with tubes, yet punctured with holes that have yet to heal.

The video ends as it began, with a long static shot of a small piece of agarwood that burns down to a charcoal husk. Like the first chapter of *Sites of Wounding*, the agarwood tree and its incense are not a part of the work, only their ashen remains. The beginning and end of this long shot of burning wood have been reversed: the video opens with wood almost completely burned, only with a small lick of a flame, while the video closes with the wood enveloped in a larger flame amid smoke. What might seem like the end of the video is actually its opening, or beginning. For Fan, as for an oyster and a tree, the opening of a wound—a hole, a burn—is never quite closed or healed, yet such opening makes regeneration possible if not necessary. Fan draws resonances between himself and Hong Kong's native species as well as the sites of wounding they share. Fan depends on analogy in order to make something like a postcolonial subjectivity in Hong Kong appear. At the same time, as with Fan's other works, the analogies drawn do not construct a legible human subject by way of injury. If a reliance on analogy is always subject to failure, exposed to the nonequivalence of differences, then Fan's work must end in ashes, without pearls, incense, or figure. The act of relating, of drawing comparisons, remains destructive and ephemeral.

Hostile Conditions

In *The Order of Things*, Foucault writes that up until the end of the sixteenth century, Western knowledge was organized by forms of resemblance. One of those forms was analogy. Analogy "speaks . . . of adjacencies, of bonds and joints," through which "all the figures in the whole universe can be drawn together."[89] As an example, Foucault describes "the old analogy of plant to animal (the vegetable is an animal living head down, its mouth—or roots—buried in the earth)," which the sixteenth-century philosopher and botanist Andrea Cesalpino turned upside down with "the discovery that a plant is an upright animal."[90] Through this analogy, Foucault notes that man, as a primary subject and object of knowledge, has become "the fulcrum upon which all these relations turn."[91] An "upright animal" is presumed to be human, as a category constructed to bolster the figure of man and what he knows. Man, or what Lisa Lowe describes as the "ideal type" of the civilized, rational man of modern Western industrial society, becomes the central point of reference against and through which difference is conceived of, related to, and produced.[92]

In Foucault's example, we can only grasp the parts of a plant when analogized to the anatomy of the human. Rather than attempt to reverse the gravitational pull of the human by saying that a human is like a plant and not the other way around, Shin revisits this old analogy in their project and exhibition *The Vegetarian*, letting the radiation and resonance of its logic render the human into something polluted, contaminated, and intoxicated. Mel Chen describes the intoxicated as a debilitating "violent reflex of pollution, coming on like a wave from elsewhere," which, at the same time, "has been welcomed, even desired" with "capabilities" that "enable taking leave of a flattening, even murderous present, to a temporal and sensory otherwise, to a place of tolerability."[93] Intoxication interrupts processes of healing and repair, and yet it does not inevitably lead to utter destruction and ruin, for intoxication "carries sensibilities of freedom, gentle excess, or moderation."[94] In *The Vegetarian*, Shin's experiments with how a plant intoxicates the human, and how the human intoxicates a plant, lets us consider the intoxication of analogy. They address the ways a dependence on analogy gestures to a susceptibility to intoxication.

For *The Vegetarian*, Shin wondered what it would be like to be a plant, not as an idealized queer ecological form in peaceful symbiosis with its surrounds, so much as a perverse form in turmoil, in hostile conditions. While Fan works with native species like the agarwood tree and its capacity to withstand injury and create something beautiful in the process, Shin turns to the invasive non-native species of the mugwort plant and its capacity for contamination and intoxication, inspired by Han Kang's novel *The Vegetarian*, translated by Deborah Smith. The novel begins with a man, Mr. Cheong, trying to describe how his wife, Yeong-hye, had recently changed. "Before my wife turned vegetarian," he explains, "I'd always thought of her as completely unremarkable in every way."[95] He continues, "The passive personality of this woman in whom I could detect neither freshness nor charm, or anything especially refined, suited me down to the ground."[96] But one night Yeong-hye had a dream, and she had not been the same since. The next morning, Mr. Cheong found his wife throwing out all the meat, eggs, and milk in their fridge. From then on, she would not have any meat in the house. She refused to cook it or eat it.

Thus begins the novel told in three parts, each narrated by people in Yeong-hye's life: her husband, her brother-in-law, and her sister, all of whom either inflict violence on her or are complicit bystanders. Throughout, they are by turns disgusted, curious, frightened, and resentful of her changes. Italicized passages are interspersed throughout the text, offering a glimpse into Yeong-hye's dreams and other visions, bored down to images and sensations in fragmented form. In these sequences, she sees blood, tastes it, feels her clothes soaked in it, feels the squish of raw meat in her mouth, and the terror of running in a dark wood, like an animal hunted. Not much is given about her past, except a childhood memory of her father killing a dog that the family eats—a violence he exacts on the dog that blurs into his abuse of Yeong-hye and her sister.

Although we are permitted these brief stays in Yeong-hye's interiority, critics have noted the opacity of her "passive personality," but also her impassivity in the midst of her experiences of sexual assault and abuse, as well as her acts of self-harm and purging. Yeong-hye's painful experiences are told from the point of view of those whose actions, or inactions, straddle the difference between the human and inhuman(e), between humans and the animals they eat. So while her husband, brother-in-law, and sister view her vegetarianism as "against human nature," by the end of the novel, Yeong-hye has, in a way, confirmed their suspicions by turning away from the human, and instead, turning into a tree.[97] Scholars have read Yeong-hye's transformation as the enactment of ecofeminist critique through interrogations of the relation between meat-eating and masculinity, gender norms and eating disorders.[98] When met with the brutality and force of patriarchal violence, Yeong-hye remains unmoved, without appetite. Her impassivity as a woman or a tree is interpreted as a response to violence and a form of resistance and refusal.

Kang was inspired to write *The Vegetarian*—initially a short story titled "The Fruit of My Woman"—after reading the Korean modernist poet Yi Sang. Under Japanese occupation in the 1920s, and in Hangul—the Korean script banned at the time—he wrote, "I believe that humans should be plants." For Sang, the qualities of a plant—of a rooted stasis, catatonia, and muted withdrawal—characterized Korean people's collective response to violence and censorship under Japanese imperial rule. In the analogy drawn between human and plant, there is the implication that humans, in the face of the traumatic, shut down and become akin to plants as a means of self-preservation. To understand plant life is to understand, in this context, a traumatized way of living and a form of life thought to occupy the lower end of the animacy hierarchy.[99] Therefore, while plants represent something purifying, natural, and clean, the plant, as an object made analogous to an injured, traumatized person, becomes something corrupt, spoiled by the connections being made. I look to Shin's work with Kang's novel and with mugwort because of how the relations they draw between plant and human shed light on analogy's capacity to spoil what might otherwise aspire to something neatly contained and whole.

Yeong-hye's metamorphosis makes a case for spoilage, or as Alexis Shotwell puts it, a case "against purity."[100] "Being against purity," Shotwell writes, "means that there is no primordial state we might wish to get back to, no Eden we have desecrated, no pretoxic body we might uncover."[101] Shin considers the possibility of becoming a toxic body and the impossibility of becoming or remaining a pretoxic one in *The Vegetarian*, their multisensory exhibition based on Kang's novel shown at The Bows in Calgary in 2022.[102] Shin's *The Vegetarian*, composed of a fourteen-minute video essay, herbarium collages, incense, and digital prints, ruminates on the intoxication of plant life. Shin's work seems to follow a realization had by Yeong-hye's older sister, In-hye, while tending to her sister, who has been placed in a psychiatric hospital due to her refusal to eat. In-hye acknowledges that although she had been spared their father's abuse, Yeong-hye had not:

> Only Yeong-hye, docile and naive, had been unable to deflect their father's temper or put up any form of resistance. Instead, she had merely absorbed all her suffering inside her, deep into the marrow of her bones. Now, with the benefit of hindsight, In-hye could see that the role that she had adopted back then of the hard-working, self-sacrificing eldest daughter had been a sign not of maturity but of cowardice. It had been a survival tactic.[103]

In-hye survived by way of deflection and detachment, but Yeong-hye carved out another way of living through her affectability and susceptibility. In-hye's reflections express, with bitterness, how Yeong-hye pushed for more than what In-hye could imagine for herself within the constraints of her life. While the novel centers on Yeong-hye's vegetarianism as a diet constituted by lack—by what she refuses and gives up—her impassivity and inaction can also be interpreted as an absorptive capacity, as a dangerously indiscriminate openness to the toxicity of others. In-hye's bitterness becomes In-hye's own to taste. Yeong-hye disturbs the people in her life—provokes their ire and antagonizes them—because despite her obtuseness, there is the sense that something is teeming within her, that the violence she has experienced is just underneath the surface, growing into something frightening and strange. Her withholding feels like evidence of hostility more so than inscrutable resilience—it becomes an expression of self-absorption, a quality usually saved for the spoiled, like, for instance, a housewife who makes food that only she would want to eat, like someone who tends to her own appetite rather than someone else's.

Yeong-hye's metamorphosis is neither complete nor literal. Since Yeong-hye's transformation comes with the relinquishment of speech, we are not given an account of what her nature is, human or not. Her metamorphosis feels unfinished and thus compromised, and for that reason, all the more perverse. By the end of the novel, she becomes an unsettling abomination rather than the ideality and beauty of a hybridized form. Yeong-hye has not returned to a pure state of an untouched, unviolated body, so much as she has been altered by what she has taken in, metabolized, and stored, in addition to what she has cast out and refused. Her transformation cannot be seen as solely a symptom of repressed trauma, but it can certainly be understood as that which has taken place in the wake of violence, as its spoiled trace.

Shin gleans this trace of Yeong-hye's life in their iteration of *The Vegetarian*. Like their source material, Shin's *The Vegetarian* starts with a dream brought on by the consumption of mugwort. Mugwort, also known as *Artemisia vulgaris* or wormwood, is an aromatic flowering plant considered native to Northeast Asia and North Africa, but invasive to North America. It is a medicinal herb used for moxibustion in traditional Chinese medicine, and when consumed, its hallucinogenic properties can help with sleep and lucid dreaming. As an incense, it is burned for purification and warding off malevolent spirits. Named after Artemis, the Greek goddess, the plant is associated with the moon's cycles, women's health, and childbirth.

Shin's video essay *Anthropology of a Phytomorphist* silently, with captions, like Fan's *Palimpsest* and *Viscera*, tells the Korean myth of the creation of the human. In the myth, a bear eats mugwort and turns into a woman, who gives birth to the first king of Koreans. Mugwort opens a pathway between the heavenly and earthly, the royal and common, human and animal. Shin's video begins with magnified microscopic scans of a mugwort leaf's surface, visible as a downy, textured bed of green. These images are accompanied by a moist soundscape of a tropical region, like wet soil gurgling and droplets of water falling off vegetation onto fertile, damp ground. The video cuts to harvested mugwort branches and leaves leaning against a wall in a lab, then to Shin and a biologist, Solon Morse, who handle lab materials in preparation for the mugwort's transfection.

Captions continue to tell the story of mugwort. In 1827, Scottish geologist John MacCulloch introduced the term "malaria" to describe an unseen, undetectable airborne disease—"an insensible and imponderable poison"—capable of attaching itself to solid substances, like vegetation and human bodies. As the video's captions explain, MacCulloch posited that malaria was "one of the three mysteries of the world, alongside odor and contagion." The word "malaria" is rooted in nineteenth-century miasma theory, which touted the belief that diseases spread through air filled with particles of decomposing matter.[104] Although germ theory came to replace miasma theory in the late nineteenth century, Hsuan L. Hsu writes that anxieties and fears around what spreads in the air persist particularly in popular representations of contagious Asiatic subjects and toxic Asiatic atmospheres.[105] What persists of racial difference, as the toxicity of Asianness, hangs in the air like a threat, like dread.

In 1967, malaria spread among the Chinese and North Vietnamese armies during the Vietnam War. It was attributed to a mosquito that hosted the parasitic disease and transmitted it to the soldiers they feasted on. To mitigate these environmental risks faced by soldiers fighting wars waged throughout Southeast Asia's tropical climates, China and the United States sought medical advancements as a solution. To remain global powers, they needed to protect and fortify their military bodies. As Thuy Linh Nguyen Tu notes in her study of the development of dermatology and pharmaceutical cosmetics by US scientists during the Vietnam War, treatments and cures became necessary for the purposes of preserving US military force.[106] In attempts to strengthen its military, the Chinese initiated a secret project called Project 523. A pharmaceutical chemist in the project, Tu Youyou, was tasked with studying traditional Chinese medicine, and from there, isolated the bioactive compounds of mugwort to create a pharmacological drug called artemisinin, which became the basis for antimalarial drugs. The World Health Organization (WHO) reports that the most widely used antimalarial treatments to this day are artemisinin-based combination therapies (ACTs), which are produced using pure artemisinin compound extract from mugwort. All current strains of malaria can be treated with at least one of the ACTs the WHO recommends.[107]

Shin began working on *The Vegetarian* during an artist residency at the University of Buffalo. While Shin felt like other artists in the residency were interested in the experimentation of the human body as a means of optimization, Shin was interested in the body's compromise, as well as its sacrifice. Mugwort, as the captions of Shin's video reads, is "an Asiatic cure or an Asiatic pest depending on one's allegiance." Shin draws out the plant's indifference to national borders and its invasion of regions, at the same time that they consider what more can be done with its promise to heal and relieve the pain and discomfort of disease, war, and restless dreams. If, like Yeong-hye, mugwort could be corrupted by way of its self-absorption, Shin wanted to see if it could absorb a part of them, too. Shin extracted their DNA from their saliva, and with a gene gun—primarily used in agricultural studies for the optimization of crops—they blasted particles coated with their DNA onto foraged mugwort.[108] "From the moment of contact," Shin writes, "the plant consumes my DNA from its pores called stomata and metabolizes me from its tissues, revealing its vascular, nervous system."[109] The moment of contact between Shin and mugwort becomes one of intoxicating analogy, where mugwort is made to become like Shin, and Shin like mugwort. Shin is transmitted virally in the air, they exchange gases with the plant, and the plant metabolizes Shin.

Shin tracked how the plant absorbed their DNA over time. Fluorescent microscopic scans reveal Shin's DNA working its way throughout the veins of the plant's vascular, nervous system. In these series of images described as self-portraits, also included in *Anthropology of a Phytomorphist*, Shin's DNA glows a neon green. Reduced to their DNA, Shin appears in their self-portraits as something toxic, sickly, or envious, eager to spoil its host, pooling in some spots, appearing like small freckles, moles, or lesions threatening to expand and grow on the mugwort's leafy plane.

Like the Akoya oyster with its pearls and the agarwood tree with its tears, mugwort's absorption of Shin's DNA can be understood as a defense mechanism, a response to hostile conditions and the intrusion of foreign objects. Shin's relationship with the mugwort is one of consumption, convergence, and compromise. They do not view the plant as a collaborator, as something on equal footing with them; they know where they are on the animacy hierarchy. Shin is made like mugwort, and mugwort is made like Shin, but such likeness does not operate on a relation of equivalence, or on the assumption of shared ground. Instead, their likeness—the way they are made analogous to each other echoing Foucault's use of the analogy between human and plant—draws attention to the hostility of their relation of nonequivalence.

In *Anthropology of a Phytomorphist*, Shin discloses that given the potential for "adverse side effects from mutagenesis," the lab's safety and health policies required them to destroy the contaminated mugwort leaves. Upon completion of the project, Shin let the mugwort leaves die. However, they found another use for what remained. Once the mugwort leaves dried out, they ground them up and mixed their remains with cinchona, makko, oak, wild cherry, sandalwood, ash, and diatomaceous earth to create an incense. For the installation *Untitled (100 days of solemnity)*, Shin laid out the incense into trails, which, like the outline of the plant's vascular system, trace the human body's nervous system. The nerves Shin tracks with incense unfurl and air out in a form mirroring the body meridians in traditional Chinese medicine. The body meridians connect the material body to its Qi, or energy, and moxibustion's use of mugwort along the pathways of the meridians aid in the flow of energy and blood, providing warmth and dispelling coldness.

Given these uses of mugwort incense, Shin's installation might promise a therapeutic scene of repair. But when I saw the work in Shin's studio, what caught my eye was the gray and black ash of the incense after it had been burned. These scorched materials, laid out to suggest a sensuous figure, mark the impossibility of Shin's body cohering within contaminated mugwort, dried out and grounded down to dust, which, with the softest breeze from an open door, or a sneeze, can blow away. The ash in Shin's installation brings to mind the piece of agarwood that burns in Fan's *Viscera*. In its temporal loop and inversion of time, Fan's video is a reminder that the site of burning remains open, like a wound, but also like the meridians through which energy flows.

A trail of the incense from *Untitled (100 days of solemnity)* is lit each day it rests on display. Shin's trace, as hazardous biological matter, threatens to become akin to the bad air mugwort is tasked with clearing and purifying. The lit incense intoxicates the air, as "imponderable" and "invisible" particulates—a hazy, smoky, mind-altering contaminant. With the scent of incense wafting throughout the space, *The Vegetarian* can be thought of alongside the work of artists such as Anicka Yi and Candice Lin, whose use of smell in their installations, made and collected from bacteria samples, fat, shrimp, and other decaying animals and vermin, render bodies and art spaces porous and vulnerable to one another, to the possibility of unfriendly, hostile conditions and atmospheric surrounds.[110] In olfactory art, smell decenters the primacy of the visual within an aesthetic encounter, pushing a viewer to experience what cannot be contained within the sterility of a deodorized art space. Olfactory art also, as Hsu writes, serves as "a visceral yet uncertain index of environmental toxicity."[111] "Insofar as its transmission involves such risky, trans-corporeal exchanges," Hsu continues, "smell violates the ideal of purity that governs both visual perception and conventional attitudes about environmental conservation."[112] Shin extends the impure afterlife of the mugwort leaves, as diffuse and affectable, corrupt in form and composition.

Malaria, like other diseases, does away with fantasies of national boundaries and bodily containment. This is what MacCullough was afraid of, and it is why the Centers for Disease Control and Prevention (CDC) is adamant in their warnings to travelers about the contraction of malaria if and when they venture outside of the United States. The CDC currently reports that while there are around two thousand cases of malaria in the United States, the vast majority of cases come from travelers, or more pointedly, from immigrants arriving from countries where transmission occurs throughout sub-Saharan Africa and South Asia.[113] In preparation for travel to these and other regions, people—as dutiful US citizens—are required to take antimalarial drugs to defend the body and the nation.

Shin's burning of mugwort materializes the racializing effects of what Hsu calls "atmo-orientalism," which associates Asiatic subjects with "atmospheric toxicity" produced by modernity, and "Asiatic atmospheres" with "biochemical threats to the integrity of white bodies and minds."[114] As Shin's video essay captions state, "Some bodies are soiled, an imponderable poison, bereft of habitation." The soiled cannot be tethered to a figure; it drifts in space as a biohazard. Shin aggravates the paranoia that constructs the spoiled Asiatic body as a noxious crisis for public health. They create a compromised species of mugwort inextricable from the legacies of colonialism and war, a species that has to be destroyed and yet continues to live another insidious life by burning and dissipating into the air.

Burning incense is an offering to the spirits that guides them back to the corporeal world. It cleanses and detoxifies a space. What clouds also clears. Burning mugwort also soothes, helping with general feelings of unease or malaise. Rather than say that mugwort heals, we might also say that it keeps channels and pathways open, receptive to whatever can be let in. Mugwort aids in perilous transmissions and connections. "Mal aria, bad air, miasm, a stain, I contaminate . . ." Shin's video essay trails off, suggestively, not without some malice. Throughout the video, captions make lists of people, places, and things made analogous to one another, shaped by repetition, variation, translation, etymological roots, and word play. Accompanying these captions are images of different parts of mugwort leaves captured at varying scales of magnification. The video zooms in and out, switching from the green surface of mugwort leaves to the glow of microscopic scans. The transition from near to nearer visually and temporally matches the pace at which the video draws associations from one thing to the next. A "malarious body" becomes a "malarious landscape" and a "malarious prognosis"; the malarious is "a swamp, a bat, mosquitos, the air, the droplets, the yellow, the brown, the black." The body and landscape are vulnerable to animals, natural elements, and the racialized. Everything collides into one another. Conflation becomes a risk that offends. Shin cultivates modes of recognition that depend on comparisons drawn between human and plant, flesh and meat, leaf and ash. Like an odor that lingers for too long, the relations wrought by analogy hang in the air, intoxicating the discrete boundaries between comparable person and things.

On the Matter of Meat

With the burning of incense, laid out like a human body, I cannot help but think of how the work invokes the meatiness of the body in its fleshy absence. Fan and Shin's work do not make a body appear, but they do attend to its materials and incongruous parts. It is this inability to separate flesh from the vegetal, the body from the plant, that brings me to briefly consider the matter of meat. "Meat is a truly weird thing," Mel Chen muses. It is "itself a nonintegrity. It is a substance whose member categories seem to vary . . . as to whether they include insects, chicken, pork, or fish. It can be a cut of an animal, and these days what one calls 'meat' can also be a vegetarian product shaped into . . . a turkey."[115] Chen meditated on meat as fire raged throughout California during the summer of 2020. They write, "I don't want to be overly sweeping, but it really feels as if California's air has become something like meat."[116] That summer had been the worst wildfire season in California's recorded history.[117] By the end of 2020, there had been nearly ten thousand fires that had burned over 4.2 million acres—more than 4 percent of the state's land.[118] Many fires were stoked by thunderstorms, and evacuation and other contingency plans were difficult to implement because of the COVID-19 pandemic. In January 2025, drought conditions, extreme windstorms, and low humidity contributed to the rapid spread of up to 359 fires in the Los Angeles metropolitan area, the largest of which destroyed thousands of homes and businesses in the neighborhoods of Altadena and Pacific Palisades, and burned an estimated 57,660 acres.[119] At the time of writing this, the fires have only recently been adequately contained, but the question of how to rebuild, and what has been left in the air, remains.

Not so dissimilar from a slaughterhouse, where animals are prepared to be made into ground-up meat and become airborne particulates, what burns in wildfires is a dangerous meeting of unknowable "substance" and "air."[120] This meaty, bad air is composed of bodies transformed into ash and smoke—it is thick, sticky, and moist with heat. The air shuttles from the concrete to the abstract, from solid to vaporous. Purity is not possible in everyday hostile conditions. I think about this as friends in California in 2020, and again in 2025, posted photos on social media of a dim, gray sky smothering a red sun, or shared, in shock and sorrow, the news that their homes and belongings have all burned and are gone. I also think about this as I drive on the freeway at night and see the glow of a fire in the mountains in the distance, or when I research which air filters and face masks are best to buy, not just for the time being but as long-term investments. We are implicated disparately, across contaminating connections between person and plant, animal and meat, smoke and air. The nonintegrity of analogy lets us know, as Chen writes, "what connections have no business being made," and yet have been made anyway.[121]

"Are you sensitive to smell?" Shin asked. We were in their studio at UCLA, standing over *Untitled (100 days of solemnity)*. I said no. They knelt down to light the incense. As we talked about the work in their studio, the smoke wafted around us. After I left, I wondered if asking about a sensitivity to smell technically went against Shin's interest in contamination. If the work intended to be hostile, where does permission and consent fit in? Or sensitivity for that matter? Sensitivity would seem to go against hostility and vice versa. But I want to compare Shin's question with a previous one: "Who hurt you?" The question—posed rather *in*sensitively—relinquishes the person asking from any role they might have played in hurting you. They are not responsible for the damage, but they are ready to come to your defense. Shin's question, though, comes with the acknowledgment that they are the person who made the work that requires asking the question in the first place. They asked if I am sensitive to smell because they made connections between harm and their own capacity, connections which depend on the wounds of analogy that spoil the space, them, their work, and me.

CODA

SWEET, SELFISH ENDS

While this book has indulged in the bitter hostility of the spoiled, here I savor sweetness. As taste and temperament, sweetness can overwhelm the necessity of nourishment, the niceties of tact and decorum. Sweetness can be pleasant and agreeable in moderation, but when there is too much of it, it can become cloying, saccharine, and contrived, enabling gratuitous kinds of craving. Julie Tolentino's durational performance *HONEY* offers a way of thinking about what the spoilage of sweetness does to the body and the self over time, furnishing it with luxury but damaging it, too, causing it to burst, leak, turn. The spoiled wants more of everything: someone's attention, too much of a good thing, a sweet thing. But what happens in the long run? How can the spoiled sustain itself and endure its earnest commitment to its own appetite? The spoiled might initially be in pursuit of an ideal, but due to overzealousness, such pursuits, over time, can lead to an ideal's ruin. I am interested in the duration of the spoiled as the time of wanting too much for too long, as the time wherein an ideal—like an identity accessed through affect or a sense of self secured through healing affirmation—is spoiled. Ultimately, this is what happens to an ideal. But when you spoil an ideal, you risk ruining something for the rest of us. You are left open to the accusation that you are only acting for your own selfish ends. I'm interested in these sweet, selfish ends, which actually have no end, and instead are constituted by their ongoingness.

"The world does not revolve around you." My mother used to tell me this when I was younger, particularly when I took too long to set the table so that we could eat dinner together. Sometimes, when my mother told me dinner was ready and I did not come, she did not want to wait. Frustrated with me and exhausted from work, she ate without me. I would have to realize on my own, belatedly, that I had taken too long, and when I did I would rush to the table to find my dinner sitting there, cold. Out of hunger, guilt, and a little bit of spite, I would eat quickly and as much as I could. I thought I could make up for lost time and catch up to the moment when my mother had also been eating at the table alone.

As a child (and an Aries), I did not have moderation on my mind. I would always eat until I felt very full, near bursting. I assumed that eating was supposed to make you feel that way. This full feeling commingled with the love and annoyance of my mother, which altogether bore a kind of sweetness that did not destroy my appetite but redirected it, causing it to change its orbit, to revolve around the thought of my mother, around someone other than myself. For Sigmund Freud, one of humankind's "outrages against its naive self-love" is the shift from a Ptolemaic to Copernican cosmology.[1] Children are confronted with the realization that the world does not revolve around them, in the same way that the sun does not revolve around the earth.

The other affronts to humankind that Freud mentions are evolution and psychoanalysis, the latter of which is the "most irritating insult" because of how it proves by way of the unconscious that the "I," the ego, "is not even master in its own home."[2] Jean Laplanche describes this cosmological shift as "the first narcissistic wound" of humankind.[3] However, Laplanche points out that this cosmological shift within psychoanalysis is not seamless. Rather, it is "an alternation between relapses into Ptolemaism and resurgences of the Copernican."[4] People shift back and forth, gravitating toward the "strangerness" of the other within the self but also the "strangerness" of other people.[5] The revolution of the Copernican, then, is never complete. The "narcissistic wound" never heals—it remains open, and so does the self.

I like to think that in Tolentino's *HONEY*, the world revolves around her at the same time that she is pulled into the orbit of other people, alternating between different kinds of "strangerness." Tolentino's lover and collaborator, Stosh Fila (also known as Pigpen), pours fifty pounds of honey into her mouth for anywhere from three to five hours. Together, they have performed *HONEY* at several gallery and museum events and academic conferences at universities in and outside the United States. While Tolentino pulls our attention as the figure taking in all the honey, Pigpen has the power to determine how much Tolentino can take. In the cosmology of the performance, two figures, like planets, turn toward one another. Each is confronted with their own decentering and reopening, given and giving over to the other. There is no closure and consolidation of the self, only its spoilage in bending toward another, again and again.

Tolentino is a Filipinx-Salvadoran interdisciplinary artist, dancer, choreographer, and activist from an earlier generation than many of the artists in this book. She lived in New York City from the 1980s to the early 2000s, before moving to the West Coast and living between Los Angeles and Joshua Tree. Her work is shaped by her community of queer artists and activists formed out of necessity, survival, love, rage, and grief during the AIDS crisis, as well as by a changing New York City, which, due to then-mayor Rudy Giuliani's "quality of life" campaign in the 1990s, cracked down on porn theaters, clubs, cruising spaces, and other public sites vital to queer nightlife and queer sex. As a member of ACT UP and one of the founding members of the pro-sex lesbian nightclub Clit Club (1990–2012), Tolentino hosted and threw parties, cowrote the Lesbian AIDS Project's *Women's Safer Sex Handbook* (1993) with Cynthia Madansky, and performed many collaborative durational works.[6] All that Tolentino's body can withstand, lend, and hold is done with the exertion and trust required to commit to loved ones who are here and no longer here, and the collective memory forged with and between them. Tolentino's body is pushed, pierced, bound, and made to shed blood, done by or on behalf of those she works to be in relation to. She inhabits and embodies the pain and difficulty of loss in her community, along with the pain and difficulty of staying in it—of keeping companions close, continuing to be with and around others, who she might harm and who might harm her.

Tolentino's *HONEY* allows me—briefly, selfishly—to recall my time as a graduate student, when I saw Tolentino and Pigpen perform *HONEY* twice: in 2012 at the academic conference "The Affect Factory: Precarity, Labor, Gender, and Performance," organized by *Women & Performance: a journal of feminist theory* and held at New York University, and in 2013 at the Performance Studies international conference hosted by Stanford University.[7] Throughout this book, I have been loosely orbiting around the figure of the student. This allows me to think about the duration of the life of the student, who always has more to learn. It is my hope that there is something to be learned from the spoiled as a site of pedagogy, constituted by the movement between the Ptolemaic and Copernican, within a classroom thrown off its axis from time to time, revolving around a teacher, like Tolentino, and what she knows, then revolving around what students learn, in turn. Maybe this is what Barbara Johnson meant when she told her students that "teaching is teaching people to think as themselves. Which means the teacher has to try to think as herself."[8] A class orbits around what the teacher is thinking as herself, and students interrupt that orbit, causing the teacher to be led astray, pulled into their orbit, into their way of thinking as themselves.

In the performances of *HONEY* that I have seen, Tolentino stands upright with her head tilted back with mouth open. She wears a strapless dress made of nude-colored leather, like a second supple layer of skin. Pigpen sits ten feet above Tolentino on a hunting blind, where he squeezes honey from condiment bottles onto a gold thread that draws a line from Pigpen's hand to Tolentino's mouth.[9] The thread is a tether and a pathway of communication, like a telephone wire or a string between two tin cans that can send messages from mouth to ear, from hand to mouth. Tolentino describes the drops of honey as "little globes."[10] In an interview with Alex Fialho, Tolentino explains, "There's just one action, you know: Craft the globes. And I just wait with my mouth open for the honey to drop into my mouth."[11] Pigpen crafts the globes, like small planets traversing their allotted path along the thread into Tolentino's open mouth.

What do these globes carry? Following Laplanche, perhaps these crafted globes of honey contain messages that Tolentino and Pigpen communicate to each other in excess of language, wherein the excess materializes as the dripping decadence of honey. Pigpen and Tolentino work at handling and consuming that excess: Pigpen focuses on the pacing of his feeding, and Tolentino focuses on waiting, remaining open to more honey that will come. Tolentino understands her role as one of a supplicant. "My head is in a receiving position," she says, "my mouth is in a receiving position, my mouth is open. But it's in the shape of an O, which is both an ecstatic, orgasmic, . . . receiving state, but it's also the exact state of one's mouth when you die."[12] Tolentino is ready to receive pleasure in sweetness that comes with finitude—the vitality of a body with an appetite converges with that body's demise. The orbit of the O, of the mouth, is the site of jouissance. Tolentino's open mouth is a plea and a posture of unconditional acceptance. She explains,

> I am trying to articulate the kind of directness of communication between people. And the loss of information, the stickiness of it, the libidinal quality and the kind of sensuality of what communication can be like or what communication offers. And also, I think that I'm expressing the opposite of that, which is the difficulty of being able to speak, the distance between people, the ways that you can hear what you want to hear. You know, like it can just be a one-way receipt. The way that the thing that you're crafting kind of ends up in a whole other state.[13]

In *HONEY*, communication is made possible through the practice of feeding a lover honey for hours, of being fed honey for hours. What is communicated can be direct—like the straight line of thread between Pigpen to Tolentino—yet there is also the possibility of a message getting stuck or distorted, leading to "a whole other state" that could be called miscommunication or else the difficult challenge of a new mode of communication. Tolentino and Pigpen's communication through globes of honey on the line, of working to sync up with each other's timing that requires Pigpen to decide how much Tolentino can take, are reminders that love, and the processes of repair that encompass all that love promises, comes with the damage of the spoiled: the honey that falls and fills, the struggle and suffering in wanting and receiving too much, stuck in the golden thick of communication and all that could go wrong.

There are other vital lines of communication in the performance, too. In the performances I have seen, Tolentino holds an analog tape recorder in each hand. One recorder plays the Costa Rican singer Chavela Vargas's song "Soledad," or "Loneliness." With desire running through the deep grooves of her voice—a voice known for lending its rich grain to the Mexican ranchera—Vargas sings of a lover who has left, leaving behind pain, a sacred silence, starless nights, and stream beds that have run dry. In the song, Soledad becomes the name of Vargas's familiar companion, to whom she sings. "[Vargas] spends most of her time in the O sound," Tolentino states, "So it sometimes gives me a lot of comfort to hear that. Like, the support of the O just goes right into my jaw."[14] One "O," resonant with sorrowful sound, loosens a clenched jaw that shapes another "O," filled with the mute sweetness of honey.

Tolentino creates a feedback loop, pressing play, record, and rewind back and forth from one recorder to another. She describes the practice as "trying to fill up" each recorder, feeding each one while she, too, is fed and filled.[15] "But it takes a little bit of my mind to have to remember who is the recorder and who is the receiver," Tolentino says, "And it starts to get mixed up."[16] Tolentino's attempts to fill the recorders leads to the song's distortion, not only because each recorder picks up other sounds with each exchange, but also because honey starts to get into the crevices of the recorders, cramming the tapes' spools of film. The multiplication of Vargas's voice across recorders and between hands obstructs distinctions between giving and receiving, between self and other. Strangerness is found in the globes of honey, in the feedback between recorders, and in the sound of Vargas's voice that fleshes out the company loneliness affords. Honey and voice become unwieldy adhesives keeping Tolentino, Pigpen, and Vargas stuck to one another, returning to each other in a way that keeps track of time passing and also loses it, letting it slip and drip by.

In preparation for Tolentino's 2012 performance in New York, a couple of graduate students on the conference organizing committee, me included, went to Astoria, Queens, to buy samples of different kinds of honey at Greek grocery stores. In preparation, Tolentino needed to taste and select specific kinds of honey for the performance. She chose two different kinds of honey: one with a better taste to start, followed by another kind, with a less distinct taste, to be used toward the end. I like knowing that Tolentino's taste was a necessary part of the performance. In addition to nourishing and conditioning her body by eating chicken for protein before the performance, she also anticipated what her body might like during the performance—what she might be able to tolerate and also find pleasurable, what kind of consistency and texture could create the globes she could consume, and which kinds of honey should be used at what time during the performance.

Durational performance puts pressure on distinctions between capacity and debility, control and powerlessness. Under constraint, Tolentino's taste preference asserts her skill and technique, as well as the possibility of her pleasure in having Pigpen feed her the honey she chose to swallow. And yet, Tolentino clarifies,

> Other things that are happening is that—you know, the sweetness is probably [laughs] the least thing that I am thinking of because it's almost as if the honey starts to move past my palate and it moves just directly into my—like, it's more about it going into my body, and also it falling out in a way, and also covering the palate and the taste buds and the place where you would actually taste the honey.[17]

Such preparation and selection are not wholly about Tolentino exercising her agential capacity, but that capacity's limit, where the inability to taste after so many hours engenders a different relationship to her body, to embodied pleasure. My preoccupation with sweetness, and what I imagine to be Tolentino's preoccupation with it, is contradicted by the moment Tolentino describes, when sweetness becomes "the least thing," and what comes first is the matter of it going on and into her body, covering "the place where you would actually taste." Sweetness is overtaken by inappropriate quantity, yet there is still some orientation to pleasure, tethered to Pigpen, by a string.

This pleasure in the consumption of too much honey is found in that inappropriate quantity of "more," which, as Ianna Hawkins Owen writes, "unfold[s] in excess of its bounded social role."[18] Owen considers the unknowable quantity of "more" in the relationship between asexuality's nonsexual pleasures—the sentiment that one would rather have cake more than sex—and feedism's sexual pleasures drawn from eating. In both contexts, as well as in *HONEY*, "more" becomes "an antihierarchical framework to think about pleasure and appetite," according to "how much and how often rather than how good or how successful."[19] "More" honey becomes honey that relishes its own sweetness for too long, as a quantity of the spoiled, which, in its inappropriateness, seeks pleasure from and in its own deviance.

Tolentino's performance deviates from the ameliorative properties and palatability of honey. To me, it also spoils familiar, nostalgic, healing Asian American narratives about food and the social worlds it affords. I do not deny the importance and pleasures of such worlds, nor our appetites in and for them. But the timing of the tense yet luxurious relation between Tolentino and Pigpen alter such narratives, interrupting them with different enactments and expressions of nurturance and love, and what it feels like to be full but not whole. When watching *HONEY*, either standing or sitting down on the floor to watch, walking away and coming back again, I think about what it is that we do in attempts to make amends for the kinds of harm or disappointment we might cause by not showing up when someone is trying to feed us, by having to eat too much when we do.

What sticks is the feeling of a disproportionate appetite and the honey accumulating on the thread, clinging in and on Tolentino's throat, face, and body. The stickiness of the honey that stalls the tape recorders also jams up idealized notions of abundance, perverting plenitude with scenes of overconsumption as the expression of the desire to be in another's company for one's own sweet, selfish ends. Acts of feeding someone more, and the act of eating more of what someone feeds you, are bound to produce the lavishness of waste. Tolentino cannot eat all the honey Pigpen pours, and as the performance continues, the honey drips onto her arms, shoulders, chest, face, and legs, pooling beneath her feet. She becomes a glistening, golden figure, enveloped by the surplus of her spoilage, a body caught between preservation and saturation.

In October 2024, I saw Tolentino and Pigpen perform *HONEY* at Brown University, as a part of the Queer Durations symposium. Tolentino announced that this iteration of *HONEY* would be its last. Thus, another sweet, selfish end. The performance was a little over three hours. During past performances of *HONEY*, I had watched intermittently, leaving and coming back as the hours passed. This time, I stayed for the entire performance. Many people in the room did the same. Tolentino later told me that during the performance she felt like she was fighting. She said what kept her fighting was the thought of who was with her in the room. I do not think we, as an audience, alleviated her suffering. Rather, we became a part of her suffering because she suffered to be in relation to us. The world revolves around her, and her world spins outward. She is not fighting against the duration of the performance so much as she is fighting to stay in it, with Pigpen and with us. What Tolentino endures throughout the performance is the experience of alternating between the Ptolemaic and Copernican cosmologies, between the strangerness of one's self and the strangerness of others.

At the end of this final performance, Pigpen climbed down from above, wrapped Tolentino in a blanket and towel, took her hands, and led her to a chair. Awash in warm light, Tolentino glowed as she wordlessly wiped her face with a towel. After she had cleaned her face and hands, Tolentino and Pigpen stood up and held hands as people applauded. Everyone exited the room and turned away from the honey, leaving it behind, sitting in the shallow bin where Tolentino had stood. The excess had been abandoned. When giving and taking "more" becomes too much, there is the matter of letting go. Over the years, I think this is what I have learned from Tolentino's sweet, selfish ends, lying in the glimmering path of her orbit, and everything that revolves around her for a time. This path and these golden dregs of globes are what I leave here with you, from the openness of a wound that never quite heals.

NOTES

INTRODUCTION

1. On beauty as that which we turn to in order to make sense of and move through crisis and catastrophe, see Nguyen, *Promise of Beauty*.

2. I am thinking with Cato Ouyang's single-channel video *THREE BETRAYALS* (2021), which was a part of their exhibition of the same name that included *Scorn of God* and *Kicked Madonna*, shown at No Place Gallery in Columbus, Ohio, January 15, 2021–March 5, 2022. In their press release for their exhibition *forgive everything* at Night Gallery in Los Angeles, November 12, 2022–January 21, 2023, which they describe as a sequel to *THREE BETRAYALS*, Ouyang invites us to think of betrayal "not only as a violation of trust, but as a generative act that passes forth and thus preserves information." Ouyang, *THREE BETRAYALS*, 2021; Ouyang, *forgive everything*, 2023.

3. Sexton, "In Excelsis."

4. Sexton, "In Excelsis."

5. Barbara Johnson reads this well-known line from John Keats's "Ode on a Grecian Urn" as pointing to the aesthetic value ascribed to a woman whose illegible yet seductive muteness renders her violation indistinguishable from her pleasure. See Johnson, "Muteness Envy."

6. I am thinking of Jillian Hernandez's work on the aesthetics of excess, as that which adorns the racialized, gendered bodies of Black and Latina women. Hernandez, *Aesthetics of Excess*.

7. Goffman, *Stigma*, 5. Also see Heather Love on midcentury sociology's study of deviance and queer theory. Love, *Underdogs*.

8. See Love, "Spoiled Identity," in *Feeling Backward.*

9. I am thinking of Veruca's appearance in the 1971 film *Willy Wonka and the Chocolate Factory* (dir. Mel Stuart), adapted from Roald Dahl's 1964 children's novel. Played by Julie Dawn Cole, Veruca sings the musical number "I Want It Now."

10. Evelyn Hammonds argues that Black feminist theorists need to reclaim Black women's bodies and Black women's sexuality via a "politics of articulation" in the face of what Evelyn Brooks Higginbotham describes as a "politics of silence" and what Darlene Clark Hines calls a "culture of dissemblance." In the nineteenth century, strategies of silence and dissemblance offered a means of combating negative stereotypes as well as claiming Black women's dignity and personhood. However, as Hammonds writes, both sedimented in the twentieth century into a heteronormative respectability politics that has limited Black women's expression as desiring sexual subjects. See Hammonds, "Black (W)holes"; Higginbotham, "African-American Women's History"; Hine, "Rape and the Inner Lives."

11. For Freud, "the polymorphously perverse disposition" is that of the child's, whose "mental dams against sexual excesses—shame, disgust and morality—have either not yet been constructed at all or are only in course of construction, according to the age of the child." He continues, "In this respect children behave in the same kind of way as an average uncultivated woman in whom the same polymorphously perverse disposition persists" (57). Freud, *Three Essays*, 57.

12. In the film *Willy Wonka and the Chocolate Factory*, Veruca's musical number ends with her falling down a garbage chute—"Where all the other bad eggs go," Willy Wonka explains. In the tradition of bad eggs, the band Veruca Salt's first 1994 single, "Seether," personifies an uncontrollable temper as a girl you cannot fight or see "till I'm foaming at the mouth."

13. In J M de Leon's dissertation "'Let Me Listen to Me,'" self-indulgence is a survival strategy for non-normative subjects, in which value is conferred on the subject in the face of its devaluation within regulatory structures of power. Here I am interested in forms of indulgence that trouble affirmations of the subject, to the extent that the subject cannot be sure of what it can call proper to itself. De Leon, "'Let Me Listen to Me.'"

14. Manalansan, "'Stuff' of Archives"; Vargas, "Ruminations on Lo Sucio."

15. Stallings, *Funk the Erotic*, xii.

16. On queer negativity, see Bersani, *Homos*; Bersani, *Is the Rectum a Grave?*; Edelman, *No Future.*

17. Saketopoulou, *Sexuality Beyond Consent*, 180–83.

18. The exhibition included Ouyang's installation, *otherwise, spite: 1. whores at the end of the world / 2. from every drop of his blood another demon arose (1829–1840)* (2020), inspired by a nineteenth-century colonial sketch of an attack on travelers by Indian "Thugs," as well as their series *Terrarium* (2017), consisting of sculptures imagining the lotus foot of their great-grandmother hand-carved from varieties of stone like alabaster and soapstone. Ouyang and I talk about *otherwise, spite* in an interview published in April 2023. Kim Lee, "Finding One Another in Recognition."

19. Lim, "Wonder Woman," 25.

20. Lim, "Wonder Woman," 25.

21. Lim, "Wonder Woman," 25.

22. Lim, "Wonder Woman," 25.

23. Lim, "Wonder Woman," 26.

24. My skepticism around *Wonder Women* does not mark the first time a group exhibition of Asian American artists has received scrutiny or critique from Asian American and non–Asian American viewers alike. Susette Min offers a historical account of the curation, organization, and reception of group exhibitions of Asian American artists at major art institutions in the United States throughout the 1990s and early 2000s. She documents how these exhibitions spoke to the shifting, contradictory interests and investments of museums, curators, artists, critics, and viewers over time. The exhibitions, and the artists they included, make evident the differences between generations of Asian American artists, which I address in this introduction. See Min, "Unnamable Encounters," in *Unnamable*.

25. Huang, *Surface Relations*, 28. I am also thinking of Laura Hyun Yi Kang's critical reading of Mitsuye Yamada's essay "Invisibility Is an Unnatural Disaster." See Kang, *Compositional Subjects*; Yamada, "Invisibility Is an Unnatural Disaster."

26. Huang, *Surface Relations*, 28.

27. Press release for *Wonder Women* at Jeffrey Deitch New York, May 7–June 25, 2022, https://deitch.com/new-york/exhibitions/wonder-women-curated-by-kathy-huang.

28. Kang, *Compositional Subjects*, 5. Kang writes that "Asian American woman" and "Asian woman" have become objects of knowledge that lend authority to academic disciplines, as well as to modes of regulation, surveillance, protection, and adjudication in US foreign policy, immigration laws, and intergovernmental organizations. Also see Kang, *Traffic in Asian Women*.

29. Zuo, *Vulgar Beauty*, 17.

30. Saketopoulou, *Sexuality Beyond Consent*, 2. I am also referring to the way Freud's theorizations of the unconscious changed over time. As Saketopoulou points out, Freud initially understood the unconscious as the container for repressed memories of trauma, which, through treatment—the "working through" of traumatic memory—could be cured. Later, Freud came to believe—as he posited in his writing about transference between analysand and analyst—that the unconscious cannot be done away with but instead always resurfaces. Saketopoulou, *Sexuality Beyond Consent*, 4–5. Also see Freud, "Remembering, Repeating, and Working Through"; Freud, "Observations on Transference-Love."

31. Doyle, *Hold It Against Me*.

32. Livien Yin (@livienyin), "'Dreaming Host' was on view at Wonder Women."

33. Eng and Han, *Racial Melancholia, Racial Dissociation*. Elsewhere, erin Khuê Ninh has mined the psychic and social pressures of the immigrant nuclear Asian American family and the model minority myth. While the former paradigmatically produces the docile, hardworking daughter driven to madness, bitterness, and even suicide due to her feelings of indebtedness and inadequacy, the latter drives some Asian Americans college students, as impostors, to violence. See Ninh, *Ingratitude*; Ninh, *Passing for Perfect*.

34. See Shimakawa, *National Abjection*; Eng, *Racial Castration*; Cheng, *Melancholy of Race*.

35. Khúc, *dear elia*, 5. Mimi Khúc also edited a collaborative hybrid art project, curated by erin Khuê Ninh, Eliza Noh, Tamara Ho, and Long Bui, titled "Open in Emergency: A Special Issue on Asian American Health," and published through the *Asian American Literary Review* in 2016. An expanded second edition followed in 2019. See Khúc, "Open in Emergency."

36. On anticure politics, see Clare, *Brilliant Imperfection*. Also see Kim, *Curative Violence*.

37. Lee, *Pedagogies of Woundedness*, 8. See also Chen et al., "Work Will Not Save Us."

38. Baik et al., "To Write in Unwellness," 494.

39. Baik et al., "To Write in Unwellness," 495.

40. Hedva, *How to Tell When We Will Die*, 29.

41. See Rivera, *Model Minority Masochism*.

42. Eng and Han, *Racial Melancholia, Racial Dissociation*, 19.

43. Johnson, "Nothing Fails Like Success," 16.

44. Johnson, "Nothing Fails Like Success," 16.

45. Sedgwick, "Paranoid Reading," in *Touching Feeling*, 128.

46. Sedgwick, "Paranoid Reading," 128.

47. Sedgwick, "Paranoid Reading," 128.

48. Sedgwick, "Paranoid Reading," 128.

49. Klein, "Love, Guilt and Reparation," 312.

50. Sedgwick, "Paranoid Reading," 128.

51. See Wilson, *Gut Feminism*; Berlant and Edelman, *Sex, or the Unbearable*; Love, "Truth and Consequences," 236.

52. Sedgwick, "Paranoid Reading," 149.

53. Eng and Han, *Racial Melancholia, Racial Dissociation*, 58.

54. See Eng and Han, *Racial Melancholia, Racial Dissociation*; Love, "Truth and Consequences"; Chambers-Letson, "Homegrown Terror"; Wilson, *Gut Feminism*; Chambers-Letson, "Reparative Feminisms"; Diaz, "Melancholic Maladies."

55. Wilson, *Gut Feminism*, 71.

56. Eng, "Colonial Object Relations," 11.

57. Eng, "Colonial Object Relations," 11.

58. Stuelke, *Ruse of Repair*, 17.

59. Stuelke, *Ruse of Repair*, 17.

60. Stuelke, *Ruse of Repair*, 4.

61. Eng, "Reparations and the Human," 582. See Jacques Derrida, *On Cosmopolitanism and Forgiveness*. Eng also turns to Judith Butler's work on forgiveness; see Butler, *Giving an Account of Oneself*.

62. Eng, "Reparations and the Human," 583.

63. Klein, "Study of Envy and Gratitude," 212, 213.

64. Ngai, *Ugly Feelings*, 128.

65. Ngai, *Ugly Feelings*, 129.

66. Hong, *Minor Feelings*, 3.

67. Hong, *Minor Feelings*, 4.

68. Hong, *Minor Feelings*, 5.

69. Hong, *Minor Feelings*, 6.

70. Hong, *Minor Feelings*, 7.

71. Chin and Chan, "Racist Love"; Rivera, *Model Minority Masochism*, xxv.

72. Eng and Han, *Racial Melancholia, Racial Dissociation*, 3.

73. Hong, *Minor Feelings*, 9–10.

74. Hong, *Minor Feelings*, 29.

75. Hong, *Minor Feelings*, 55; see also Ngai, *Ugly Feelings*.

76. Chang, "Poet Pundit."

77. In *The Protestant Ethnic*, Rey Chow critiques Georg Lukács's argument that modernist narratives of violence posit a binary relation between captivity and emancipation in which humanity, at first held captive under a primitive barbarism, progresses toward an emancipatory modern civilization. Chow writes, "If captivity itself is a historical, discursive construct—in what may be termed a modernist imaginary—then the idea of resistance that is hitherto considered such a natural and logical, because 'human,' response to captivity would also need to be rehistoricized as a modernist invention" (39). Chow, *Protestant Ethnic*.

78. As an alternative to understanding racial feeling as the provenance of racialized subjects, Jeffrey Santa Ana turns to the ways Euro-American or white feelings of happiness that bolster ideals of liberal personhood and individualism are contingent on the denigration, use, and objectification of Asian Americans, as figures who represent capital accumulation and labor abstraction. See Santa Ana, *Racial Feelings*.

79. Song, quoted by Chang, "Poet Pundit."

80. Liu, *Feeling Asian American*, 6.

81. Liu, *Feeling Asian American*, 2–3.

82. See Muñoz, "Feeling Brown, Feeling Down."

83. Muñoz, "'Chico, What Does It Feel Like to Be a Problem?,'" in *Sense of Brown*, 36.

84. Scholarship on queer temporality in the early 2000s overlapped with the affective turn, addressing what it felt like to live out of time, behind the times, and in another time, in ways that felt dissonant, out of touch, and mismatched with one's present. See Cvetkovich, *Archive of Feelings*; Halberstam, *In a Queer Time and Place*; Luciano, *Arranging Grief*; Love, *Feeling Backward*; Muñoz, *Cruising Utopia*; Freeman, *Time Binds*; Dinshaw, *How Soon Is Now?*; Cvetkovich, *Depression*.

85. Berlant, *Female Complaint*, 20.

86. Berlant, *Female Complaint*, viii.

87. See Zauner, *Crying in H Mart*; Shi, *Turning Red*; Song, *Past Lives*; Sung Jin, *Beef*.

88. See Mayer and Park, *Feeling Asian*, https://www.feelingasian.com/about.

89. See Mayer and Park, *Feeling Asian*.

90. See Kwan and Scheinert, *Everything Everywhere All at Once*; Zornosa, "How 'Everything Everywhere All at Once' Helps"; Koul, "I Made My Mom."

91. Zornosa, "How 'Everything Everywhere All at Once' Helps." For some, the film also offered a meaningful representation of the experience of having ADHD. Fisher, "Everything Everywhere All at Once."

92. Dango, *Crisis Style*, 7.

93. Muñoz, "'Chico, What Does It Feel Like to Be a Problem?,'" 40.

94. Muñoz, "'Chico, What Does It Feel Like to Be a Problem?,'" 40.

95. Cathy Park Hong describes getting angry with a young Asian nail technician giving her a pedicure, who accidentally (but was it? Her paranoid mind races) burned her with hot water, clipped her toes, and tore her cuticles. Hong, *Minor Feelings*, 11–12.

96. See Winnicott, "The Roots of Aggression."

97. See León, "Forms of Opacity"; Mengesha and Padmanabhan, "Introduction to *Performing Refusal/Refusal to Perform*"; Chung, "Defiant Still Worker"; Léon, "Curious Entanglements"; Yao, *Disaffected*; Huang, *Surface Relations*; Post, *Deadpan*.

98. Winnicott, "Hate in the Counter-Transference," 350. Winnicott's essay addresses the need for analysts to become conscious of their own hatred in the treatment of patients.

99. I am referring to Shoshana Felman's reading of analytic pedagogy and didactic analysis as "the interminable task." See Felman, "Psychoanalysis and Education," 35.

100. Viet Thanh Nguyen describes an "economy of narrative plenitude" as the proliferation of Asian American stories and representations that would counter "the economy of narrative scarcity," wherein a film like *Crazy Rich Asians* (2018), for example, could afford to be "mediocre," rather than a film that must be exceptionally good (or bad). This mediocrity, then, is a "luxury." Nguyen, "Asian-Americans Need More Movies, Even Mediocre Ones."

101. Nguyen, "Asian-Americans Need More Movies, Even Mediocre Ones."

102. On the ways insurgent modes of articulating minoritized difference have been incorporated into the university and the workplace by way of conditional inclusion, administration, and management, see Gordon, "Work of Corporate Culture"; Gordon and Newfield, *Mapping Multiculturalism*; Ahmed, *On Being Included*; Ferguson, *Reorder of Things*.

103. Chuh, "Asians Are the New . . . What?," 223.

104. Pew Research Center, "Rise of Asian Americans."

105. Chuh, "Asians Are the New . . . What?," 226. Relatedly, Takeo Rivera argues that the figure of the model minority cannot be dispelled as a myth because it has played a crucial role in forming Asian American subjectivities, whether embraced via a self-subjugating relation to capital and whiteness, or disavowed via self-punishment and an aspiration to an idealized blackness. Rivera, *Model Minority Masochism*.

106. Chuh, "Asians Are the New . . . What?," 222, 223.

107. Chuh, "Asians Are the New . . . What?," 224.

108. See Nguyen, *Race and Resistance*; Koshy, "Morphing Race into Ethnicity;" Lee, *Semblance of Identity*. It is worth also mentioning Nick Mitchell's critique of the figure of the critical intellectual, who bolsters ethnic studies' institutionalization within the university and is imagined as a radical figure pitted against the institution while securing that very institution's image of itself. Mitchell, "(Critical Ethnic Studies) Intellectual."

109. I have written elsewhere about how one's areas of study determine how one chooses their objects, and I have tried to see what might happen when one decides, from within one's own area of study, to choose someone else's object instead. See Kim Lee, "Introduction."

110. Chuh, *Imagine Otherwise*, 9.

111. For a critique of "aboutness," see Chuh, "It's Not About Anything."

112. Min, *Unnamable*, 3.

113. Susette Min notes that although the term "Asian American" can trace its origins to radical social movements in the late 1960s and '70s, intertwined with the field of Asian American studies, it was not until the late 1980s and '90s that "Asian American art" was named and exhibited as such in major art institutions. Min, *Unnamable*, 16. Before that, there was the Asian American community arts movement of the late 1960s and '70s, founded and influenced by the Basement Workshop in New York City (which included the folk band Yellow Pearl), the Kearney Street Workshop in San Francisco, and the Japantown Art and Media Workshop in San Francisco. In her catalog essay for *One Way or Another: Asian American Art Now*—a 2006 exhibition at the Asia Society in New York City cocurated by Min, Melissa Chiu, and Karin Higa—Min writes, "The naming or categorizing of art as Asian American began as a historical and sociopolitical project to challenge racial oppression, secure parity of representation, and represent the specificities and contributions of the Asian American experience." Min, "Last Asian American Exhibition," 35. Also see Machida, *Unsettled Visions*.

114. Song, *Children of 1965*, 8. This was noticeable in the framing around the group exhibition *One Way or Another: Asian American Art Now*, which featured artists representative of a new generation of Asian Americans born both in and outside the United States between 1966 and 1980. In her essay for the exhibition catalog, journalist Helen Zia writes that for the post-1965 generations of Asian Americans, "the social attitude is significantly more visible and affirmative to their Asian Americanness." Zia, "Asian American," 13. For Min, also in the exhibition catalog, "What characterizes much of their art, as distinguished from its predecessors in the 1990s, is a *freedom* to pick, choose, manipulate, and reinvent different kinds of languages and issues, both formal and political." Min, "Last Asian American Exhibition," 36.

115. On the post-1965 boom in Asian American literature, see Song, *Children of 1965*. In the 1990s, notable sites of Asian American artistic production included group exhibitions of Asian American artists. The group exhibition *Asia/America: Identities in Contemporary Asian American Art*, at the Asia Society in 1994, preceded *One Way or Another: Asian American Art Now*, also at the Asia Society, in 2006. Additionally, there was the group exhibition *The Curio Shop* at Artists Space in New York City in 1993—organized by the Asian American art collective Godzilla, founded in New York City—and *Uncommon Traits: Re/Locating Asia* (1997–98) at the CEPA Gallery in Buffalo, New York. Throughout the 1990s, gender- and race-specific group exhibitions started appearing in major art institutions in the United States. These exhibitions overlapped with, and directly spoke to, artists and organizations forming coalitions and collectives putting pressure on art institutions, calling for more inclusivity in the art world. Exhibitions of note include: *The Decade Show: Frameworks of Identity in the 1980s* (1990) in New York City, presented at the Museum of Contemporary Hispanic Art, the New Museum of Contemporary Art, and the Studio Museum in Harlem (1990), and the 1993 Whitney Biennial at the Whitney Museum in New York City. On the history of race- and ethnic-specific group exhibitions, particularly in relation to Asian American art

and its curation and reception, see Min, "Unnamable Encounters." On the art collective Godzilla and *The Curio Shop*, see Chen, *Godzilla*. On *Uncommon Traits*, see Marilyn Jung et al., *Uncommon Traits*.

116. In February 2024, I attended a panel at the Institute of Contemporary Arts, Los Angeles (ICA LA), with artists Patty Chang, Vishal Jugdeo, and Miljohn Ruperto, moderated by Anuradha Vikram. The panel was organized in conjunction with the group exhibition *Scratching at the Moon*, cocurated by artist Anna Sew Hoy and Anne Ellegood, described as "the first focused survey of Asian American artists in a major Los Angeles contemporary art museum." ICA LA, *Scratching at the Moon*, accessed February 20, 2025, https://www.theicala.org/en/exhibitions/133-scratching-at-the-moon. During the panel, the artists and the moderator acknowledged that they were a part of the same generation. (Although Hoy did not speak at this panel, she is also a part of the same generation.) When discussing their experience of making work in the 1990s, they recalled how their work was not initially read as Asian American art and how the naming of their work as such felt retroactive, and to some extent still did, at the panel itself. I did not read their conversation as a resistance to the moniker but more so an attempt to make sense of their experience as it converged and diverged from recent historicizations of Asian American art. See Ellegood and Hoy, *Scratching at the Moon*.

117. Chiang, *Cultural Capital*.

118. Eng and Han, *Racial Melancholia, Racial Dissociation*, 178.

119. As one example, an article in the *New York Times* from 2022 reported the efforts of faculty and students at Dartmouth College to build an Asian American studies program. To make a case for the field's relevancy and exigency, faculty and students addressed anti-Asian violence and discrimination while also communicating to the administration that, though Asian Americans' presence on college campuses continues to grow, Asian Americans are still a minority group. See Kambhampaty, "Fight for Asian American Studies."

120. Eng and Han, *Racial Melancholia, Racial Dissociation*, 179.

121. Foucault, *History of Sexuality*, 59.

122. Chow, *Face Drawn in Sand*, 145.

123. Chow, *Face Drawn in Sand*, 150.

124. Chow, *Face Drawn in Sand*, 150.

125. Chow, *Face Drawn in Sand*, 152. Here, "voicing bitterness" is Chow's translation of *suku*, "a kind of speech act that lowly peasants in Communist China were once encouraged actively to practice" (152).

126. Berlant, *Female Complaint*, vii.

127. Berlant, *Female Complaint*, 1.

128. Chow, *Face Drawn in Sand*, 19.

129. Muñoz, "Teaching, Minoritarian Knowledge, and Love," 119.

130. Muñoz, "Teaching, Minoritarian Knowledge, and Love," 119.

131. Cheng, *Ornamentalism*.

132. Cheng, *Ornamentalism*; Chen, *Animacies*; Shimakawa, *National Abjection*; Shah, *Contagious Divides*.

133. Huang, *Surface Relations*; Kang, *Compositional Subjects*; Hayot, *Hypothetical Mandarin*; Sohn, "Introduction."

134. Fung, "Looking for My Penis." Also see Huang, *Surface Relations*; Zuo, *Vulgar Beauty*; Cheng, *Ornamentalism*; Nguyen, *View from the Bottom*; Shimizu, *Hypersexuality of Race*; Eng, *Racial Castration*.

135. Ngai, *Ugly Feelings*, 182.

136. Amin et al., "Queer Form," 230.

137. Sedgwick, *Touching Feeling*, 3. Also quoted by Amin et al., "Queer Form," 230.

138. Sedgwick, *Touching Feeling*, 13.

139. Hong and Ferguson, "Introduction," 18. Additionally, Lisa Lowe attributes the limits of theorizing and thinking about "difference"—which, as she sees it, can sometimes feel like an exhausted and banal term—to comparative methods of analysis with origins in Max Weber's interpretative sociology that operated according to a preexisting "ideal type" of "rational action" within Western modern society, against which all else is measured. See Lowe, "Insufficient Difference," 410.

140. Musser, *Sensational Flesh*, 1; Moraga and Anzaldúa, "Entering the Lives of Others," 23.

141. Ngai, *Ugly Feelings*, 188.

142. Rancière, *Dissensus*.

143. Chuh, *Difference Aesthetics Makes*, 3.

144. Amin, *Disturbing Attachments*, 11.

145. Amin, *Disturbing Attachments*, 10.

146. Amin, *Disturbing Attachments*, 10.

147. Love, *Underdogs*, 17.

148. Edwards, "Ethnics of Surrealism," 96.

149. Edwards, "Ethnics of Surrealism," 96, 109.

150. Tompkins, "Crude Matter," 264.

151. Edwards, "Ethnics of Surrealism," 109. In his review of Yve-Alain Bois and Rosalind Krauss's *Formless: A User's Guide*, Edwards distinguishes *informe* from Julia Kristeva's theorization of abjection. While abjection implies the return of what has been repressed and jettisoned from the self, *informe* names waste that is in excess of systems of meaning. Edwards, "Ethnics of Surrealism," 109. See also Krauss, "Destiny of the *Informe*."

152. Tompkins, "Crude Matter," 264–65.

CHAPTER 1. STAYING IN

A version of chapter 1 appeared in "Staying In: Mitski, Ocean Vuong, and Asian American Asociality," *Social Text* 37, no. 1 (2019): 27–50, https://doi.org/10.1215/01642472-7286252.

1. Miyawaki, "Your Best American Girl."

2. Miyawaki, "Your Best American Girl."

3. On the confessional voice in singer-songwriter/popular music, see Dougher, "Authenticity, Gender, and Personal Voice."

4. Nersessian, *Keats's Odes*, 16.

5. Vuong, "Ode to Masturbation" (video).

6. Vuong, "Ode to Masturbation" (video).

7. McAdory, "Gay Sincerity Is Scary."

8. Vuong, "Ode to Masturbation," in *Night Sky with Exit Wounds*, 61.

9. I cannot help thinking of Tony Tulathimutte's short story "Ahegao, or, The Ballad of Sexual Repression" and its protagonist, Kant, a sadist who describes a pornographic fantasy in excruciating detail, wherein he, more or less, takes over the world with his insatiable desire. See Tulathimutte, "Ahegao."

10. See Freud, "On Narcissism"; Freud, *Three Essays*.

11. Freud, *Three Essays*, 47–49.

12. In psychoanalyst Wilhelm Stekel's study of autoeroticism, he disagrees with Sigmund Freud by positing that a child's masturbation is not followed by a period of latency, as that which should be given up or else a symptom of neurosis. Instead, a person continues to masturbate throughout their adult life with brief pauses now and then (as opposed to with a pathological compulsiveness). For Stekel, masturbation is not neurotic, whereas abstinence from it is. Stekel, *Auto-eroticism*.

13. Phillips, *One Way and Another*, 143.

14. Phillips, *One Way and Another*, 130.

15. Gopinath, *Impossible Desires*, 14.

16. I am thinking of Adriana Cavarero's work on inclination as a feminized position and ethical form. See Cavarero, *Inclinations*.

17. Scott, "Evidence of Experience."

18. Nguyen, "Blunt-Force Ethnic Credibility."

19. For scholarship on Ocean Vuong's work in relation to his own personal experience, placed within a broader historical context of the Vietnamese diaspora and the afterlives of the Vietnam War, see Nguyen, "Queering Telemachus"; Chavez and Lin, "Faithful Work of Drowning.'"

20. See Mercer, "Black Art."

21. On "modern peculiarity," see Zimmer, "Origins of 'Relatable'"; on "scourge," see Mead, "Scourge of 'Relatability'"; Orange, "And This Is Word for Word."

22. Zimmer, "Origins of 'Relatable.'"

23. Garber, "Relatable," 113–14.

24. Mead, "Scourge of 'Relatability.'"

25. Glavey, "Having a Coke," 997.

26. Garber, "Relatable," 115.

27. Mead, "Scourge of 'Relatability.'"

28. Salisbury, "Relatable," 1157.

29. Laura Salisbury suggests that such fantasies are not far off from what Lauren Berlant calls the good life at the center of cruel optimism, wherein relatability promises that what one needs—what will make one feel affirmed—is readily within one's grasp at the same time that it is always just out of reach. There's the good life, and there's the good object, or good text, too. Salisbury, "Relatable," 1157. See also Berlant, *Cruel Optimism*.

30. I find it amusing that Rebecca Mead and Marjorie Garber address the use of "relatable" in a post on Twitter (now X) by the public radio host and producer Ira Glass, who is himself known for popularizing another iteration of the therapeutic confession with his radio show, *This American Life*. After seeing a production of *King Lear* at Shakespeare

in the Park starring actor John Lithgow in July 2014, Glass posted, "@JohnLithgow as Lear tonight: amazing. Shakespeare: not good. No stakes, not relatable. I think I'm realizing: Shakespeare sucks." See Mead, "Scourge of 'Relatability'"; Garber, "Relatable."

31. North, "Should Literature Be 'Relatable'?"

32. Mead, "Scourge of 'Relatability'"; Onion, "Awful Emptiness of 'Relatable.'"

33. Garber is not taking issue with her students, so much as she takes issue with how the academy's division of fields, particularly in its distribution of curricular requirements that silo fields from one another (such as the sciences from the humanities), have a hand in determining what is relatable to which students and their studies.

34. Garber, "Relatable," 125.

35. Glavey, "Having a Coke," 996.

36. Glavey, "Having a Coke," 996.

37. Dancer, "Being Kathy H."

38. Glavey, "Having a Coke," 999.

39. Tongson, *Relocations*, 23.

40. O'Hara, "Having a Coke with You," in *Collected Poems*, 360.

41. O'Hara, "Having a Coke with You," 360.

42. José Esteban Muñoz reads O'Hara's poem alongside Andy Warhol's silk screens and drawings of Coke bottles. Muñoz quotes Andy Warhol: "A Coke is a Coke and no amount of money can get you a better Coke than the one the bum on the corner is drinking. All the Cokes are the same and all the Cokes are good." Muñoz, *Cruising Utopia*, 7–8.

43. Chiu, "Conversation on Today's Asian America," 28.

44. Musser, *Sensual Excess*, 4–5. Musser is in conversation with Alexander Weheliye's *Habeas Viscus*, where hunger is "not about the possibility of fulfillment or nurturance." She writes, "This form of hunger, I argue, is constitutive of a type of selfhood that coalesces—even as it gnaws at the edges—in this state of openness and insatiability." See Weheliye, *Habeas Viscus*, 5.

45. Oishi, "Interview with Patty Chang," 128.

46. Oishi, "Interview with Patty Chang,"125.

47. Musser, *Sensual Excess*, 139.

48. Freud, "On Narcissism," 90–91.

49. Bersani and Phillips, *Intimacies*, 43; Dean, *Unlimited Intimacy*. Leo Bersani and Adam Phillips propose that the "impersonality of mothering, one might say, is the precursor, the precondition of an impersonal narcissism." Bersani and Phillips, *Intimacies*, 104.

50. Bersani and Phillips, *Intimacies*, 107.

51. On Marina Abramovic's *The Onion* and tears, see Doyle, *Hold It Against Me*, 85–86.

52. Oishi, "Interview with Patty Chang," 124.

53. Oishi, "Interview with Patty Chang," 124–25.

54. Rey Chow writes about the "the pattern of a thwarted narcissism" (143) of autobiographical writing in contemporary ethnic literature, wherein narcissism, as a kind of "self-regard" that operates as a form of social belonging, is always already a lost object, and as such, becomes the source of a self-regard that turns into a "self-hatred—into just

another round of internalization of the exclusion [the self] experiences from society at large" (143). See Chow, *Protestant Ethnic.*

55. Oishi, "Interview with Patty Chang," 124.

56. Chang, quoted by Cheung, "Abject, Exposed, and Potential Desires," 64.

57. Amin, *Disturbing Attachments*, 6.

58. Berlant, *Cruel Optimism*, 4.

59. Berlant, *Cruel Optimism*, 10.

60. Yapp, "Feeling Down(town Julie Brown)," 6.

61. Amin, *Disturbing Attachments*, 4.

62. For scholarship that mines the relation between Asian bodies/subjects, racial form, and labor, see Day, *Alien Capital*; Manalansan, "Servicing the World"; Lye, *America's Asia*; Kang, *Compositional Subjects.*

63. Huang, *Surface Relations*, 54; Prashad, *Karma of Brown Folk*, 6.

64. Harney and Moten, *Undercommons*, 26.

65. Wiegman, *Object Lessons*, 6.

66. See Nguyen, *Race and Resistance*; Chiang, *Cultural Capital.*

67. Demers, "@mitskileaks how do u feel."

68. Miyawaki, "I prefer to go alone."

69. Miyawaki, "you can go to shows alone!"

70. I am referring to Shane Vogel's reading of Lena Horne's "impersona." See Vogel, *Scene of Harlem Cabaret.*

71. Ao, "Distant Mitski."

72. Ao, "Distant Mitski."

73. Eng and Han, "Dialogue on Racial Melancholia," 351.

74. Eng and Han, "Dialogue on Racial Melancholia," 351.

75. I am thinking of the lawsuit against Harvard University filed in 2014 by the right-wing nonprofit organization Students for Fair Admissions (SFFA), which accused Harvard of using affirmative action admission policies that discriminate against Asian American and white students. The case was brought to the US Supreme Court in 2021, alongside another lawsuit filed by SFFA against the University of North Carolina for its affirmative action admission policies. Both lawsuits were argued before the court in October 2022. The cases were decided in June 2023, with the court ruling that affirmative action admission policies at both schools were unconstitutional under the Equal Protection Clause of the Fourteenth Amendment. As a part of the initial Harvard lawsuit, records of the admissions process showed that while Asian American students scored the highest out of other racial and ethnic groups on grades, test scores, and extracurricular activities, they scored lower with regard to personal traits. Much like the concerns around not being "well-rounded," Asian American students were perceived as, ultimately, less relatable. It is troubling yet important to mention how the relatability of Asian American students—or lack thereof—was used by SFFA for the purposes of asserting and protecting white students' privilege at the expense of Black and Latinx students. Given this, rather than insist on Asian Americans' relatability, we should interrogate the category of relatability and how it is constituted in relation to, and by way of, whiteness. See "Asian Americans Advancing Justice"; Hartocollis, "Asian-Americans Suing Harvard"; Hartocollis, "Harvard

Rated Asian-American Applicants"; Hartocollis and Saul, "Affirmative Action Battle"; Gersen, "Uncomfortable Truth."

76. See the now-broken link for the blog: asianssleepinginthelibrary.tumblr.com. Screenshots of the blog can be found here: "Asians Sleeping in the Library," Asian American TV.

77. *KoreAm Journal*, "Asians Sleeping in the Library."

78. I keep in mind the work of Kevin Quashie, Sarah Jane Cervenak, and Shoniqua Roach on the significance of and insistence on Black psychic interiority and Black privacy as quiet, wandering, and fugitive, particularly in the face of anti-Black imaginings of Black subjects that reduce them to the materiality and surface of the body. I write this acknowledging that while Asian American subjects in their perceived invisibility and racialized asociality can stay in, Black subjects, in their hypervisibility, subject to surveillance and policing, are not able to stay in, in the same way. See Quashie, *Sovereignty of Quiet*; Cervenak, *Wandering*; Roach, "Black Sex in the Quiet." See also Hilton, "Avonte's Law."

79. Vuong, "Someday I'll Love Ocean Vuong," in *New Yorker*.

80. O'Hara, "Katy," in *Collected Poems*, 242.

81. Reeves, "Someday I'll Love Roger Reeves," 73.

82. O'Hara, "Katy," 242.

83. O'Hara, "Katy," 242.

84. Vuong, "Someday I'll Love Ocean Vuong," in *Night Sky with Exit Wounds*, 82–83.

85. Vuong, "Someday I'll Love Ocean Vuong," 82–83.

86. Vuong, "Someday I'll Love Ocean Vuong," 82–83.

87. Nick Salvato writes about "cringe criticism," which emerges out of embarrassment, in conversation with Erving Goffman's study of embarrassment. See Salvato, *Obstruction*; Goffman, "Embarrassment and Social Organization."

88. Jennifer Doyle writes of performance artist Franko B's "bleeding performances" that present the "difficulty of sentimentality" insofar as they are both aggressive and earnest, provoking what Lauren Berlant calls the "countersentimental." Doyle, *Hold It Against Me*, 73, 82. Also see Berlant, *Female Complaint*, 56.

89. Mitski, quoted by Zoladz, "Mitski Is More than TikTok."

90. Miyawaki, "Working for the Knife."

91. Goffman, "Embarrassment and Social Organization," 268.

92. Goffman, "Embarrassment and Social Organization," 266.

93. Goffman, "Embarrassment and Social Organization," 266.

94. Han and Hsu, "jas lin in Conversation."

95. Goffman, "Embarrassment and Social Organization," 267.

96. Goffman, "Embarrassment and Social Organization," 268.

97. See Brazil, "Whatever Happened to Queer Happiness"; McAdory, "Gay Sincerity Is Scary."

98. On tact, see Russell, *Tact*.

99. In her 2022 profile of Mitski, Lindsay Zoladz writes of Mitski's newfound "social media stardom," particularly on TikTok, which has led to fans getting upset with her when and if she attempts to express any "boundaries." See Zoladz, "Mitski Is More Than TikTok."

100. Zoladz, "Mitski Is More Than TikTok."

101. Miller, "Secret Subjects, Open Secrets," 18. Thank you to Tony Wei Ling for pointing me to this essay and this quotation.

CHAPTER 2. USING QUOTATIONS

An earlier iteration of chapter 2 appeared in "Borrowed Speech: Giving an Account of Another with Wu Tsang's Full Body Quotation," special issue, *ASAP/Journal* 6, no. 3 (2021): 679–706, https://doi.org/10.1353/asa.2021.0036.

1. McLuhan, *Understanding Media.*

2. I am thinking of Eve Kosofsky Sedgwick's axiom "People are different from each other." Sedgwick, *Epistemology of the Closet*, 22.

3. Muñoz, *Sense of Brown*, 138.

4. Hilderbrand, *Paris Is Burning*, 40–41.

5. Hilderbrand, *Paris Is Burning*, 27.

6. Hilderbrand, *Paris Is Burning*, 42.

7. Philbrick, *Group Works*, 25.

8. Tsang, quoted in Gonzalez, "Speech Acts," 26.

9. Cavarero, *For More Than One Voice*, 4. On the voice in relation to embodiment and techniques of ventriloquism and lip-synching in a performance and audiovisual context, see Chion, *Voice in Cinema*; Dolar, *Voice and Nothing More*. On the voice in music, in feminist critiques of sound studies' devaluation of the voice, as it is associated with the woman's body, see Fiol-Matta, *Great Woman Singer*; Vazquez, *Listening in Detail.*

10. Cavarero, *For More Than One Voice*, 6.

11. Cavarero, *For More Than One Voice*, 9.

12. Gonzalez, "Speech Acts," 26.

13. Pérez, "Proximity," 281–92.

14. In *Citizen*, Claudia Rankine writes, "it is difficult not to think that if Serena lost context by abandoning all rules of civility, it could be because of her body, trapped in a racial imaginary, trapped in disbelief—code for being black in America—is being governed not by the tennis match she is participating in but by a collapsed relationship that had promised to play by the rules. Perhaps this is how racism feels no matter the context—randomly the rules everyone else gets to play by no longer apply to you, and to call this out by calling out 'I swear to God!' is to be called insane, crass, crazy. Bad sportsmanship." Rankine, *Citizen*, 30.

15. Nyong'o, *Afro-Fabulations*, 2.

16. On the "diva tantrum," see Hilderbrand, *Paris Is Burning*, 47; on the "epic 'read,'" see Nyong'o, *Afro-Fabulations*, 2; and on LaBeija's handling of the cinematic gaze, see Nyong'o, *Afro-Fabulations*, 3.

17. Post, *Deadpan*, 4.

18. Gill-Peterson, *A Short History*, 23.

19. Prosser, *Second Skins*; Namaste, *Invisible Lives*; Heaney, *New Woman.*

20. Gill-Peterson, *Short History*, 124.

21. Heaney, *New Woman*, 5.

22. bell hooks, "Is Paris Burning?"

23. Butler, *Bodies That Matter*, 137.

24. Butler, *Bodies That Matter*, 137.

25. Butler, *Bodies That Matter*, 137.

26. Butler, "Critically Queer," in *Bodies That Matter*.

27. Gill-Peterson, *Short History*, 12.

28. Awkward-Rich, *Terrible We*, 3.

29. Awkward-Rich, *Terrible We*, 16.

30. Awkward-Rich, *Terrible We*, 6.

31. Awkward-Rich, *Terrible We*, 7. Cameron Awkward-Rich is in conversation with Rosemarie Garland-Thomson's conceptualization of "misfit." See Garland-Thomson, "Misfits."

32. Awkward-Rich, *Terrible We*, 120. On the "wrong body" model and trans studies critiques of it, see Prosser, *Second Skins*; Serano, *Whipping Girl*; Salamon, *Assuming a Body*; Bettcher, "Trapped in the Wrong Theory"; Meyerowitz, *How Sex Changed*; Heaney, *New Woman*.

33. Awkward-Rich, *Terrible We*, 6.

34. I am also thinking of what Hil Malatino calls "side affects," or the negative, bad feelings that persist within the "trans mundane." Malatino, *Side Affects*, 6.

35. Gill-Peterson, *Short History*, 20.

36. Gill-Peterson, *Short History*, 27.

37. Gill-Peterson, *Short History*, 12.

38. Harney and Moten, *Undercommons*, 61.

39. Awkward-Rich, *Terrible We*, 6.

40. Gonzalez, "Speech Acts," 27.

41. Green, "Paris Has Burned."

42. Rich, *New Queer Cinema*,

43. In 2019 the film was restored by the UCLA Film and Television Archive and released by the Criterion Collection as a Blu-Ray DVD with select footage from the archive.

44. Gonzalez, "Speech Acts," 27; Nyong'o, *Afro-Fabulations*, 7–9.

45. Mervosh et al., "Debate over Plagiarism."

46. Serpell, "Plagiarism thing."

47. Serpell, "I say this."

48. Wyma, "'I Dislike the Word Visibility.'"

49. Ahmed, "Feminist Shelters." Also see Ahmed, *Living a Feminist Life*.

50. McKittrick, *Dear Science*, 22.

51. McKittrick, *Dear Science*, 22.

52. McKittrick, *Dear Science*, 16.

53. Alexandra Vazquez writes of the aside within and between songs in live music performance. See Vazquez, "Salon Philosophers."

54. Nelson, *Argonauts*.

55. Nash, "Citational Desires."

56. Moraga, "Entering the Lives of Others," 23. Rich, "Notes Toward a Politics of Location"; Miller, "Untitled Work"; Butler, "Imitation and Gender Insubordination."

57. Smith, *Enacting Others*; Chen, "'Speaking Nearby'"; Alcoff, "Problem of Speaking for Others."

58. José Esteban Muñoz writes on Wu Tsang, and he, too, does not engage with her work to debate whether or not it is appropriative. Muñoz, "Sense of *Wildness*," in *Sense of Brown*. Meanwhile, Cathy Park Hong's reading of Tsang's *Wildness* is "hypercritical" of Tsang's guilt in contributing to the gentrification of the Silver Lake neighborhood in Los Angeles. Hong admits to how her hypercriticality "comes from a selfish place, since an artist's guilt is a contagion that I want to swat away so it doesn't infect me." Perhaps we might think of Tsang's work as purposively inhabiting that "selfish place," as a space of social contagion. Hong, *Minor Feelings*, 108.

59. Montez, *Keith Haring's Line*, 10.

60. Montez, *Keith Haring's Line*, 11.

61. Johnson, "Using People," 262.

62. Johnson, "Using People," 262.

63. Johnson, "Using People," 263. See Winnicott, *Playing and Reality*.

64. Johnson, "Using People," 265.

65. Johnson, "Using People," 273.

66. Tsang, *Wildness*.

67. Cheh, "Artists at Work."

68. Muñoz, "Sense of *Wildness*," 138.

69. On the racialized, gendered, classed constructions of "safe space," see Hanhardt, *Safe Space*.

70. Baggs, "In My Language."

71. Baggs, "In My Language."

72. Baggs, "In My Language."

73. Yergeau, *Authoring Autism*, 2.

74. Yergeau, *Authoring Autism*, 3.

75. Yergeau, *Authoring Autism*, 2.

76. Baggs, "In My Language."

77. Tsang, quoted in Wyma, "I Dislike the Word Visibility."

78. Tsang and Moten, "All Terror, All Beauty," 344.

79. Doyle, *Hold It Against Me*, 84.

80. Musser, *Sensual Excess*, 120.

81. Yergeau, *Authoring Autism*, 25, 176.

82. Glavey, "Lyric Wilt," 583.

83. Muñoz, "Teaching, Minoritarian Knowledge, and Love," 118.

84. Muñoz, "Teaching, Minoritarian Knowledge, and Love," 118.

85. Austin, quoted in Muñoz, "Teaching, Minoritarian Knowledge, and Love," 118. See Austin, *How to Do Things with Words*; Felman, *Scandal of the Speaking Body*.

86. Muñoz, "Teaching, Minoritarian Knowledge, and Love," 118.

87. Muñoz, "Teaching, Minoritarian Knowledge, and Love," 119.

88. Browning, *Gift*, 201.

89. Browning, *Gift*, 201.

90. Browning, *Gift*, 202.

91. Browning, *Gift*, 202. See Lauren Berlant's essay on the work of artist William Pope.L, titled "Showing Up to Withhold." I am also thinking of artist Riva Lehrer's mixed-media charcoal portrait of Berlant; see Lehrer and Berlant, *Risk Pictures*.

92. Lax, "Adjacencies," 38.

93. I am thinking of Mel Heberer's articulations of "the logic of Asians on Demand," which "renders Asian people, and sometimes even Asian states . . . into ready-made exemplars: a seamlessly accessible representational function, an on-demand figure set up to serve. . . . The Asian on Demand heralds a series of familiar and far-reaching expectations of *readiness on demand*, the expectation that Asians appear seamlessly accessible in ways that please and satisfy their audience—and to remain invisible otherwise." Heberer, *Asians on Demand*, 4.

94. Chuh, *Imagine Otherwise*, 8.

95. Huang, "Inscrutably, Actually," 192.

96. Lax, "Adjacencies," 39.

CHAPTER 3. COLD LEFTOVERS

1. Hwang, *M. Butterfly*, 4.

2. Hwang, *M. Butterfly*, 4.

3. Hwang, *M. Butterfly*, 94.

4. Chow, *Protestant Ethnic*, 66.

5. Bradley, *Anteaesthetics*, 96. In her theorizations of touch, Rizvana Bradley offers a reading of a quotation from Hortense Spillers included in artist Arthur Jafa's 2014 film *Dreams Are Colder Than Death*: "We were available in the flesh to slave masters. In the flesh. Immediate; hands on . . . I can pluck your little nappy head from wherever it is. Bang! . . . That's flesh." Spillers, quoted by Bradley, *Anteaesthetics*, 94.

6. Bradley, *Anteaesthetics*, 96.

7. I am thinking of Homay King's work on Orientalist tropes in Western film as enigmatic signifiers. See King, *Lost in Translation*.

8. Tompkins, "Crude Matter," 265.

9. Tompkins, "Crude Matter," 266.

10. Tompkins, "Crude Matter," 266.

11. For instance, Amy Sueyoshi considers the construction and denigration of the American "Oriental" as a pan–Asian American stereotype that bolsters white gender and sexual liberation in San Francisco at the turn of the twentieth century; see Sueyoshi, *Discriminating Sex*. Additionally, Fiona Ngô addresses how, during the Jazz Age of the 1920s and 1930s, white women cultivated their own imperial selfhood via Orientalist performances of Salomé and sheiks. See Ngô, "Orienting Subjectivities," in *Imperial Blues*.

12. Shimizu, *Hypersexuality of Race*, 6.

13. Huang, "Silence and Parasitic Hospitality," in *Surface Relations*.

14. Cheng, *Ornamentalism*, xii.

15. Cheng, *Ornamentalism*, x.

16. Cheng, *Ornamentalism*, 3, xii.

17. Cheng, *Ornamentalism*, 3. Cheng is referencing Allewaert, *Ariel's Ecology*. With regard to interstitial life, particularly in Cheng's engagement with Black feminist theory, also see Spillers, "Interstices."

18. Cheng, *Ornamentalism*, 2.

19. Cheng, *Ornamentalism*, 19.

20. Cheng, *Ornamentalism*, 5.

21. Alarcón, quoted by Muñoz, *Disidentifications*, 7. See Alarcón, "Conjugating Subjects," 129.

22. Cheng, *Ornamentalism*, 14.

23. Shimizu, *Hypersexuality of Race*, 1. See Zuo, *Vulgar Beauty*, 39–40, 113–14.

24. Wilson, *Gut Feminism*, 69–70.

25. Gina Marchetti views the Butterfly as a figure of assimilation, whose romance with a white man serving in the military during or after war time covers over the violence of Western military intervention in Asian countries. See Marchetti, *Romance and the Yellow Peril*.

26. Shimakawa, *National Abjection*, 120–27.

27. Eng, *Racial Castration*, 1–5, 137–66.

28. Cheng, *Melancholy of Race*, 106.

29. In his 1991 essay, "Come All Ye Asian American Writers of the Real and the Fake," Frank Chin associated *M. Butterfly* with Amy Tan's *The Joy Luck Club* and Maxine Hong Kingston's *Woman Warrior*—notably, works addressing gender and sexuality written either by or about women—as "boldly fake" Asian American cultural productions. Chin, "Come All Ye," 3.

30. As scholars like Hazel Carby, Roderick Ferguson, and Jodi Melamed note, representation of minoritized subjects and conservative beliefs were not wholly in opposition to each other, as assumed. Hollow gestures of inclusion and recognition became concessions to more radical demands in the post–civil rights era. Such gestures were made in institutionalized spaces like the university, where the canon wars, as Carby notes, were in fact "the multicultural wars" enabled by what Ferguson describes as the "incorporation of minority difference." See Carby, "Multicultural Wars"; Melamed, *Represent and Destroy*; Ferguson, *Reorder of Things*.

31. Musser, *Sensational Flesh*, 2.

32. A range of scholarship theorizes sensation in relation to minoritarian difference and identitarian categories. On plasticity, see Jackson, *Becoming Human*, Schuller and Gill-Peterson, "Introduction"; on capacity and debility, see Puar, *Right to Maim*; on animacy, see Chen, *Animacies*; on the visceral, see Khanna, *Visceral Logics of Decolonization*; Holland et al., "On the Visceral"; on impressibility, see Schuller, *Biopolitics of Feeling*.

33. Clare, "Feeling Cold," 169. S. Brook Corfman also writes about heat as a form of bodily knowledge in the durational performances of the artist Cassils. See Corfman, "Melting Muscles."

34. Beauvoir, *Second Sex*, 399.

35. Beauvoir, *Second Sex*, 399.

36. Beauvoir, *Second Sex*, 393.

37. Beauvoir, *Second Sex*, 400.

38. See Ellis, *Studies in the Psychology of Sex*; Stekel, *Frigidity in Women*.

39. Yao, *Disaffected*, 111, 114.

40. Yao, *Disaffected*, 112.

41. Zuo, *Vulgar Beauty*, 98.

42. Zuo, *Vulgar Beauty*, 74.

43. Musser, *Sensational Flesh*, 69.

44. Deleuze, *Masochism*, 53.

45. Musser, *Sensational Flesh*, 71.

46. León, "Caribbean Conflagrations."

47. Deleuze writes, "The coldness is both protective milieu and medium, cocoon and vehicle: it protects supersensual sentimentality as inner life, and expresses it as external order, as wrath and severity." Deleuze, *Masochism*, 52.

48. Ellis, *Studies in the Psychology of Sex*, 203.

49. Musser, *Sensational Flesh*, 63.

50. Cheng reads the quality of shine and "gleaming things" in relation to the actress Anna May Wong on screen and Afong Moy, a young Chinese woman put on display as the "Chinese Lady" by the Carne Brothers and later by P. T. Barnum throughout the 1830s–1850s in the United States. Cheng writes, "Orientalized femininity . . . has always relied on the spectacularization not of naked skin but of ornament: the excessive coverings and decorations that supposedly symptomize the East's overdeveloped and hence feminized and corrupt civilization." See Cheng, "Gleaming Things," in *Ornamentalism*, 69.

51. On "a sheer dressing gown," see Hwang, *M. Butterfly*, 38; on "a sheer robe," see Hwang, *M. Butterfly*, 25; on "simple baggy clothes," see Hwang, *M. Butterfly*, 20; and on an "elegant black gown," see Hwang, *M. Butterfly*, 27.

52. See Cheng, "Gleaming Things"; Cheng, *Second Skin*.

53. Hwang, *M. Butterfly*, 39–40.

54. McMillan, *Embodied Avatars*.

55. Hwang, *M. Butterfly*, 91.

56. Hwang, *M. Butterfly*, 93.

57. Tompkins, *Racial Indigestion*, 92.

58. Kristeva, *Powers of Horror*, 3.

59. Shimakawa, *National Abjection*, 8.

60. Shimakawa, *National Abjection*, 8.

61. Shimakawa, *National Abjection*, 8.

62. Day Above Ground, "Asian Girlz."

63. Mila Zuo, correspondent, email message to author, November 15, 2017.

64. Mel Chen analyzes the discourse on lead, as a toxin animated by race, particularly in the context of the US lead panic of 2007 surrounding toys produced in and associated with China. See Chen, "Lead's Racial Matters," in *Animacies*.

65. Tompkins, *Racial Indigestion*, 103.

66. Zuo, *Vulgar Beauty*, 116.

67. On animatedness, see Ngai, "Animatedness," in *Ugly Feelings*.

68. Johnson, "Muteness Envy," 131.

69. Johnson, "Muteness Envy," 137.

70. Johnson, "Muteness Envy," 135.

71. I am thinking, too, of Bernini's *The Rape of Proserpina* (1621–22), which depicts the Roman myth of the abduction of Proserpina by Pluto, the god of the underworld. One can see the pressure of Pluto's grasp digging into Proserpina's thigh and torso, much like how we can see Apollo's grip in Bernini's *Apollo and Daphne*.

72. Keats, quoted in Johnson, "Muteness Envy," 134.

73. Johnson, "Muteness Envy," 135.

74. Chion, *Voice in Cinema*.

75. Dolar, *Voice and Nothing More*, 60–61.

76. Dolar, *Voice and Nothing More*, 30.

77. Saketopoulou, *Sexuality Beyond Consent*, 171.

78. Saketopoulou, *Sexuality Beyond Consent*, 182.

79. Saketopoulou, *Sexuality Beyond Consent*, 183.

80. Saketopoulou, *Sexuality Beyond Consent*, 183.

81. Dolar, *Voice and Nothing More*, 31.

82. Dolar, *Voice and Nothing More*, 20.

83. Hwang, *M. Butterfly*, 92.

84. Tompkins, *Racial Indigestion*, 5.

85. Dolar, *Voice and Nothing More*, 24.

86. Sedgwick, *Weather in Proust*, 79.

87. A similar version of this essay can be found in "Come as You Are," a published, edited version of a talk Sedgwick gave at a conference, "Transforming the Culture of Death and Dying in America," at SUNY Stony Brook in 1999. See Sedgwick, "Come as You Are," in *Come as You Are*.

88. Sedgwick, *Weather in Proust*, 69.

89. Sedgwick, *Weather in Proust*, 71.

90. Sedgwick, *Weather in Proust*, 71–75.

91. Sedgwick, *Weather in Proust*, 71.

92. See Sedgwick's chapter "Pedagogy of Buddhism," in *Touching Feeling*.

93. Sedgwick, *Weather in Proust*, 83.

94. Sedgwick, *Weather in Proust*, 83.

95. Phillips, *On Giving Up*, 13.

96. "Alison Kuo," Abron Arts Center.

97. Hollibaugh and Moraga, "What We're Rollin," 59. Hollibaugh describes femme sexuality as active rather than passive, and she is insistent and careful not to conflate femme sexuality with masochism. I keep this in mind while also thinking of Trisha Low's articulation of masochism in *Socialist Realism*. She writes, "An acknowledgment of how impossible it is to escape the power structures that hold us, the pleasure of masochism is in unconditional *letting*." Low, *Socialist Realism*, 149. On femme receptivity, see Cvetkovich, "Trauma and Touch: Butch-Femme Sexualities," in *Archive of Feelings*. On femme sexuality, see MacCowan, "Re-Collecting History, Renaming Lives"; Nestle, "Femme Question"; Davis et al., "Femme Tapes."

98. Phillips, *On Giving Up*, 5.

99. Chuh, "It's Not About Anything," 127.

100. Healy, "Seat at the Table."

101. Healy, "Seat at the Table."

102. Tompkins, *Deviant Matter*, 176.

103. Tompkins, *Deviant Matter*, 176.

104. Alison Kuo, quoted in Wilkinson, *Extremely absorbent and increasingly hollow*.

105. In her *Catalysis* series, Piper made herself into an art object in public spaces, subject to the confused and at times antagonistic reactions of the people around her. In Piper's texts accompanying the *Catalysis* series, she explains, "I define the work as the viewer's reaction to it: to me the strongest, most complex, and most esthetically interesting catalysis is the one that occurs in uncategorised, undefined and non-human confrontation." Piper, quoted by Bowles, *Adrian Piper*, 181. Also see Lippard, "Catalysis"; McMillan, "Plastic Possibilities: Adrian Piper's Adamant Self-Alienation," in *Embodied Avatars*; Moten, "Resistance of the Object: Adrian Piper's Theatricality," in *In the Break*.

106. Berg, "History of 'Death Avenue.'"

107. "History," *High Line*.

108. Kuo, "Bone Bath."

109. Tompkins, *Deviant Matter*, 177. On animacy hierarchies, see Mel Chen, *Animacies*.

110. Tompkins, *Deviant Matter*, 194.

111. Tompkins, *Deviant Matter*, 194, 195.

112. Tompkins, *Deviant Matter*, 182.

113. Gallagher, "Eliciting Euphoria Online."

114. Gallagher, "Eliciting Euphoria Online."

115. "Somatic's Grocery," CCS Bard.

116. Alison Kuo, correspondent, email message to author, April 30, 2024.

117. Alison Kuo, correspondent, email message to author, April 30, 2024.

118. Alison Kuo, correspondent, email message to author, April 30, 2024.

119. Alison Kuo, correspondent, email message to author, April 30, 2024.

120. Alison Kuo, correspondent, Zoom meeting with author, July 27, 2022.

121. Wiegman, *Object Lessons*.

122. Zuo, *Vulgar Beauty*, 112.

CHAPTER 4. INJURED ENOUGH

1. See Chuh, "Asians Are the New . . . What?"

2. Harper, *Abstractionist Aesthetics*, 9.

3. Harper, *Abstractionist Aesthetics*, 3.

4. Chin and Chan, "Racist Love," 68.

5. Chin and Chan, "Racist Love," 69.

6. Throughout their essay, Frank Chin and Jeffery Paul Chan accuse other Chinese American writers—almost all women—of falling for racist love, confirming existing racial stereotypes, and "find[ing] Chinese-America repulsive." Chin and Chan, "Racist Love," 68.

7. Cheng, *Ornamentalism*, 2.

8. Cheng, *Ornamentalism*, xi.

9. Cheng, *Ornamentalism*, 4.

10. Bow, *Racist Love*, 5; on cuteness, also see Ngai, *Our Aesthetic Categories*.

11. Bow, *Racist Love*, 2.

12. Bow, *Racist Love*, 17.

13. Bow, *Racist Love*, 3.

14. Jackson, *Becoming Human*, 1.

15. McMillan, *Embodied Avatars*, 9.

16. Moten, *In the Break*, 1.

17. See Fanon, *Black Skin, White Masks*; Spillers, "Mama's Baby, Papa's Maybe."

18. Cheng, *Ornamentalism*, 4. For a critique of Anne Anlin Cheng's engagements with Frantz Fanon and Hortense Spillers, see Bradley, *Anteaesthetics*, esp. 157–69.

19. Cheng, *Ornamentalism*, 5.

20. Bow, *Racist Love*, 70–72.

21. Lye, "Afro-Asian Analogy," 1732, 1733.

22. Kim, "Racial Triangulation of Asian Americans," 106.

23. Lye, "Afro-Asian Analogy," 1733.

24. Lye, "Afro-Asian Analogy," 1735.

25. Wilderson, *Red, White, and Black*, 37.

26. Wilderson, *Red, White, and Black*, 37.

27. Lye, "Afro-Asian Analogy," 1733.

28. Wilderson, *Red, White, and Black*, 38.

29. Lye, "Afro-Asian Analogy," 1733.

30. Cheng, *Ornamentalism*, 4.

31. Cheng, *Ornamentalism*, 5.

32. Cheng, *Ornamentalism*, 153. Spillers's "Mama's Baby, Papa's Maybe" begins: "Let's face it. I am a marked woman, but not everybody knows my name: 'Peaches' and 'Brown Sugar,' 'Sapphire' and 'Earth Mother,' 'Aunty,' 'Granny,' God's 'Holy Fool,' a 'Miss Ebony First,' or 'Black Woman at the Podium': I describe a locus of confounded identities, a meeting ground of investments and privations in the national treasury of rhetorical wealth. My country needs me, and if I were not here, I would have to be invented." Spillers, "Mama's Baby, Papa's Maybe," 65. Meanwhile, Anne Anlin Cheng introduces the figure of the yellow woman by stating, "She goes by many names: Celestial Lady, Lotus Blossom, Dragon Lady, Yellow Fever, Slave Girl, Geisha, Concubine, Butterfly, China Doll, Prostitute. She is carnal and delicate, hot and cold, corporeal and abstract, a full and empty signifier." Cheng, *Ornamentalism*, 4.

33. Cheng, *Ornamentalism*, 154.

34. Lye, "Afro-Asian Analogy," 1733.

35. Goyal, *Runaway Genres*, 5.

36. Goyal, *Runaway Genres*, 8.

37. On Third World studies and the Third World Liberation Front in 1968 at San Francisco State University, see Okihiro, *Third World Studies*. On Afro-Asian solidarities, see Prashad, *Everybody Was Kung Fu Fighting*; Ho and Mullen, *Afro Asia*; Raphael-Hernandez and Steen, *AfroAsian Encounters*.

38. Okihiro, *Third World Studies*.

39. Cheng, "Yellow Skin, White Gold." I am thinking of Candice Lin's *Hard White Body* (2017–18). Across three exhibitions, Lin worked with porcelain at many stages: the unfired, stained, and cracked; the fired, durable, and strong; and the diluted, decayed, and destroyed. See Arndt and Umolu, *Candice Lin*; Byers and Sung, *Candice Lin*.

40. Cheng, "Yellow Skin, White Gold."

41. Cheng, "Yellow Skin, White Gold."

42. Storti, "Half and Both," 105.

43. Storti, "Half and Both," 105.

44. Hayot, *Hypothetical Mandarin*, 167.

45. Heinrich, *Afterlife of Images*.

46. Shah, *Contagious Divides*.

47. Liu, "Lab-Leak Theory."

48. TJ Shin's works, *Universal Skin Salvation* (2018) and *Universal Skin Salvation 2.0* (2019), constructed an immersive sauna using the production and commercial use of lactic acid. Shin created a custom line of K-beauty products that play on lactic acid as a whitening agent and an active bacterial agent that promotes bodily rehabilitation. See Shin, "Universal Skin Salvation"; Shin, "Universal Skin Salvation 2.0."

49. Lee, *Exquisite Corpse*, 5.

50. Lee, *Exquisite Corpse*, 7–8.

51. Lee, *Exquisite Corpse*, 7.

52. Lee, *Exquisite Corpse*, 20.

53. Lee, *Exquisite Corpse*, 8.

54. Chang, *Inhuman Citizenship*, 1.

55. Chang, *Inhuman Citizenship*, 3.

56. Castro, "States of Flux."

57. As a part of Jes Fan's 2018 exhibition *Obscure Functions: Experiments in Decolonizing Melanin* at Recess Art in Brooklyn, New York, visitors were invited to experiment with melanin as sculpting material and a coating agent outside of the human body and form. For more on the exhibition and Fan's engagement with melanin, see Heinrich, "Applied Co-Enmeshment." Also see Henrich, "Ejecta."

58. Fan, "Infectious Beauty."

59. Chang, *Inhuman Citizenship*, 5.

60. Kingston, *Woman Warrior*, 172.

61. Kingston, *Woman Warrior*, 173.

62. Chang, *Inhuman Citizenship*, 6.

63. Tulathimutte, "cover of books by asian writers."

64. Asian Americanist scholars have also included the Asian head on their book's covers, critically gesturing to this tendency of equating the Asian head with the inscrutability and abstraction of the Asian woman. See Kang, *Compositional Subjects*; Bow, *Racist Love*.

65. Brown, *States of Injury*.

66. Brown, *States of Injury*, 74.

67. Muñoz, *Sense of Brown*, 116.

68. Muñoz, *Cruising Utopia*, 93.

69. Muñoz, *Sense of Brown*, 116. See Butler, "Longing for Recognition." While José Esteban Muñoz writes of the woundedness of recognition in his reading of Amiri Baraka's 1964 play *The Toilet*, via Judith Butler and G. W. F. Hegel in *Cruising Utopia*, in his reading of Nao Bustamante's work *Soldadera* (2015), published posthumously in *The Sense of the Brown*, he critiques Brown while thinking alongside Lauren Berlant's theorizations of an "intimate publics." Muñoz, *Sense of Brown*. See also Berlant, *Female Complaint*.

70. Muñoz, *Sense of Brown*, 116.

71. Gilman, "Lam Qua," 60.

72. Lam Qua's Portraits of Peter Parker's Patients, Harvey Cushing/John Hay Whitney Medical Library, Yale University, New Haven, CT, https://library.medicine.yale.edu/historical/digitized-collections/lam-qua-paintings.

73. Rachman, "Memento Morbi," 146.

74. Heinrich, *Afterlife of Images*, 42.

75. Ari Larissa Heinrich points out that in the early nineteenth century, the concept of character was more prevalent and graspable than that of race and was not tethered to the body in the same way. Heinrich, *Afterlife of Images*, 58.

76. Heinrich, *Afterlife of Images*, 58. Eric Hayot also writes about the assumption of a Chinese insensitivity to pain in relation to Lam Qua's portraits. See Hayot, *Hypothetical Mandarin*, 105–131.

77. Fan, "Infectious Beauty."

78. Fan, "Infectious Beauty."

79. Heinrich, *Afterlife of Images*, 70.

80. Heinrich, *Afterlife of Images*, 65.

81. Fan, *Sites of Wounding*.

82. Saketopoulou, *Sexuality Beyond Consent*, 134.

83. Saketopoulou, *Sexuality Beyond Consent*, 132–33.

84. Yan et al., "Problems and Prospects," 2.

85. Fan, *Sites of Wounding*.

86. Yan, quoted in McGill, "Hong Kong Scientist Pins Hopes."

87. Buchanan, "Plant of the Month."

88. Naziz et al., "Scent of Stress"; Zeiba, "Jes Fan."

89. Foucault, *Order of Things*, 21, 22.

90. Foucault, *Order of Things*, 21.

91. Foucault, *Order of Things*, 22.

92. Lowe, "Insufficient Difference," 410.

93. Chen, *Intoxicated*, 4.

94. Chen, *Intoxicated*, 6.

95. Kang, *Vegetarian*, 11.

96. Kang, *Vegetarian*, 11.

97. Kang, *Vegetarian*, 31.

98. See Stobie, "Good Wife?"; Casey, "Willed Arboreality."

99. Chen, *Animacies*.

100. Shotwell, *Against Purity*, 4.

101. Shotwell, *Against Purity*, 4.

102. A second iteration of the exhibition was included in *The Vegetarian: the Swamp, the Swarm & the Cross* at the Buffalo Institute for Contemporary Art in 2023.

103. Kang, *Vegetarian*, 163.

104. On miasma theory, see Corbin, *Foul and the Fragrant*; Kiechle, *Smell Detectives*.

105. Hsu, *Smell of Risk*. On germ theory, see Tomes, *Gospel of Germs*.

106. Tu, *Experiments in Skin*.

107. "Use of Non-Pharmaceutical Forms of Artemisia," World Health Organization.

108. Shin, *Vegetarian*.

109. Shin, *Vegetarian*.

110. I am thinking of Anicka Yi's *You Can Fall Me F* (2021) and Candice Lin's *Swamp Fat* (2021). On olfactory art, see Drobnick, "Toposmia"; De Cupere, *Peter de Cupere*; Drobnick, *Smell Culture Reader*; Jones, *Eyesight Alone*; Drobnick, "Towards an Olfactory Art History."

111. Hsu, *Smell of Risk*, 101.

112. Hsu, *Smell of Risk*, 94.

113. "About Malaria," Centers for Disease Control and Prevention.

114. Hsu, *Smell of Risk*, 115.

115. Chen, "Fire and Ash," 280–81.

116. Chen, "Fire and Ash," 282.

117. "2020 Incident Archive," California Department of Forestry and Fire Protection.

118. "2020 Incident Archive," California Department of Forestry and Fire Protection.

119. "2025 Incident Archive," California Department of Forestry and Fire Protection.

120. Chen, *Intoxicated*, 91.

121. Chen, *Intoxicated*, 4.

CODA

1. Freud, *General Introduction*, 246.

2. Freud, *General Introduction*, 247.

3. Laplanche, *Unfinished Copernican Revolution*, 4.

4. Laplanche, *Unfinished Copernican Revolution*, 13.

5. Laplanche, *Unfinished Copernican Revolution*, 19.

6. Madansky and Tolentino, *Safer Sex Handbook for Lesbians*.

7. See, respectively, "Final Schedule," "The Affect Factory" and "PSi Conferences Archive," Performance Studies international.

8. Johnson, quoted in Feuerstein et al., "Editors' Preface," in *Barbara Johnson Reader*, xv.

9. In other iterations of the performance that I have not seen, Julie Tolentino and Pigpen have used eleven gold threads.

10. "Oral History Interview with Julie Tolentino," Archives of American Art, Smithsonian Institution.

11. "Oral History Interview with Julie Tolentino," Archives of American Art, Smithsonian Institution.

12. "Oral History Interview with Julie Tolentino," Archives of American Art, Smithsonian Institution.

13. "Oral History Interview with Julie Tolentino," Archives of American Art, Smithsonian Institution.

14. "Oral History Interview with Julie Tolentino," Archives of American Art, Smithsonian Institution.

15. "Oral History Interview with Julie Tolentino," Archives of American Art, Smithsonian Institution.

16. "Oral History Interview with Julie Tolentino," Archives of American Art, Smithsonian Institution.

17. "Oral History Interview with Julie Tolentino," Archives of American Art, Smithsonian Institution.

18. Owen, "More," 94.

19. Owen, "More," 94, 93.

BIBLIOGRAPHY

"2020 Incident Archive." California Department of Forestry and Fire Protection. Accessed December 19, 2024. https://www.fire.ca.gov/incidents/2020.

"2025 Incident Archive." California Department of Forestry and Fire Protection. Accessed February 18, 2025. https://www.fire.ca.gov/incidents/2025.

"About Malaria." Centers for Disease Control and Prevention. Accessed December 19, 2024. https://www.cdc.gov/malaria/about/index.html.

Ahmed, Sara. "Feminist Shelters." *feministkilljoys*. December 30, 2015. https://feministkilljoys.com/2015/12/30/feminist-shelters.

Ahmed, Sara. *Living a Feminist Life*. Durham, NC: Duke University Press, 2017.

Ahmed, Sara. *On Being Included: Racism and Diversity in Institutional Life*. Durham, NC: Duke University Press, 2012.

Alarcón, Norma. "Conjugating Subjects in the Age of Multiculturalism." In *Mapping Multiculturalism*, edited by Avery F. Gordon and Christopher Newfield, 127–48. Minneapolis: University of Minnesota Press, 1996.

Alcoff, Linda. "The Problem of Speaking for Others." *Cultural Critique* 20 (1991–92): 5–32.

Allewaert, Monique. *Ariel's Ecology: Plantations, Personhood, and Colonialism in the American Tropics*. Minneapolis: University of Minnesota Press, 2013.

"Alison Kuo: The New Joys of Gellies." Abron Arts Center. January 29, 2019. www.abronsartscenter.org/programs/alison-kuo-the-new-joys-of-gellies.

Amin, Kadji. *Disturbing Attachments: Genet, Modern Pederasty, and Queer History*. Durham, NC: Duke University Press, 2017.

Amin, Kadji, Amber Jamilla Musser, and Roy Pérez. "Queer Form: Aesthetics, Race, and the Violences of the Social." *ASAP/Journal* 2, no. 2 (2017): 227–39.

Ao, Bethany. "A Distant Mitski Doesn't Move the Larimer Lounge." *Denver Post*, November 17, 2021. https://www.denverpost.com/2016/07/18/a-distant-mitski-doesnt-move-the-larimer-lounge/.

Arndt, Lotte, and Yesomi Umolu, eds. *Candice Lin, a Hard White Body*. Chicago: University of Chicago Press, 2019.

"Asian Americans Advancing Justice Denounces Supreme Court Decision on Affirmative Action." Asian Americans Advancing Justice. June 29, 2023. https://www.advancingjustice-aajc.org/press-release/asian-americans-advancing-justice-denounces-supreme-court-decision-affirmative-action.

"'Asians Sleeping in the Library' Is a Racist Website!" Asian American TV. December 25, 2010. https://asianamericantv.blogspot.com/2010/12/asians-sleeping-in-libary-is-racist.html (open to invited readers only).

Austin, J. L. *How to Do Things with Words*. Cambridge, MA: Harvard University Press, 1975.

Awkward-Rich, Cameron. *The Terrible We: Thinking with Trans Maladjustment*. Durham, NC: Duke University Press, 2022.

Baggs, Mel (silentmiaow). "In My Language." YouTube video, 8 minutes, 36 seconds, January 14, 2007. https://www.youtube.com/watch?v=JnylM1hI2jc.

Baik, Crystal, Diane Wong, Vivian Truong, et al. "To Write in Unwellness: Documenting A/P/A Voices." *Journal of Asian American Studies* 25, no. 3 (2022): 493–515.

Beauvoir, Simone de. *The Second Sex*. Translated by H. M. Parshley. New York: Vintage Books, 1989.

Berg, Madeline. "The History of 'Death Avenue.'" High Line, October 28, 2021. https://www.thehighline.org/blog/2021/10/28/the-history-of-death-avenue-2/.

Berlant, Lauren. *Cruel Optimism*. Durham, NC: Duke University Press, 2011.

Berlant, Lauren. *The Female Complaint: The Unfinished Business of Sentimentality in American Culture*. Durham, NC: Duke University Press, 2008.

Berlant, Lauren. "Showing Up to Withhold: On Pope.L's Deadpan Aesthetic." In *Pope.L: Showing Up to Withhold*, 107–35. Chicago: University of Chicago Press, 2014.

Berlant, Lauren, and Lee Edelman. *Sex, or the Unbearable*. Durham, NC: Duke University Press, 2014.

Bersani, Leo. *Homos*. Cambridge, MA: Harvard University Press, 1995.

Bersani, Leo. *Is the Rectum a Grave? And Other Essays*. Chicago: University of Chicago Press, 2009.

Bersani, Leo, and Adam Phillips. *Intimacies*. Chicago: University of Chicago Press, 2008.

Bettcher, Talia Mae. "Trapped in the Wrong Theory: Rethinking Trans Oppression and Resistance." *Signs* 39, no. 2 (2014): 383–406.

Bow, Leslie. *Racist Love: Asian Abstraction and the Pleasures of Fantasy*. Durham, NC: Duke University Press, 2022.

Bowles, John P. *Adrian Piper: Race, Gender, and Embodiment*. Durham, NC: Duke University Press, 2011.

Bradley, Rizvana. *Anteaesthetics: Black Aesthesis and the Critique of Form*. Stanford, CA: Stanford University Press, 2023.

Brazil, Kevin. "Whatever Happened to Queer Happiness?" *Granta*, June 24, 2020. https://granta.com/whatever-happened-to-queer-happiness.

Brown, Wendy. *States of Injury: Power and Freedom in Late Modernity*. Princeton, NJ: Princeton University Press, 1995.

Browning, Barbara. *The Gift*. Minneapolis: Coffee House Press, 2017.

Buchanan, Ashley. "Plant of the Month: Agarwood." *JSTOR Daily*, January 20, 2021. https://daily.jstor.org/plant-of-the-month-agarwood.

Butler, Judith. *Bodies That Matter: On the Discursive Limits of "Sex."* New York: Routledge, 1993.

Butler, Judith. *Giving an Account of Oneself*. New York: Fordham University Press, 2003.

Butler, Judith. "Imitation and Gender Insubordination." In *The Lesbian and Gay Studies Reader*, edited by Henry Abelove, Michèle Aina Barale, and David M. Halperin, 307–20. New York: Routledge, 1993.

Butler, Judith. "Longing for Recognition." In *Undoing Gender*, 131–51. New York: Routledge, 2004.

Byers, Dan, and Victoria Sung, eds. *Candice Lin: Sleeping, Rotting, Resting*. Cambridge, MA: Carpenter Center for the Visual Arts and Harvard University; Minneapolis: Walker Art Center, 2021.

Carby, Hazel. "The Multicultural Wars." *Radical History Review* 54, no. 7 (1992): 7–18.

Casey, Rose. "Willed Arboreality: Feminist Worldmaking in Han Kang's *The Vegetarian*." *Critique: Studies in Contemporary Fiction* 62, no. 3 (2020): 347–60.

Castro, Jan Garden. "States of Flux: A Conversation with Jes Fan." *Sculpture Magazine*, April 15, 2020. https://sculpturemagazine.art/states-of-flux-a-conversation-with-jes-fan/.

Cavarero, Adriana. *For More Than One Voice: Toward a Philosophy of Vocal Expression*. Stanford, CA: Stanford University Press, 2005.

Cavarero, Adriana. *Inclinations: A Critique of Rectitude*. Stanford, CA: Stanford University Press, 2016.

Cervenak, Sarah Jane. *Wandering: Philosophical Performances of Racial and Sexual Freedom*. Durham, NC: Duke University Press, 2014.

Chambers-Letson, Joshua. "Homegrown Terror: Projective Identification and Wafaa Bilal's Domestic Tension." *Journal of Asian American Studies* 19, no. 2 (2016): 169–92.

Chambers-Letson, Joshua. "Reparative Feminisms, Repairing Feminism—Reparation, Postcolonial Violence, and Feminism." *Women and Performance: a journal of feminist theory* 16, no. 2 (2006): 169–89.

Chang, Clio. "The Poet Pundit: How Cathy Park Hong Became Liberal America's Go-To Thinker." *New York Magazine*, September 28, 2022. https://www.vulture.com/article/cathy-park-hong-minor-feelings-profile.html.

Chang, Juliana. *Inhuman Citizenship: Traumatic Enjoyment and Asian American Literature*. Minneapolis: University of Minnesota Press, 2012.

Chavez, Jeremy De, and Cassie Jun Lin. "'The Faithful Work of Drowning': A Reparative Reading of Ocean Vuong's 'Telemachus.'" *Explicator* 78, no. 2 (2020): 66–70.

Cheh, Carol. "Artists at Work: Wu Tsang." *East of Borneo*, June 30, 2014. https://eastofborneo.org/articles/artists-at-work-wu-tsang/.

Chen, Howie, ed. *Godzilla: Asian American Arts Network*. Brooklyn, NY: Primary Information, 2021.

Chen, Mel Y. *Animacies: Biopolitics, Racial Mattering, and Queer Affect*. Durham, NC: Duke University Press, 2012.

Chen, Mel Y. "Fire and Ash." In *Meat! A Transnational Analysis*, edited by Sushmita Chatterjee and Banu Subramaniam, 279–87. Durham, NC: Duke University Press, 2021.

Chen, Mel Y. *Intoxicated: Race, Disability, and Chemical Intimacy Across Empire*. Durham, NC: Duke University Press, 2023.

Chen, Mel Y., Mimi Khúc, and Jina B. Kim. "Work Will Not Save Us: An Asian American Crip Manifesto." *Disability Studies Quarterly* 43, no. 1 (2023). https://dsq-sds.org/index.php/dsq/article/view/9652/8014.

Chen, Nancy N. "'Speaking Nearby': A Conversation with Trinh T. Minh-ha." *Visual Anthropology Review* 8, no. 1 (1992): 82–91.

Cheng, Anne Anlin. *The Melancholy of Race: Psychoanalysis, Assimilation, and Hidden Grief*. Oxford: Oxford University Press, 2000.

Cheng, Anne Anlin. *Ornamentalism*. Oxford: Oxford University Press, 2018.

Cheng, Anne Anlin. *Second Skin: Josephine Baker and the Modern Surface*. Oxford: Oxford University Press, 2010.

Cheng, Anne Anlin. "Yellow Skin, White Gold." *Asia Art Archive*, January 9, 2020. https://aaa.org.hk/en/ideas-journal/ideas-journal/yellow-skin-white-gold.

Cheung, Ysabelle. "Abject, Exposed, and Potential Desires." *ArtAsiaPacific* 114 (July–August 2019): 60–69.

Chiang, Mark. *The Cultural Capital of Asian American Studies: Autonomy and Representation in the University*. New York: New York University Press, 2009.

Chin, Frank. "Come All Ye Asian American Writers of the Real and the Fake." In *The Big Aiiieeeee! An Anthology of Chinese American and Japanese American Literature*, edited by Jeffery Paul Chan, Frank Chin, Lawson Fusao Inada, and Shawn Wong, 1–92. New York: Meridian Books, 1991.

Chin, Frank, and Jeffery Paul Chan. "Racist Love." In *Seeing Through Shuck*, edited by Richard Kostelanetz, 65–79. New York: Ballantine Books, 1972.

Chion, Michel. *The Voice in Cinema*. Translated by Claudia Gorben. New York: Columbia University Press, 1999.

Chiu, Melissa. "A Conversation on Today's Asian America." In *One Way or Another: Asian American Art Now*, edited by Melissa Chiu, Karin Higa, and Susette Min, 26–33. New Haven, CT: Yale University Press, 2006.

Chiu, Melissa, Karin Higa, and Susette Min, eds. *One Way or Another: Asian American Art Now*. New Haven, CT: Yale University Press, 2006.

Chow, Rey. *A Face Drawn in the Sand: Humanistic Inquiry and Foucault in the Present*. New York: Columbia University Press, 2021.

Chow, Rey. *The Protestant Ethnic and the Spirit of Capitalism*. New York: Columbia University Press, 2022.

Chuh, Kandice. "Asians Are the New . . . What?" In *Flashpoints for Asian American Studies*, edited by Cathy J. Schlund-Vials, 220–38. New York: Fordham University Press, 2017.

Chuh, Kandice. *The Difference Aesthetics Makes: On the Humanities "After Man."* Durham, NC: Duke University Press, 2019.

Chuh, Kandice. *Imagine Otherwise: On Asian Americanist Critique*. Durham, NC: Duke University Press, 2003.

Chuh, Kandice. "It's Not About Anything." *Social Text* 32, no. 121 (2014): 125–34.

Chung, Kelly. "The Defiant Still Worker: Ramiro Gomez and the Expressionism of Abstract Labor." *Women and Performance: a journal of feminist theory* 29, no. 1 (2019): 62–76.

Clare, Eli. *Brilliant Imperfection: Grappling with Cure*. Durham, NC: Duke University Press, 2017.

Clare, Stephanie. "Feeling Cold: Phenomenology, Spatiality, and the Politics of Sensation." *differences* 24, no. 1 (2013): 169–91.

Corbin, Alain. *The Foul and the Fragrant: Odor and the French Social Imagination*. Cambridge, MA: Harvard University Press, 1986.

Corfman, S. Brook. "Melting Muscles: Cassils's *Tiresias* at the Intersection of Affect and Gendered Embodiment." *TSQ* 7, no. 1 (2020): 5–19.

Cvetkovich, Ann. *An Archive of Feelings: Trauma, Sexuality, and Lesbian Public Cultures*. Durham, NC: Duke University Press, 2003.

Cvetkovich, Ann. *Depression: A Public Feeling*. Durham, NC: Duke University Press, 2012.

Dahl, Roald. *Charlie and the Chocolate Factory*. New York: Alfred A. Knopf, 1964.

Dancer, Thom. "Being Kathy H.: Relatability in *Never Let Me Go*." *MFS: Modern Fiction Studies* 67, no. 1 (2021): 149–70.

Dango, Michael. *Crisis Style: The Aesthetics of Repair*. Stanford, CA: Stanford University Press, 2022.

Davis, Madeline, Amber Hollibaugh, and Joan Nestle. "The Femme Tapes." In *The Persistent Desire: A Femme-Butch Reader*, edited by Joan Nestle, 254–67. Boston: Alyson Publications, 1992.

Day, Iyko. *Alien Capital: Asian Racialization and the Logic of Settler Colonial Capitalism*. Durham, NC: Duke University Press, 2016.

Day Above Ground. "Asian Girlz with Lyrics (Explicit)—Day Above Ground." YouTube video, 5 minutes, 4 seconds, August 3, 2013. https://www.youtube.com/watch?v=1KgnlTdmmkE&t=14s.

Dean, Tim. *Unlimited Intimacy: Reflections on the Subculture of Barebacking*. Chicago: University of Chicago Press, 2009.

De Cupere, Peter. *Peter de Cupere: Scent in Context*. Antwerp: Stockmans, 2016.

de Leon, J M. "'Let Me Listen to Me': The Politics and Aesthetics of Self-Indulgence." PhD diss., New York University, 2016.

Deleuze, Gilles. *Masochism: Coldness and Cruelty*. New York: Zone Books, 1992.

Demers, Lauren (@laurendemers). "@mitskileaks how do u feel about going to shows by yourself?" Twitter, September 6, 2016, 9:42 p.m. twitter.com/laurendemers/status/773335687290576896.

Derrida, Jacques. *On Cosmopolitanism and Forgiveness*. New York: Routledge. 2001.

Diaz, Robert G. "Melancholic Maladies: Paranoid Ethics, Reparative Envy, and Asian Americanist Critique." *Women and Performance: a journal of feminist theory* 16, no. 2 (2016): 201–19.

Dinshaw, Carolyn. *How Soon Is Now? Medieval Texts, Amateur Readers, and the Queerness of Time*. Durham, NC: Duke University Press, 2012.

Dolar, Mladen. *A Voice and Nothing More*. Cambridge, MA: MIT Press, 2006.

Dougher, Sarah. "Authenticity, Gender, and Personal Voice: She Sounds Sad, Do You Think She Really Is?" In *This Is Pop: In Search of the Elusive at Experience Music Project*, edited by Eric Weisbard, 145–54. Cambridge, MA: Harvard University Press, 2004.

Doyle, Jennifer. *Hold It Against Me: Difficulty and Emotion in Contemporary Art*. Durham, NC: Duke University Press, 2013.

Drobnick, Jim, ed. *The Smell Culture Reader*. New York: Berg, 2006.

Drobnick, Jim. "Toposmia: Art, Scent, and Interrogations of Spatiality." *Angelaki* 7, no. 1 (2002): 31–47.

Drobnick, Jim. "Towards an Olfactory Art History." *Senses and Society* 7, no. 2 (2012): 196–208.

Edelman, Lee. *No Future: Queer Theory and the Death Drive*. Durham, NC: Duke University Press, 2004.

Edwards, Brent Hayes. "The Ethnics of Surrealism." *Transition*, no. 78 (1998): 84–135.

Ellegood, Anne, and Anna Sew Hoy, eds. *Scratching at the Moon*. Los Angeles: DoPe Press, 2024.

Ellis, Havelock. *Studies in the Psychology of Sex*. Vol. 3, *Analysis of the Sexual Impulse, Love and Pain, The Sexual Impulse in Women*. Philadelphia: F. A. Davis, 1913.

Eng, David L. "Colonial Object Relations." *Social Text* 34, no. 1 (March 2016): 1–19.

Eng, David L. *Racial Castration: Managing Masculinity in Asian America*. Durham, NC: Duke University Press, 2001.

Eng, David L. "Reparations and the Human." *Columbia Journal of Gender and Law* 21, no. 2 (2011): 561–83.

Eng, David L., and Shinhee Han. "A Dialogue on Racial Melancholia." In *Loss: The Politics of Mourning*, edited by David L. Eng and David Kazanjian, 343–71. Berkeley: University of California Press, 2003.

Eng, David L., and Shinhee Han. *Racial Melancholia, Racial Dissociation: On the Social and Psychic Lives of Asian Americans*. Durham, NC: Duke University Press, 2019.

Fan, Jes. "Infectious Beauty." *New York Close Up*, Art21, May 20, 2020. https://art21.org/watch/new-york-close-up/jes-fan-infectious-beauty.

Fan, Jes. *Sites of Wounding: Chapter 1*. Hong Kong: Empty Gallery, 2023. Exhibition brochure. https://emptygallery.com/exhibitions/eg27-jes-fan/.

Fanon, Frantz. *Black Skin, White Masks*. Translated by Richard Philcox. New York: Grove Press, 2008.

Felman, Shoshana. "Psychoanalysis and Education: Teaching Terminable and Interminable." *Yale French Studies*, no. 63 (1982): 21–44.

Felman, Shoshana. *The Scandal of the Speaking Body: Don Juan with J. L. Austin, or Seduction in Two Languages*. Stanford, CA: Stanford University Press, 2003.
Ferguson, Roderick A. *The Reorder of Things: The University and Its Pedagogies of Minority Difference*. Minneapolis: University of Minnesota Press, 2012.
Feuerstein, Melissa, Bill Johnson González, Lili Porten, and Keja Valens, eds. *The Barbara Johnson Reader: The Surprise of Otherness*. Durham, NC: Duke University Press, 2014.
"Final Schedule." Affect Factory. January 24, 2012. https://affectfactory.blogspot.com.
Fiol-Matta, Licia. *The Great Woman Singer: Gender and Voice in Puerto Rican Music*. Durham, NC: Duke University Press, 2017.
Fisher, Ariel. "Everything Everywhere All at Once Or: How I Stopped Fighting and Learned to Love My Brain." */Film*, January 9, 2023. https://www.slashfilm.com/1157086/everything-everywhere-all-at-once-or-how-i-stopped-fighting-and-learned-to-love-my-brain.
Foucault, Michel. *The History of Sexuality*. Translated by Robert Hurley. New York: Vintage Books, 1990.
Foucault, Michel. *The Order of Things*. Translated by Alan Sheridan. New York: Vintage Books, 1994.
Freeman, Elizabeth. *Time Binds: Queer Temporalities, Queer Histories*. New York: New York University Press, 2010.
Freud, Sigmund. *A General Introduction to Psychoanalysis*. Translated by G. Stanley Hall. New York: Boni and Liveright, 1920.
Freud, Sigmund. "Observations on Transference-Love." In *The Standard Edition of the Complete Psychological Works of Sigmund Freud*, vol. 12 *(1911–1913): The Case of Schreber, Papers on Technique and Other Works*, translated and edited by J. Strachey, 157–71. London: Hogarth Press, 1958.
Freud, Sigmund. "On Narcissism." In *The Standard Edition of the Complete Psychological Works of Sigmund Freud*, vol. 14 *(1914–1916): On the History of the Psycho-Analytic Movement, Papers on Metapsychology and Other Works*, translated and edited by J. Strachey, 67–102. London: Hogarth Press, 1957.
Freud, Sigmund. "Remembering, Repeating, and Working Through." In *The Standard Edition of the Complete Psychological Works of Sigmund Freud*, vol. 12 *(1911–1913): The Case of Schreber, Papers on Technique and Other Works*, translated and edited by J. Strachey, 145–56. London: Hogarth Press, 1958.
Freud, Sigmund. *Three Essays on the Theory of Sexuality*. Translated and edited by James Strachey. New York: Basic Books, 1975.
Fung, Richard. "Looking for My Penis: The Eroticized Asian in Gay Video Porn." Accessed March 30, 2025. http://www.richardfung.ca/index.php?/articles/looking-for-my-penis-1991.
Gallagher, Rob. "Eliciting Euphoria Online: The Aesthetics of 'ASMR' Video Culture." In "The Aesthetics of Online Videos," edited by Stephen Groening, special issue, *Film Criticism* 40, no 2 (2016).
Garber, Marjorie. "Relatable." *Raritan* 38, no. 4 (2019): 113–29.
Garland-Thomson, Rosemarie. "Misfits: A Feminist Materialist Disability Concept." *Hypatia: A Journal of Feminist Philosophy* 26, no. 3 (2011): 591–609.

Gersen, Jeannie Suk. "The Uncomfortable Truth About Affirmative Action and Asian-Americans." *New Yorker*, August 10, 2018. https://www.newyorker.com/news/news-desk/the-uncomfortable-truth-about-affirmative-action-and-asian-americans.

Gill-Peterson, Jules. *A Short History of Trans Misogyny*. New York: Verso Books, 2024.

Gilman, Sander L. "Lam Qua and the Development of Westernized Medical Iconography in China." *Medical History* 30 (1986): 57–69.

Glavey, Brian. "Having a Coke with You Is Even More Fun Than Ideology Critique." *PMLA* 134, no. 5 (2019): 996–1011.

Glavey, Brian. "Lyric Wilt, or, The Here and Now of Queer Impotentiality." *New Literary History* 51, no. 3 (2020): 567–86.

Goffman, Erving. "Embarrassment and Social Organization." *American Journal of Sociology* 62, no. 3 (1956): 264–71.

Goffman, Erving. *Stigma: Notes on the Management of Spoiled Identity*. New York: Touchstone, 1963.

Goldberg, Jonathan, ed. *Come as You Are: After Eve Kosofsky Sedgwick*. Brooklyn, NY: Punctum, 2021.

Gonzalez, Rita. "Speech Acts." In *Wu Tsang: Not in My Language*. Cologne: Buchhandlung Walther König, 2015.

Gopinath, Gayatri. *Impossible Desires: Queer Diasporas and South Asian Public Cultures*. Durham, NC: Duke University Press, 2005.

Gordon, Avery. "The Work of Corporate Culture: Diversity Management." *Social Text*, no. 44 (1995): 3–30.

Gordon, Avery, and Christopher Newfield, eds. *Mapping Multiculturalism*. Minneapolis: University of Minnesota Press, 1966.

Goyal, Yogita. *Runaway Genres: The Global Afterlives of Slavery*. New York: New York University Press, 2019.

Green, Jesse. "Paris Has Burned." *New York Times*, April 18, 1993. https://www.nytimes.com/1993/04/18/style/paris-has-burned.html.

Halberstam, Jack. *In a Queer Time and Place: Transgender Bodies, Subcultural Lives*. New York: New York University Press, 2005.

Hammonds, Evelyn. "Black (W)holes and the Geometry of Black Female Sexuality." *differences* 6, nos. 2–3 (1994): 126–45.

Han, Madeleine, and Irene Hsu. "jas lin in Conversation with Madeleine Han and Irene Hsu." *Fruit: Queer Literary Journal* 5 (July 2022): 6–12. https://fruitjournal.co.uk/2022/07/07/jas-lin-in-conversation-with-madeleine-han-and-irene-hsu.

Hanhardt, Christina. *Safe Space: Gay Neighborhood History and the Politics of Violence*. Durham, NC: Duke University Press, 2013.

Harney, Stefano, and Fred Moten. *The Undercommons: Fugitive Planning and Black Study*. New York: Minor Compositions, 2013.

Harper, Phillip Brian. *Abstractionist Aesthetics: Artistic Form and Social Critique in African American Culture*. New York: New York University Press, 2015.

Hartocollis, Anemona. "Asian-Americans Suing Harvard Say Admissions Files Show Discrimination." *New York Times*, April 4, 2018. https:// www.nytimes.com/2018/04/04/us/harvard-asian-admission.html.

Hartocollis, Anemona. "Harvard Rated Asian-Americans Lower on Personality Traits, Suit Says." *New York Times*, June 15, 2018. https:// www.nytimes.com/2018/06/15/us /harvard-asian-enrollment-applicants.html.

Hartocollis, Anemona, and Stephanie Saul. "Affirmative Action Battle Has a New Focus: Asian-Americans." *New York Times*, August 2, 2017. https:// www.nytimes.com/2017 /08/02/us/affirmative-action-battle-has-a-new-focus-asian-americans.html.

Hayot, Eric. *The Hypothetical Mandarin: Sympathy, Modernity, and Chinese Pain*. Oxford: Oxford University Press, 2009.

Healy, Clare Marie. "A Seat at the Table." *Dazed*, January 5, 2018. https://www .dazeddigital.com/artsandculture/article/38490/1/food-art-new-york.

Heaney, Emma. *The New Woman: Literary Modernism, Queer Theory, and the Trans Feminine Allegory*. Evanston, IL: Northwestern University Press, 2017.

Hedva, Johanna. *How to Tell When We Will Die: On Pain, Disability, and Doom*. New York: Hillman Grad Books, 2024.

Heinrich, Ari Larissa. *The Afterlife of Images: Translating the Pathological Body Between China and the West*. Durham, NC: Duke University Press, 2008.

Heinrich, Ari Larissa. "Applied Co-Enmeshment." Recess. October 2018. https://www .recessart.org/projects/122-applied-co-enmeshment.

Heinrich, Ari Larissa. "Ejecta." In *Cookie Jar 1: Home Is a Foreign Place*. New York: Andy Warhol Foundation Arts, Writers Grant, 2022. https://cookiejar.artswriters .org/.

Heberer, Mel. *Asians on Demand: Mediating Race in Video Art and Activism*. Minneapolis: University of Minnesota Press, 2023.

Hernandez, Jillian. *Aesthetics of Excess: The Art and Politics of Black and Latina Embodiment*. Durham, NC: Duke University Press, 2020.

Hilderbrand, Lucas. *Paris Is Burning: A Queer Film Classic*. Vancouver: Arsenal Pulp Press, 2021.

Higginbotham, Evelyn Brooks. "African-American Women's History and the Metalanguage of Race." *Signs* 17, no. 2 (1992): 251–74.

Hilton, Leon J. "Avonte's Law: Autism, Wandering, and the Racial Surveillance of Neurological Difference." *African American Review* 50, no. 2 (2017): 221–35.

Hine, Darlene Clark. "Rape and the Inner Lives of Black Women in the Middle West: Preliminary Thoughts on the Culture of Dissemblance." *Signs* 14, no. 4 (1989): 915–20.

"History." High Line. Accessed December 19, 2024. https://www.thehighline.org /history/.

Ho, Fred Wei-han, and Bill Mullen, eds. *Afro Asia: Revolutionary Political and Cultural Connections Between African Americans and Asian Americans*. Durham, NC: Duke University Press, 2008.

Holland, Sharon P., Marcia Ochoa, and Kyla Wazana Tompkins. "On the Visceral." *GLQ* 20, no. 4 (2014): 391–406.

Hollibaugh, Amber, and Cherríe Moraga. "What We're Rollin Around in Bed With: Sexual Silences in Feminism: A Conversation Toward Ending Them." *Heresies* 12 (1981): 58–62.

Hong, Cathy Park. *Minor Feelings: An Asian American Reckoning*. New York: One World, 2020.

Hong, Grace Kyungwon, and Roderick A. Ferguson. "Introduction." In *Strange Affinities: The Gender and Sexual Politics of Comparative Racialization*, coedited by Hong and Ferguson, 1–22. Durham, NC: Duke University Press, 2011.

hooks, bell. "Is Paris Burning?" In *Black Looks: Race and Representation*, 145–56. Boston: South End Press, 1992.

Hsu, Hsuan L. *The Smell of Risk: Environmental Disparities and Olfactory Aesthetics*. New York: New York University Press, 2020.

Huang, Vivian L. "Inscrutably, Actually: Hospitality, Parasitism, and the Silent Work of Yoko Ono and Laurel Nakadate." *Women and Performance: a journal of feminist theory* 28, no. 3 (2018): 187–203.

Huang, Vivian L. *Surface Relations: Queer Forms of Asian American Inscrutability*. Durham, NC: Duke University Press, 2022.

Hwang, David Henry. *M. Butterfly*. New York: Penguin, 1993.

Jackson, Zakiyyah Iman. *Becoming Human: Matter and Meaning in an Antiblack World*. New York: New York University Press, 2020.

Jin, Lee Sung, dir. *Beef*. Aired April 6, 2023, on Netflix.

Johnson, Barbara. "Muteness Envy." In *The Feminist Difference: Literature, Psychoanalysis, Race, and Gender*, 129–54. Cambridge, MA: Harvard University Press, 1998.

Johnson, Barbara. "Nothing Fails Like Success." In *A World of Difference*, 11–16. Baltimore, MD: Johns Hopkins University Press, 1987.

Johnson, Barbara. "Using People: Kant with Winnicott." In *The Barbara Johnson Reader: The Surprise of Otherness*, edited by Melissa Feuerstein, Bill Johnson González, Lili Porten, and Keja Valens, 262–74. Durham, NC: Duke University Press, 2014.

Jones, Caroline A. *Eyesight Alone: Clement Greenberg's Modernism and the Bureaucratization of the Senses*. Chicago: University of Chicago Press, 2008.

Jung, Marilyn, Monica Chau, and Margo Machida, eds. *Uncommon Traits: Re/locating Asia*. Buffalo, NY: CEPA Gallery, 1997.

Kambhampaty, Anna P. "The Fight for Asian American Studies." *New York Times*, January 13, 2022. https://www.nytimes.com/2022/01/13/style/asian-american-studies-dartmouth.html.

Kang, Han. *The Vegetarian*. Translated by Deborah Smith. New York: Hogarth, 2015.

Kang, Laura Hyun Yi. *Compositional Subjects: Enfiguring Asian/American Women*. Durham, NC: Duke University Press, 2022.

Kang, Laura Hyun Yi. *Traffic in Asian Women*. Durham, NC: Duke University Press, 2020.

Khanna, Neetu. *The Visceral Logics of Decolonization*. Durham, NC: Duke University Press, 2020.

Khúc, Mimi. *dear elia: Letters from the Asian American Abyss*. Durham, NC: Duke University Press, 2024.

Khúc, Mimi, ed. "Open in Emergency: A Special Issue on Asian American Mental Health." *Asian American Literary Review* 10, no. 2 (2019).

Kiechle, Melanie A. *Smell Detectives: An Olfactory History of Nineteenth-Century Urban America*. Seattle: University of Washington Press, 2017.

Kim, Claire Jean. "The Racial Triangulation of Asian Americans." *Politics and Society* 27, no. 1 (1999): 105–38.

Kim, Eunjung. *Curative Violence: Rehabilitating Disability, Gender, and Sexuality in Modern Korea*. Durham, NC: Duke University Press, 2017.

Kim Lee, Summer. "Finding One Another in Misrecognition: Summer Kim Lee Meets Catalina Ouyang." *Momus*, April 28, 2023. https://momus.ca/finding-one-another-in-misrecognition-summer-kim-lee-meets-catalina-ouyang/.

Kim Lee, Summer. "Introduction." In "Someone Else's Object," edited by Summer Kim Lee. *Post45 Contemporaries* (2019). https://post45.org/2019/12/introduction-someone-elses-object/.

King, Homay. *Lost in Translation: Orientalism, Cinema, and the Enigmatic Signifier*. Durham, NC: Duke University Press, 2010.

Kingston, Maxine Hong. *The Woman Warrior: Memoirs of a Girlhood Among Ghosts*. New York: Alfred A. Knopf, 1976.

Klein, Melanie. "Love, Guilt and Reparation." In *Love, Guilt and Reparation and Other Works 1921–1945*, 306–43. New York: Free Press, 1975.

Klein, Melanie. "A Study of Envy and Gratitude." In *The Selected Melanie Klein*, edited by Juliet Mitchell, 211–29. New York: Free Press, 1986.

KoreAm Journal. "Asians Sleeping in the Library." CharacterMedia. December 23, 2010. https://charactermedia.com/asians-sleeping-in-the-library/.

Koshy, Susan. "Morphing Race into Ethnicity: Asian Americans and Critical Transformations of Whiteness." *boundary 2* 28, no. 1 (Spring 2001): 153–94.

Koul, Scaachi. "I Made My Mom See 'Everything Everywhere All at Once' and We Both Cried." *Buzzfeed News*, April 27, 2022. https://www.buzzfeednews.com/article/scaachikoul/everything-everywhere-all-at-once-intergenerational-trauma.

Krauss, Rosalind E. "The Destiny of the *Informe*." In *Formless: A User's Guide*, 235–52. New York: Zone Books, 1997.

Kristeva, Julia. *Powers of Horror: An Essay on Abjection*. Translated by Leon S. Roudiez. New York: Columbia University Press, 1982.

Kuo, Alison. "Bone Bath." Artist website. Accessed December 19, 2024. http://www.kuospace.com/#/bone-bath.

Kwan, Daniel, and Daniel Scheinert, dirs. *Everything Everywhere All at Once*. Santa Monica, CA: Lionsgate, 2022.

Laplanche, Jean. *The Unfinished Copernican Revolution: Selected Works, 1967–1991*. Translated by Luke Thurston. New York: The Unconscious in Translation, 2020.

Lax, Thomas J. "Adjacencies: Wu Tsang in Conversation with Thomas J. Lax." In *Wu Tsang: Not In My Language*, 33–42. Cologne: Buchhandlung Walther König, 2015.

Lee, Christopher. *The Semblance of Identity: Aesthetic Mediation in Asian American Literature*. Stanford, CA: Stanford University Press, 2012.

Lee, James Kyung-Jin. *Pedagogies of Woundedness: Illness, Memoir, and the Ends of the Model Minority*. Philadelphia: Temple University Press, 2022.

Lee, Rachel C. *The Exquisite Corpse of Asian America: Biopolitics, Biosociality, and Posthuman Ecologies*. New York: New York University Press, 2014.

León, Christina A. "Caribbean Conflagrations: Camouflage, Ambivalence, and Anti-Analogical Entanglements." In "Ambivalent Criticism," edited by Michael Dango and Tina Post, special issue, *Post45*, no. 8 (2022). https://post45.org/2022/10/caribbean-conflagrations.

León, Christina A. "Curious Entanglements: Opacity and Ethical Relation in Latina/o Studies." In *Curiosity Studies: A New Ecology of Knowledge*, edited by Perry Zurn and Arjun Shankar, 167–87. Minneapolis: University of Minnesota Press, 2020.

León, Christina A. "Forms of Opacity: Roaches, Blood, and Being Stuck in Xandra Ibarra's Corpus." *ASAP/Journal* 2, no. 2 (2017): 369–94.

Lim, Genny. "Wonder Woman." In *This Bridge Called My Back: Writings by Radical Women of Color*, edited by Cherríe Moraga and Gloria Anzaldúa, 25–26. 2nd ed. New York: Kitchen Table Press, 1983.

Lippard, Lucy. "Catalysis: An Interview with Adrian Piper." *TDR/The Drama Review* 16, no. 1 (March 1972): 76–78.

Liu, Andrew. "Lab-Leak Theory and the 'Asiatic' Form." *n+1* 42 (Spring 2022). https://www.nplusonemag.com/issue-42/politics/lab-leak-theory-and-the-asiatic-form.

Liu, Wen. *Feeling Asian American: Racial Flexibility Between Assimilation and Oppression*. Urbana: University of Illinois Press, 2024.

Lorde, Audre. "The Master's Tools Will Never Dismantle the Master's House." In *Sister Outsider: Essays and Speeches*, 110–13. Berkeley: Crossing, 1984.

Love, Heather. *Feeling Backward: Loss and the Politics of Queer History*. Cambridge, MA: Harvard University Press, 2009.

Love, Heather. "Truth and Consequences: On Paranoid Reading and Reparative Reading." *Criticism* 52, no. 2 (2010): 235–41.

Love, Heather. *Underdogs: Social Deviance and Queer Theory*. Chicago: University of Chicago Press, 2021.

Low, Trisha. *Socialist Realism*. Brooklyn, NY: Coffee House Press, 2019.

Lowe, Lisa. "Insufficient Difference." *Ethnicities* 5, no. 3 (2005): 409–14.

Luciano, Dana. *Arranging Grief: Sacred Time and the Body in Nineteenth-Century America*. New York: New York University Press, 2007.

Lye, Colleen. "The Afro-Asian Analogy." *PMLA* 123, no. 5 (2008): 1732–36.

Lye, Colleen. *America's Asia: Racial Form and American Literature, 1893–1945*. Princeton, NJ: Princeton University Press, 2005.

MacCowan, Lyndall. "Re-Collecting History, Renaming Lives: Femme Stigma and the Feminist Seventies and Eighties." In *The Persistent Desire: A Femme-Butch Reader*, edited by Joan Nestle, 299–328. Boston: Alyson Publications, 1992.

Machida, Margo. *Unsettled Visions: Contemporary Asian American Artists and the Social Imaginary*. Durham, NC: Duke University Press, 2009.

Madansky, Cynthia, and Julie Tolentino. *Safer Sex Handbook for Lesbians*. New York: Gay Men's Health Crisis, 1993.

Malatino, Hil. *Side Affects: On Being Trans and Feeling Bad*. Minneapolis: University of Minnesota Press, 2022.

Manalansan, Martin F. "Servicing the World: Flexible Filipinos and the Unsecured Life." In *Political Emotions*, edited by Janet Staiger, Ann Cvetkovich, and Ann Reynolds, 215–28. London: Taylor and Francis, 2010.

Manalansan, Martin F. "The 'Stuff' of Archives: Mess, Migration, and Queer Lives." *Radical History Review* 120 (2014): 96–107.

Marchetti, Gina. *Romance and the Yellow Peril: Race, Sex, and Discursive Strategies in Hollywood Fiction*. Berkeley: University of California Press, 1994.

Mayer, Youngmi, and Brian Park. "About." *Feeling Asian* (podcast). https://www.feelingasian.com/about.

McAdory, Paul. "Gay Sincerity Is Scary." *Gawker*, September 9, 2021. https://www.gawker.com/culture/gay-sincerity-is-scary.

McGill, Ayaka. "Hong Kong Scientist Pins Hopes to Revive 'Pearl of the Orient' Past on Cutting-Edge Technology." *Hong Kong Free Press*, June 7, 2019. https://hongkongfp.com/2019/06/07/hong-kong-scientist-pins-hopes-revive-pearl-orient-past-cutting-edge-technology/.

McKittrick, Katherine. *Dear Science and Other Stories*. Durham, NC: Duke University Press, 2021.

McLuhan, Marshall. *Understanding Media: The Extensions of Man*. Cambridge, MA: MIT Press, 1994.

McMillan, Uri. *Embodied Avatars: Genealogies of Black Feminist Art and Performance*. New York: New York University Press, 2015.

Mead, Rebecca. "The Scourge of 'Relatability.'" *New Yorker*, August 1, 2014. https://www.newyorker.com/culture/cultural-comment/scourge-relatability.

Melamed, Jodi. *Represent and Destroy: Rationalizing Violence in the New Racial Capitalism*. Minneapolis: University of Minnesota Press, 2011.

Mengesha, Lilian, and Lakshmi Padmanabhan. "Introduction to *Performing Refusal/Refusal to Perform*." *Women and Performance: a journal of feminist theory* 29, no. 1 (2019): 1–8.

Mercer, Kobena. "Black Art and the Burden of Representation." *Third Text* 4, no. 10 (1990): 61–78.

Mervosh, Sarah, Dana Goldstein, Jennifer Schuessler, and Anemona Hartocollis. "Debate over Plagiarism Allegations Against Claudine Gay Adds to Pressures at Harvard." *New York Times*, December 21, 2023. https://www.nytimes.com/2023/12/21/us/harvard-claudine-gay-plagiarism-antisemitism-israel-palestine-protests.html.

Meyerowitz, Joanne. *How Sex Changed: A History of Transsexuality in the United States*. Cambridge, MA: Harvard University Press, 2022.

Miller, D. A. "Secret Subjects, Open Secrets." *Dickens Studies Annual* 14 (1985): 17–38.

Miller, Nancy K. "Untitled Work, Or, Speaking as a Feminist. . . ." In *Getting Personal: Feminist Occasions and Other Autobiographical Acts*, 31–37. New York: Routledge Press, 2013.

Min, Susette. "The Last Asian American Exhibition." In *One Way or Another: Asian American Art Now*, edited by Melissa Chiu, Karin Higa, and Susette Min, 34–41. New Haven, CT: Yale University Press, 2006.

Min, Susette. *Unnamable: The Ends of Asian American Art*. New York: New York University Press, 2018.
Mitchell, Nick. "(Critical Ethnic Studies) Intellectual." *Critical Ethnic Studies* 1, no. 1 (2015): 86–94.
Miyawaki, Mitski. "I Love Me After You," on *The Land Is Inhospitable and So Are We*. Dead Oceans, 2023, MP3. https://www.discogs.com/master/3239857-Mitski-The-Land-Is-Inhospitable-And-So-Are-We.
Miyawaki, Mitski (@mitskileaks). "I prefer to go alone." Twitter, September 6, 2016, 9:56 p.m. twitter.com/mitskileaks/status/773339058214998016.
Miyawaki, Mitski. "Lonesome Love," on *Be the Cowboy*. Dead Oceans, 2018, MP3. https://www.discogs.com/master/1406567-Mitski-Be-The-Cowboy.
Miyawaki, Mitski. "Working for the Knife," on *Laurel Hell*. Dead Oceans, 2022, MP3. https://www.discogs.com/master/2491018-Mitski-Laurel-Hell.
Miyawaki, Mitski (@mitskileaks). "you can go to shows alone!" Twitter, June 23, 2015, 11:00 a.m. twitter.com/mitskileaks/status/613361047164993536.
Miyawaki, Mitski. "Your Best American Girl." YouTube video, 3 minutes, 33 seconds, April 13, 2016. www.youtube.com/watch?v=u_hDHm9MDoI.
Montez, Ricardo. *Keith Haring's Line: Race and the Performance of Desire*. Durham, NC: Duke University Press, 2020.
Moraga, Cherríe, and Gloria Anzaldúa. "Entering the Lives of Others." In *This Bridge Called My Back: Writings by Radical Women of Color*, edited by Cherríe Moraga and Gloria Anzaldúa, 23. 2nd ed. New York: Kitchen Table Press, 1983.
Moten, Fred. *In the Break: The Aesthetics of the Black Radical Tradition*. Minneapolis: University of Minnesota Press, 2003.
Muñoz, José Esteban. *Cruising Utopia: The Then and There of Queer Futurity*. New York: New York University Press, 2009.
Muñoz, José Esteban. *Disidentifications: Queers of Color and the Performance of Politics*. Minneapolis: University of Minnesota Press, 1999.
Muñoz, José Esteban. "Feeling Brown, Feeling Down: Latina Affect, the Performativity of Race, and the Depressive Position." *Signs* 31, no. 3 (2006): 675–88.
Muñoz, José Esteban. *The Sense of Brown*. Edited by Joshua Chambers-Letson and Tavia Nyong'o. Durham, NC: Duke University Press, 2020.
Muñoz, José Esteban. "Teaching, Minoritarian Knowledge, and Love." *Women and Performance: a journal of feminist theory* 14, no. 2 (2004): 117–21.
Musser, Amber Jamilla. *Sensational Flesh: Race, Power, and Masochism*. New York: New York University Press, 2014.
Musser, Amber Jamilla. *Sensual Excess: Queer Femininity and Brown Jouissance*. New York: New York University Press, 2018.
Namaste, Vivian. *Invisible Lives: The Erasure of Transsexual and Transgendered People*. Chicago: University of Chicago Press, 2000.
Nash, Jennifer C. "Citational Desires: On Black Feminism's Institutional Longings." In "Citation, Otherwise," edited by Annabel L. Kim, special issue, *Diacritics* 48, no. 3 (2020): 76–91.

Naziz, Pearlin Shabna, Runima Das, and Supriyo Sen. "The Scent of Stress: Evidence From the Unique Fragrance of Agarwood." *Frontiers in Plant Science* 10 (2019). https://doi.org/10.3389/fpls.2019.00840.

Nelson, Maggie. *The Argonauts*. Minneapolis: Graywolf Press, 2015.

Nestle, Joan. "The Femme Question." In *The Persistent Desire: A Femme-Butch Reader*, edited by Joan Nestle, 138–46. Boston: Alyson Publications, 1992.

Nersessian, Anahid. *Keats's Odes: A Lover's Discourse*. Chicago: University of Chicago Press, 2021.

Ngai, Sianne. *Our Aesthetic Categories: Zany, Cute, Interesting*. Cambridge, MA: Harvard University Press, 2012.

Ngai, Sianne. *Ugly Feelings*. Cambridge, MA: Harvard University Press, 2005.

Ngô, Fiona. *Imperial Blues: Geographies of Race and Sex in Jazz Age New York*. Durham, NC: Duke University Press, 2014.

Nguyen, Kelly. "Queering Telemachus: Ocean Vuong, Postmemories, and the Vietnam War." *International Journal of the Classical Tradition* 29, no. 4 (2022): 430–48.

Nguyen, Mimi Thi. *The Promise of Beauty*. Durham, NC: Duke University Press, 2024.

Nguyen, Som-Mai. "Blunt-Force Ethnic Credibility." *Astra Magazine*, June 30, 2022. https://astra-mag.com/articles/blunt-force-ethnic-credibility.

Nguyen, Tân Hoàng. *View from the Bottom: Asian American Masculinity and Sexual Representation*. Durham, NC: Duke University Press, 2014.

Nguyen, Viet Thanh. "Asian-Americans Need More Movies, Even Mediocre Ones." *New York Times*, April 21, 2018. https://www.nytimes.com/2018/08/21/opinion/crazy-rich-asians-movie.html.

Nguyen, Viet Thanh. *Race and Resistance: Literature and Politics in Asian America*. Oxford: Oxford University Press, 2002.

Ninh, erin Khuê. *Ingratitude: The Debt-Bound Daughter in Asian American Literature*. New York: New York University Press, 2011.

Ninh, erin Khuê. *Passing for Perfect: College Imposters and Other Model Minorities*. Philadelphia: Temple University Press, 2021.

North, Anna. "Should Literature Be 'Relatable'?" *New York Times*, August 5, 2014. https://archive.nytimes.com/op-talk.blogs.nytimes.com/2014/08/05/should-literature-be-relatable.

Nyong'o, Tavia. *Afro-Fabulations: The Queer Drama of Black Life*. New York: New York University Press, 2018.

O'Hara, Frank. *The Collected Poems of Frank O'Hara*. Edited by Donald Allen. Berkeley: University of California Press, 1995.

Oishi, Eve. "Interview with Patty Chang." *Camera Obscura* 56, vol. 18, no. 3 (2003): 118–29.

Okihiro, Gary Y. *Third World Studies: Theorizing Liberation*. Durham, NC: Duke University Press, 2016.

Onion, Rebecca. "The Awful Emptiness of 'Relatable.'" *Slate*, April 11, 2014. https://slate.com/human-interest/2014/04/relatable-the-adjective-is-everywhere-in-high

-scchool-and-college-discussions-of-fiction-film-and-other-popular-culture-but-it-doesn-t-mean-anything.html.

"Oral History Interview with Julie Tolentino, 2018 April 11–12." Archives of American Art, Smithsonian Institution. https://www.aaa.si.edu/collections/interviews/oral-history-interview-julie-tolentino-17564.

Orange, Michelle. "And This Is Word for Word: The Theory of Relatability and Rethinking Justin Long's Face." *Rumpus*, October 26, 2010. https://therumpus.net/2010/10/26/and-this-is-word-for-word-the-theory-of-relatability-and-rethinking-justin-long%E2%80%99s-face.

Ouyang, Cato. "forgive everything." Night Gallery. Accessed June 2024. https://www.nightgallery.ca/exhibitions/catalina-ouyang/about.

Ouyang, Cato. "*THREE BETRAYALS*." Artist website. Accessed June 2024. https://catalinaouyang.com/three-betrayals.

Owen, Ianna Hawkins. "More: Cake, Feedism, and Asexuality." *Social Text* 40, no. 2 (2022): 93–111.

Pérez, Roy. "Proximity: On the Work of Mark Aguhar." In *Trap Door: Trans Cultural Production and the Politics of Visibility*, edited by Johanna Burton, Tourmaline, and Eric Stanley, 281–92. Cambridge, MA: MIT Press and The New Museum, 2017.

Philbrick, Ethan. *Group Works: Art, Politics, and Collective Ambivalence*. New York: Fordham University Press, 2023.

Phillips, Adam. *On Giving Up*. New York: Farrar, Straus and Giroux, 2024.

Phillips, Adam. *One Way and Another: New and Selected Essays*. New York: Penguin, 2018.

Post, Tina. *Deadpan: The Aesthetics of Black Inexpression*. New York: New York University Press, 2022.

Prashad, Vijay. *Everybody Was Kung Fu Fighting: Afro-Asian Connections and the Myth of Cultural Purity*. Boston: Beacon Press, 2001.

Prashad, Vijay. *The Karma of Brown Folk*. Minneapolis: University of Minnesota Press, 2001.

Prosser, Jay. *Second Skins: The Body Narratives of Transsexuality*. New York: Columbia University Press, 1998.

"PSi Conferences Archive." Performance Studies international. https:// www.psi-web.org/psi-archive-project/psi-conferences-archive.

Puar, Jasbir K. *The Right to Maim: Debility, Capacity, Disability*. Durham, NC: Duke University Press, 2017.

Quashie, Kevin. *The Sovereignty of Quiet: Beyond Resistance in Black Culture*. New Brunswick, NJ: Rutgers University Press, 2012.

Rachman, Stephen. "Memento Morbi: Lam Qua's Paintings, Peter Parker's Patients." *Literature and Medicine* 23, no. 1 (2004): 134–59.

Rancière, Jacques. *Dissensus: On Politics and Aesthetics*. Translated by Steven Corcoran. London: Bloomsbury, 2015.

Rankine, Claudia. *Citizen: An American Lyric*. Minneapolis: Graywolf Press, 2014.

Raphael-Hernandez, Heike, and Shannon Steen, eds. *AfroAsian Encounters: Culture, History, Politics*. New York: New York University Press, 2006.

Reeves, Roger. "Someday I'll Love Roger Reeves." In *King Me*, 73–74. Port Townsend, WA: Copper Canyon, 2013.

Rich, Adrienne. "Notes Toward a Politics of Location." In *Blood, Bread, and Poetry: Selected Prose*, 210–32. New York: W. W. Norton, 1986.

Rich, B. Ruby. *New Queer Cinema: The Director's Cut*. Durham, NC: Duke University Press, 2013.

"The Rise of Asian Americans." Pew Research Center. June 19, 2012. https://www.pewresearch.org/social-trends/2012/06/19/the-rise-of-asian-americans/.

Rivera, Takeo. *Model Minority Masochism: Performing the Cultural Politics of Asian American Masculinity*. Oxford: Oxford University Press, 2022.

Roach, Shoniqua. "Black Sex in the Quiet." *differences* 30, no. 1 (2019): 126–47.

Russell, David. *Tact: Aesthetic Liberalism and the Essay Form in Nineteenth-Century Britain*. Princeton, NJ: Princeton University Press, 2018.

Saketopoulou, Avgi. *Sexuality Beyond Consent: Risk, Race, Traumatophilia*. New York: New York University Press, 2023.

Salamon, Gayle. *Assuming a Body: Transgender and Rhetorics of Materiality*. New York: Columbia University Press, 2010.

Salisbury, Laura. "Relatable." In "30@30: The Future of Literary Thinking," special issue of *Textual Practice* 30, no. 7 (2016): 1157.

Salvato, Nick. *Obstruction*. Durham, NC: Duke University Press, 2016.

Santa Ana, Jeffrey. *Racial Feelings: Asian America in a Capitalist Culture of Emotion*. Philadelphia: Temple University Press, 2015.

Schuller, Kyla. *The Biopolitics of Feeling: Race, Sex, and Science in the Nineteenth Century*. Durham, NC: Duke University Press, 2018.

Schuller, Kyla, and Jules Gill-Peterson. "Introduction: Race, the State, and the Malleable Body." *Social Text* 38, no 2. (2020): 1–17.

Scott, Joan W. "The Evidence of Experience." *Critical Inquiry* 17, no. 4 (1991): 773–97.

Sedgwick, Eve Kosofsky. *Epistemology of the Closet*. Berkeley: University of California Press, 1990.

Sedgwick, Eve Kosofsky. *Touching Feeling: Affect, Pedagogy, Performativity*. Durham, NC: Duke University Press, 2003.

Sedgwick, Eve Kosofsky. *The Weather in Proust*. Durham, NC: Duke University Press, 2011.

Serano, Julia. *Whipping Girl: A Transsexual Woman on Sexism and the Scapegoating of Femininity*. Emeryville: Seal, 2007.

Serpell, Namwali (@namwalien). "I say this." X, December 11, 2023, 5:26 p.m. https://twitter.com/namwalien/status/1734384317218906210.

Serpell, Namwali (@namwalien). "The plagiarism thing." X, December 11, 2023, 5:26 p.m. https://twitter.com/namwalien/status/1734384314148642848?s=12&t=5RSQCqUF2qKEODdINXsQpA.

Sexton, Anne. "In Excelsis." In *Anne Sexton: The Complete Poems*, 608. Boston: Houghton Mifflin, 1998.

Shah, Nayan. *Contagious Divides: Epidemics and Race in San Francisco's Chinatown*. Berkeley: University of California Press, 2001.

Shi, Domee, dir. *Turning Red*. Burbank, CA: Disney, 2022.

Shimakawa, Karen. *National Abjection: The Asian American Body Onstage*. Durham, NC: Duke University Press, 2002.

Shimizu, Celine Parreñas. *The Hypersexuality of Race: Performing Asian/American Women on Screen and Scene*. Durham, NC: Duke University Press, 2007.

Shin, TJ. "Universal Skin Salvation." Artist website. https://jaeyeonshin.com/Universal-Skin-Salvation.

Shin, TJ. "Universal Skin Salvation 2.0: Strange Life: Beauty, Race & War." Artist website. https://jaeyeonshin.com/Universal-Skin-Salvation-2–0.

Shin, TJ. *The Vegetarian*. Mohkínstsis (Calgary), Alberta: The Bows, 2022. Exhibition brochure. https://jaeyeonshin.com/The-Vegetarian.

Shotwell, Alexis. *Against Purity: Living Ethically in Compromised Times*. Minneapolis: University of Minnesota Press, 2016.

Smith, Cherise. *Enacting Others: Politics of Identity in Eleanor Antin, Nikki S. Lee, Adrian Piper, and Anna Deavere Smith*. Durham, NC: Duke University Press, 2011.

Sohn, Stephen Hong. "Introduction: Alien/Asian: Imagining the Racialized Future." *Melus* 33, no. 4 (2008): 5–22.

"Somatic's Grocery." CCS Bard. Accessed December 19, 2024. https://ccs.bard.edu/museum/exhibitions/556-somatic-s-grocery.

Song, Celine, dir. *Past Lives*. Santa Monica, CA: Lionsgate, 2023.

Song, Min Hyoung. *The Children of 1965: On Writing, and Not Writing, as an Asian American*. Durham, NC: Duke University Press, 2013.

Spillers, Hortense J. "Interstices: A Small Drama of Words." In *Black, White, and in Color: Essays on American Literature and Culture*, 152–75. Chicago: University of Chicago Press, 2003.

Spillers, Hortense J. "Mama's Baby, Papa's Maybe: An American Grammar Book." *Diacritics* 17, no. 2 (1987): 65–81.

Stallings, L. H. *Funk the Erotic: Transaesthetics and Black Sexual Cultures*. Champaign: University of Illinois Press, 2015

Stekel, Wilhelm. *Auto-Eroticism: A Psychiatric Study of Onanism and Neurosis*. New York: Routledge Press, 2011.

Stekel, Wilhelm. *Frigidity in Women in Relation to Her Love Life*. New York: Boni and Liveright, 1926.

Stobie, Caitlin E. "The Good Wife? Sibling Species in Han Kang's *The Vegetarian*." *ISLE: Interdisciplinary Studies in Literature and Environment* 24, no. 4 (2017): 787–802.

Storti, Anna M. Moncada. "Half and Both: On Color and Subject/Object Tactility." *Women and Performance: a journal of feminist theory* 30, no. 1 (2020): 104–12.

Stuart, Mel, dir. *Willy Wonka and the Chocolate Factory*. Los Angeles: Paramount, 1971.

Stuelke, Patricia. *The Ruse of Repair: U.S. Neoliberal Empire and the Turn from Critique*. Durham, NC: Duke University Press, 2021.

Sueyoshi, Amy. *Discriminating Sex: White Leisure and the Making of the American "Oriental."* Chicago: University of Illinois Press, 2018.

Tan, Amy. *The Joy Luck Club*. New York: Penguin, 2006.

Tomes, Nancy. *The Gospel of Germs: Men, Women, and the Microbe in American Life*. Cambridge, MA: Harvard University Press, 1999.

Tompkins, Kyla Wazana. "Crude Matter, Queer Form." *ASAP/Journal* 2, no. 2 (2017): 264–68.

Tompkins, Kyla Wazana. *Deviant Matter: Ferment, Intoxicants, Jelly, Rot*. New York: New York University Press, 2024.

Tompkins, Kyla Wazana. *Racial Indigestion: Eating Bodies in the 19th Century*. New York: New York University Press, 2012.

Tongson, Karen. *Relocations: Queer Suburban Imaginaries*. New York: New York University Press, 2011.

Tsang, Wu, dir. *Wildness*. New York: Electronic Arts Intermix, 2012.

Tsang, Wu, and Fred Moten. "All Terror, All Beauty." In *Trap Door: Trans Cultural Production and the Politics of Visibility*, edited by Johanna Burton, Tourmaline, and Eric Stanley, 339–48. Cambridge, MA: MIT Press and The New Museum, 2017.

Tu, Thuy Linh Nguyen. *Experiments in Skin: Race and Beauty in the Shadows of Vietnam*. Durham, NC: Duke University Press, 2021.

Tulathimutte, Tony (@tonytula). "cover of books by asian writers." Twitter, September 13, 2016, 10:18 a.m. https://twitter.com/tonytula/status/775745527430385665.

Tulathimutte, Tony. *Rejection: Fiction*. New York: William Morrow, 2024.

"The Use of Non-Pharmaceutical Forms of Artemisia." World Health Organization. October 10, 2019. https://www.who.int/publications/i/item/WHO-CDS-GMP-2019.14.

Vargas, Deborah R. "Ruminations on Lo Sucio as a Latino Queer Analytic." *American Quarterly* 66, no. 3 (2014): 715–26.

Vazquez, Alexandra T. *Listening in Detail: Performances of Cuban Music*. Durham, NC: Duke University Press, 2013.

Vazquez, Alexandra T. "Salon Philosophers: Ivy Queen and Surprise Guests Take Reggaetón Aside." In *Reggaeton*, edited by Raquel Z. Rivera, Wayne Marshall, and Deborah Pacini Hernandez, 300–311. Durham, NC: Duke University Press, 2009.

Vogel, Shane. *The Scene of Harlem Cabaret: Race, Sexuality, Performance*. Chicago: Chicago University Press, 2009.

Vuong, Ocean. *The Emperor of Gladness*. New York: Penguin, 2025.

Vuong, Ocean. *Night Sky with Exit Wounds*. Port Townsend, WA: Copper Canyon, 2016.

Vuong, Ocean. "Ode to Masturbation." YouTube video, 5 minutes, 37 seconds, April 16, 2016. National Geographic Grosvenor Auditorium, Washington, DC. https://www.youtube.com/watch?v=ohY5cVvRWfU.

Vuong, Ocean. "Someday I'll Love Ocean Vuong." *New Yorker*, May 4, 2015. https://www.newyorker.com/magazine/2015/05/04/someday-ill-love-ocean-vuong.

Vuong, Ocean. "Someday I'll Love Ocean Vuong." In *Night Sky with Exit Wounds*, 82–83. Port Townsend, WA: Copper Canyon, 2016.

Vuong, Ocean. *Time Is a Mother*. New York: Penguin, 2022.

Walleston, Aimee. "In Both Bi- and Triennial, Wu Tsang Talks Community." *Art in America*, February 10, 2012. https://www.artnews.com/art-in-america/features/wu-tsang-3–58700/.

Weheliye, Alexander G. *Habeas Viscus: Racializing Assemblages, Biopolitics, and Black Feminist Theories of the Human*. Durham, NC: Duke University Press, 2014.

Wiegman, Robyn. *Object Lessons*. Durham, NC: Duke University Press, 2012.

Wilderson, Frank B. *Red, White, and Black: Cinema and the Structure of U.S. Antagonisms*. Durham, NC: Duke University Press, 2010.

Wilkinson, Alexis, curator. *Extremely absorbent and increasingly hollow*. New York: Cuchifritos Gallery + Project Space, 2018. Exhibition brochure. https://www.artistsallianceinc.org/wp-content/uploads/2021/08/CuchifritosGallery_ExtremelyAbsorbent_AlexisWilkinson.pdf.

Wilson, Elizabeth. *Gut Feminism*. Durham, NC: Duke University Press, 2015.

Winnicott, D. W. "Hate in the Counter-Transference." *Journal of Psychotherapy Practice and Research* 3, no. 4 (1994): 348–56.

Winnicott, D. W. *Playing and Reality*. London: Taylor and Francis, 2012.

Winnicott, D. W. "The Roots of Aggression." In *The Child, the Family, and the Outside World*, 232–39. Cambridge, MA: Perseus Publishing, 1964.

Wyma, Chloe. "'I Dislike the Word Visibility': Wu Tsang on Sexuality, Creativity, and Conquering New York's Museums." *Blouin Art Info International*, March 2, 2012. http://cliftonbenevento.com/wp-content/uploads/2011/08/TSA_Artinfo_Mar2012.pdf.

Yamada, Mitsuye. "Invisibility Is an Unnatural Disaster: Reflections of an Asian American Woman." In *This Bridge Called My Back: Writings by Radical Women of Color*, edited by Cherríe Moraga and Gloria Anzaldúa, 35–40. 2nd ed. New York: Kitchen Table Press, 1983.

Yan, Wa-Tat, Chi-Pang Lau, Kenneth M. Y. Leung, and Stephen N. G. Davies. "Problems and Prospects of Revitalizing Marine Pearl Cultivation in Highly Urbanized Coasts: A Case Study of Tolo Harbour in Hong Kong." *Regional Studies in Marine Science* 31 (2019): 1–16. https://doi.org/10.1016/j.rsma.2019.100756.

Yao, Xine. *Disaffected: The Cultural Politics of Unfeeling in Nineteenth-Century America*. Durham, NC: Duke University Press, 2021.

Yapp, Hentyle. "Feeling Down(town Julie Brown): The Sense of Up and Expiring Relationality." *Journal of Visual Culture* 17, no. 1 (2018): 3–21.

Yergeau, M. Remi. *Authoring Autism: On Rhetoric and Neurological Queerness*. Durham, NC: Duke University Press, 2017.

Yin, Livien (@livienyin). "'Dreaming Host' was on view at Wonder Woman." Instagram, September 4, 2022. https://www.instagram.com/p/CiF56n8px5t/?igsh=NjZiM2M3MzIxNA%3D%3D.

Zauner, Michelle. *Crying in H Mart*. New York: Doubleday, 2021.

Zeiba, Drew. "Jes Fan: The Artist Probing the Intersections of Biology, Identity and Creativity." *Wallpaper**, October 6, 2022. https://www.wallpaper.com/art/jes-fan-artist-profile.

Zia, Helen. "Asian American: An Evolving Consciousness." In *One Way or Another: Asian American Art Now*, edited by Melissa Chiu, Karin Higa, and Susette Min, 10–14. New Haven, CT: Yale University Press, 2006.

Zimmer, Ben. "The Origins of 'Relatable.'" *New York Times*, August 13, 2010. https://www.nytimes.com/2010/08/15/magazine/15onlanguage.html.

Zoladz, Lindsay. "Mitski Is More than TikTok." *New York Times*, March 11, 2022. https://www.nytimes.com/interactive/2022/03/11/magazine/mitski.html.

Zornosa, Laura. "How 'Everything Everywhere All at Once' Helps to Heal Generational Trauma." *New York Times*, April 15, 2022. https://www.nytimes.com/2022/04/15/movies/everything-everywhere-all-at-once-interviews.html.

Zuo, Mila. *Vulgar Beauty: Acting Chinese in the Global Sensorium*. Durham, NC: Duke University Press, 2022.

INDEX

Page numbers in italics refer to figures and plates.